EBook: ISBN 978-969-33-9277-7

Paperback: ISBN 978-969-33-9278-4

Hardcover: ISBN 978-969-33-9279-1

Table of Contents

INTRODUCTION –
IT'S RAINING LAWSUITS

Maybe I'm just paranoid and crazy.

After all, if I said "A stranger could show up at your door tomorrow, remove you by way of a deputy sheriff, and then auction your home to pay herself" would you believe me?

Let's begin a story that sounds like a tall tale.

There once was a Polka Queen happily squeezing her accordion, hurling fake bananas and colorful Marti-gras beads into the audience at her cheering, drunken college fans, who were singing along polka songs.

One day, the clouds opened up, and thunder bolts blasted from the heavens.

Suddenly, several greedy attorneys, crooked judges, a predatory guardian named Rebecca Fierle, and a crazy New Mexican computer hacker appeared from the skies and began tumbling down upon Angelina, the Polka Queen. She tried to run away, clad in her lace gloves, puffy-sleeved 80's prom dress, and purple bouffant wig, but the powerful, wicked people fell down upon her and then imprisoned her in front of her computer.

There was no more hopsa dancing, no more maraca-shaking, and no more happy polka singing. Instead, the Polka Queen was forced to compose a mountain of sickening, nauseating court papers.

Finally, after 15 long, exhausting years, the unscrupulous guardian, Rebecca Fierle, was suddenly arrested.

Handcuffed?!

Yep, she was shackled and placed into the back of a cop car, while visibly seen giggling. Laughing uproariously.

"This is where the fun begins!" Rebecca Fierle queerly squealed as the deputy hauled her away.

The Polka Queen gasped and pinched herself as she watched the bizarre, surreal scene on the six o'clock news.

The events you are about to read may seem too bizarre to be true. Yet, they are grounded in a very real and infamous case that made local and national headlines, centered around the professional guardian, Rebecca Fierle.

Some of the shocking headlines read:

***Disgraced Florida Guardian Rebecca Fierle Arrested**

***Guardian for elderly arrested on abuse, neglect charges**

***Trial scheduled to begin for former professional guardian accused in man's death**

On Friday, July 12, 2019, at approximately 12 noon, I received a most unusual and unexpected e-mail from Tampa investigative reporter (ABC Action News) Adam Walser* that made my heart "stop."

"REALLY??? Is this for real?" I texted him back.

Indeed. It was for real.

Rebecca Fierle had been legally removed from nearly 100 guardianship cases in Orange County, Florida!

Within a few hours, my phone was ringing off the hook, and e-mails were pouring in from across the nation. Other guardianship fraud victims were calling me to congratulate me.

"Did you hear the news?!"

It was a few days of this constant frenzy.

The name Rebecca Fierle might mean nothing to most people. But for those entangled in the twisted web of Florida's toxic guardianship system, it is a name that now carries a weighty and dark reputation.

Rebecca Fierle has come to be known as "The Nation's Most Notorious Guardian." Some refer to her as "The Al Capone of 'Professional' Guardians."

Even the Netflix movie, "I Care A Lot" is allegedly based on her infamous persona.

Good morning, Ms. Peterson, ... I'm sorry to disturb you so early. The court has ruled that you require assistance in taking care of yourself. The court has appointed me to be your legal guardian. You have to come with me. And remember . . . I'm here to help.

But, unlike the plot in "I Care A Lot," you can't call up the Russian mafia or hire a midget to get you out of a predatory guardianship. There's generally no escape.

The guardianship booby trap strikes very suddenly, like a bolt of lightning.

Marie Sandusky was in her beauty shop, fluffing up her customer's hair, when, all of a sudden, a deputy sheriff arrived and served her with legal court papers.

Within the next 24 hours, her mother was removed from her home, never to return.

Soon her mother would be dead, and all of her money would be legally transferred to strangers.

It could start with a creepy neighbor.

It could commence with a disgruntled relative.

Or it could begin with that helping non-profit organization that wants to come into your home and, oh so kindly, assist you for *free* -- volunteering to replace burned out light bulbs.

What you are about to read is not the product of a fevered imagination or a writer's creative liberties. It is the true account of my life, intertwined with the notorious figure of Rebecca Fierle.

You see, I'm not just a polka queen. I'm also a licensed private investigator.

I was the very first professional to investigate and expose Rebecca Fierle. My investigative reports commenced in early 2008 – more than 12 years before Fierle was finally arrested. In total, I discovered millions of dollars missing from the elderly and hundreds of mysterious deaths.

I screamed out to the authorities. I wrote elaborate, detailed reports alerting the FBI, the FDLE, and other agencies over and over again. Unfortunately, crimes continued to be committed for more than a decade.

No action was taken. No one seemed to care.

I felt like the frenzied character in that Nicholas Cage movie "Knowing", where he's the only one who knows that the world is going to end. He's screaming about it, but nobody seems to care.

"Cremated remains of 9 people found in office of embattled Florida guardian"

When the FDLE (Florida Department of Law Enforcement) finally raided Rebecca Fierle's Orlando guardianship office, they found the cremains of nine humans and one puppy.

One puppy?! (That's a little odd, Rebecca. I was expecting at least three puppies and one cat.)

Joking aside, despite Fierle's arrest, The Guardianship Racket continues, with minimal government oversight, and little public awareness. There are many other "Rebecca Fierle's" operating across the United States, and if you try to expose them, you might end up in jail, or charged with libel/slander.

Outspoken victims have been sued by predatory guardians and their attorneys when they dare to expose The Guardianship Hustle. Victim Lesa Martino, for example, lost her $450,000.00 home after she exposed corrupt guardian Traci

Hudson on her Facebook page. Hudson was later arrested and charged with more than 23 felonies, but Hudson still won in court when she sued Lesa Martino for libel. Additionally, whistle-blowing attorneys (the very few white hat attorneys who exist) have been systematically disbarred when trying to get victims out of unwarranted guardianships.

Even the media, who occasionally write about guardianship fraud, have been silenced. Netflix, for example, was ordered to remove its well-written, shocking documentary "Guardians, Inc." after exposing how one elderly gentleman was robbed of all of his assets and then confined against his will, to a marginal nursing home.

Netflix sued after show with Needham plot

'Dirty Money' episode leads to defamation lawsuit

Trevor Ballantyne tballantyne@wickedlocal.com
Published 3:51 p.m. ET Sept. 18, 2020

Released in late March, the episode features interviews with John Savanovich, an elderly former Needham resident who alleges local attorneys he hired in 2015 used the conservatorship system in Massachusetts to steward the sale of six run-down properties he owned near the town's border with Newton.

On Aug. 18, lawyers representing Nicholas Louisa, one of the attorneys Savanovich hired, filed a 38-page complaint claiming the episode defamed Louisa's reputation by presenting a false narrative that left out key circumstances related to the real

Finally, I decided to do the one thing I can do. Write this book. But that was easier said than done. I have written several books during my lifetime. By far, this book was the most daunting to complete. The subject matter defeated me. Fifteen years have passed. At last, after hundreds of drafts, thousands of tears, and many professional read-throughs, I completed this shocking story.

It's Raining Lawsuits in My Life, and I Just Wanna Be . .

ANGELINA, THE POLKA QUEEN, was originally commenced during my Trial-by-Fire. But I didn't want this to be just another sad story.** Today, I'm tickling the squeezebox again and going on a Polka tour – The Great American Sing-Along Show! (Hope to see you there!)

This book includes several links to many of my wacky original songs, so that readers can sing along while enjoying this sometimes quirky, sometimes hilarious, but mostly tragic fast-paced dark-humored, incredulous adventure.

The Guardianship Hustle continues nationwide. "**Guardianship exploitation is the (top) crime of the 21st Century.**" ~Dirty Money "Guardians, Inc." (aired March 11, 2020)

I wrote this book in the hopes of increasing public awareness, and making a difference.

•••●●●•••

*Adam Walser, ABC Action News, Tampa, has been bravely and tirelessly reporting and airing numerous stories on guardianship fraud for more than 15 years, despite his TV station being threatened with lawsuits from the predators.

•••●●●•••

**A well-written book that already details the basics of The Guardianship Racket is Dr. Sam Sugar's "Guardianships and the Elderly: The Perfect Crime". I would highly encourage you to read Dr. Sugar's book.

I would also encourage you to read "Oh, Florida!: How America's Weirdest State Influences the Rest of the Country" by Craig Pittman. Florida is frequently referred to as "The Most Corrupt State in the Nation," and my story here certainly backs up that unfortunate and embarrassing claim.

THANK YOU!

There are so many people I want to thank who listened to my story over the years. They were all part of the healing process from this horrific Trial-by-Fire.

First of all, I do want to thank Dr. Sam Sugar and Rick Black. These two guys have both devoted countless hours listening not only to me but to thousands of victims across the nation with stories similar to mine. Rick is the head of an organization called CEAR – Center for Estate Administration Reform.

Sam was the founder of AAAPG.net -- Americans Against Abusive Probate and Guardianships. He was one of the original movers and shakers after our original leader of guardianship reform, Latifa Ring, passed away.

Special thanks to Latifa Ring who, in 2011, took 44 of us guardianship victims to Washington, D.C., where we marched and spoke on Capitol Hill. Our testimonies are part of the permanent Congressional record.

Then there is Doug Franks – a mover and shaker, and guardianship reform victim advocate, who fought hard and actually got his mother out of a fraudulent guardianship. (Of course, shortly thereafter, his mother died, and he never got back the stolen money.)

Prior to using the internet to help free his mother, there was another victim who took the same approach -- Ray Fernandez. Ray started a website called ElderAbuse.org. Many of my investigations into Rebecca Fierle first appeared on Ray's blog.

Meanwhile, our first leader, Latifa Ring, died of colon cancer. We all felt that it was guardianship fraud and abuse that was the real cancer that had killed her. She fought with every breath until the day she died to shed light upon this horrific criminal enterprise.

I'd also like to acknowledge all of the guardianship victims I've met over the years. Your lives have been forever changed. Some events in life have ripple effects that flow for decades and in some cases, an entire lifetime. That certainly is the case for victims of guardianship fraud.

I'd also like to thank all of the people who listened over the years. Listening has certainly been a major part of the healing process.

There's my buddy, and sound engineer, Wayne Severson. Oh Wayne, you are the best guy in the whole world. You listened patiently and also helped to bring my songs to life. What would I do without you? Wayne Severson was named top guitarist 2016 in Branson, Missouri. He is also the owner of Lion Feather Recording Studio. Which leads me to remember John Wyatt, the most fabulous keyboardist on the planet! I will never forget the countless hours John, Wayne and I spent in Wayne's recording studio bringing life to hundreds of my original songs. Thank you, John and Wayne, for your wonderful talents.

I also want to thank my ex, David Newman. For 10 years, you were there with me and lived this horrific nightmare with me. You walked the hallways of nursing homes with me. You helped me while I was confined to a computer for nearly 10 years of my life. You helped photocopy and staple court documents. You listened. You cried with me. You videotaped my mom. Like me, you were in disbelief that such horrible things could happen in the USA.

I'd also like to thank the unscrupulous cast of characters that appear in this book. I couldn't ask for a more striking cast of wretched beings. You are certainly a colorful gang. But let me give you a piece of advice, because it's my turn now. I don't have to be subjected to your lies or theft any more. Yes, you got away with a million dollars and ten years of my life, but at some point, I believe justice will prevail.

Oh, and Nini, my beloved all white kitty with bright blue eyes. She sat on my shoulder every day while I typed and typed, during my ten years of court hell as I composed court papers every day, faithfully sitting there on my shoulder, purring. Nini is in kitty Heaven now. I miss you so much! I will always love you!

Special thanks, too, to Jeff Dreisin, my artist, who brought to life the Dishonorable Members of the Rebecca Fierle Probate Hall of Shame. In addition to his satirical drawings, Jeff also has spent thousands of hours listening to me over the past 20 years, laughing with me, and providing humor to my life when the outlook was bleak. Jeff has that special magic with people.

I'd also like to mention Rick Scott and Ron DeSantis, the former and current governors of Florida. You weren't addressed in my Probate Hall of Shame because we, the victims, are still waiting for you to do the right thing. Please stop allowing predatory attorneys, guardians, and judges (especially judges) to rob the elderly and slander their natural heirs via corrupt Florida courts. **Do the right thing.**

Chapter One –

Born to Squeeze

Live the life you want to live. Be as weird as you wanna be. You will never find true happiness until you can accept who you truly are. ~Weird Al Yankovick

Dressed in my sparkly, purple sequin 80's prom dress, my big, blonde bouffant wig, tiara, and fingerless, lace gloves, I walk into the dining room at the nursing home, and there is suddenly magic in the air.

Great excitement. Anticipation.

The staff is rolling in residents in their wheelchairs while I set up my musical equipment and accordion. I pass out maracas to everyone. The look of elation is in their eyes. The room begins to chatter with the shaking of maracas.

And then, it is **showtime**!

The sound of introductory trumpets can be heard on my synthesized keyboard as I dramatically introduce myself.

"Ladies and gentlemen! It is time for our fabulous show!!! Are you ready to have the FUNNEST fun?!"

Maracas are shaking wildly from the quivering hands of the assembled, mostly old ladies.

I continue my overly dramatic self-introduction.

"Folks! You saw her on the Howard Stern Show!" (a burst of cheers from the audience, although most of them have no idea what is "The Howard Stern Show").

"You saw her in the HBO movie, Recount!" (more cheers from the audience). "You saw her at the laundromat!" (more cheers and laughter).

And now, here she is -- LIVE -- to perform for you here at Palm Gardens Assisted Living Facility! WOOO—HOOOOOOOO!" The maracas are shaking wildly.

"Ladies and gentlemen!" I dramatically declare. "Please welcome the one! The only! ANGELINNNNNNNA, THE POLLLLLLKKKKKA QUEEEEEEEEEN!!!!!!

ALL BOW BEFORE THE *QUEEN*!!"

I bow my head and raise my right hand as boisterous cheers are heard from the residents and staff members! Everyone complies and dramatically uses their arms from their wheel chairs to bow before me. And then, I burst into this introductory song.

"Some think the world is made for fun and frolic!
And so do I! And so do I!
Some think it well to be all melancholic!
To pine and sigh! To pine and sigh! [BOO-HOOOOOOO!]
But I! I love to spend my time in singing!
Some joyous songs! Some joyous songs!
To set the world with music bravely ringing!
Is far from wrong! Is far from wrong!
Listen! Listen! Music from afar!
Listen! Listen! With a happy heart!
Funiculi! Funicula! Funiculi! Funicula!
Joy is everywhere!
Funiculi! Funicula!"
WOOOOOO—HOOOOO!!

We enjoy a full hour of the **funnest** fun! Indeed, as one old lady told me after the show, "This is the most fun I've ever had in my whole life!" She brushed away happy tears as I gently squeezed her hands and thanked her.

But now, it was time to put down my accordion.

There would be no more shows for a long, long time.

My mother, age 90, had come to live with me, and I dutifully and graciously would be there every day to take care of her.

I didn't realize it at the time, but . . .

My mother would soon be murdered after a court-appointed unscrupulous guardian took control of her and her million dollars of assets . . . (my stolen inheritance).

And me? It would be a long and truly bizarre nearly 15 years before I would ever pick up my beloved accordion ever again.

•••◦•◉•◦•••

While I frolicked in nursing homes, entertaining the elderly, the demented, and the bed-ridden, there was another woman who also was roaming the hallways of nursing homes. She, too, had become keenly interested in old ladies, but not for the sake of entertaining them. Clad in her gray Gucci pantsuit, and carrying her Christian Dior leather briefcase, Rebecca Fierle (a complete stranger to me, who has forever changed my life) was charmingly conniving rich old ladies to sign over powers of attorney to her. Soon, a once bankrupt divorcee who had resided in a run-down trailer with her three kids, was driving a Mercedes and now held title to hundreds of thousands of dollars of real estate.

More than three decades later, when the Florida Department of Law Enforcement finally raided her office and arrested her, they found her human trophies – victims' cremains.

One of Fierle's victims was my mother, Louise A. Falvo.

So, what led up to my suddenly and inadvertently becoming involved in five quirky, horrible, and nightmarish lawsuits – all at the same time?

I once saw a bumper sticker that read, "Interesting women live messy lives."

A wacky accordion player, suddenly confined every day to an office chair and computer screen, composing endless court papers, is the epitome of messiness!

So, let's go back in time . . . to the very beginning.

It all started with the historically famous Mafia-town's (Youngstown, Ohio) Great Snow of 1950 . . . and that first fateful car ride in a big, black hearse.

———————— ••● ●•• ————————

There's absolutely nothing – nothing -- an abused child might not do to win her mother's love. I remember being prompted by my mother, as a small child, to sing and dance for her when she was feeling blue.

"Sing for me, Ang! Dance for me!"

Of course, I will sing and dance for you, my Dear Mommy! I thought. *I will sing for you until my throat is hoarse and my feet are exhausted. And maybe, just maybe, you will <u>really</u> love me during these moments that I am singing and dancing for you.*

It didn't matter that a few minutes later, my mother might be clobbering me for singing and dancing -- because I was suddenly "giving her a headache."

We lived in the moment.

One minute, all was quiet and fine. Next minute, a war zone.

"I wish you had never been born, you little bitch and whore! If abortion had been legal in the 1950s, I would have aborted you! If it wasn't for you, I could leave this horrible, horrible, horrible marriage! You have always been such an ungrateful child! Look at all that I do for you, you little, unappreciative bitch. You whore."

A swift slap across my face, pulling my hair, pummeling my back.

An hour later, I would find a new, lavish wardrobe of fancy skirts and stylish dresses laid out upon my bed, the price tags still on them.

"Ang, try on your new outfits," my mother would chirp in the sickeningly sweetest voice.

"Tell me if you like them! If not, we can go downtown tomorrow and get some other things that you like. Did I get the right size? Do you like that color?" "Do you want to go out to eat? Let's go to your favorite pizza place."

There was never an actual apology. Instead, my mother would wrap me in her arms, shower me with hugs and kisses, and tell me how much she dearly loved me.

"You are the love of my life! Without you, I could not survive."

It was now time to put aside all bad memories and start creating new, happy memories. My mother was now 90 years old, a recent widow who had moved into my home, into my bedroom. No longer was she that chunky plus size woman who could lift an entire hefty wooden case of 48 glass Coke bottles, or beat any baseball player in an arm wrestle. She was a mere 90 pounds and covered in wrinkles from head to toe. Her stringy, thin gray hair covered one eye. And there she sat on my bed that first evening, looking so frail and terrified.

"Eternal"

My mother had always told me I was "***eternal***" --because of my unusual birth story.

She loved telling her favorite stories over and over again.

"You know, Ang, . . . we almost **died**! The doctor said **we almost died**!"

My mother's eyes grew wide as she leaned forward in my bed.

I was born during The Great Snow of 1950 in Youngstown, Ohio to my first-generation Italian parents, Carl and Louise Falvo. I was their first -- and only -- child.

It was my duty – as a child, and as an adult -- to listen to these repetitive stories and act as though I had never heard them before.

"We almost **died**, Ang!"

My mother loved repeating her most favorite, dramatic lines.

"Oh, Mom! That's really **horrible**! What happened?" I'd ask her, feigning surprise.

"Well, I was almost 36 years old, which was **really, really** old -- back then -- for giving birth to a child," my mother said. "But after **<u>seven</u>** long, painful days of loooooong labor . . . (The story was originally three days) . . . there you were!"

"Wow. That was a really, long labor, Mom. **<u>Seven</u>** days!"

My mother looked extremely pleased to know I realized how much she had suffered.

"Oh, yes! I suffered **tremendously**!" my mother assured me, cradling her abdomen, swaying back and forth. "But soon, they laid you in my arms, swaddled in a pink blanket, with a big, pink bow on top of your head! You had so much curly hair!"

Then she looked at me with soft, loving eyes, and her frown slowly evolved into a happy pout. "It was all worth it!"

"Awww!" I replied, squeezing my mother's hands.

"How high was the snow, Mom?" I inquired.

"The snow was as high as the roofs of the houses!" my mother continued, exaggerating, of course. (When I was a teenager, the familiar story was that the snow was as high as the roofs of the cars.)

I knew it was time for me to ask that all-important familiar question.

"So, Mom, how did you get to the hospital, since the snow was as high as the roofs of the houses?"

My mother sat up straight again and continued her story.

"Well, you see, back in those days, neighbors were neighborly. The hospital ambulance could not get through the streets. So, each neighbor came out and shoveled their half of the road!"

"And then did the ambulance come, Mom?"

"No! The hospital ambulance never came, Ang!" my mother declared.

"Oh! My goodness!" I interjected.

"So, how did we get to the hospital?"

"Instead, Blackstone Funeral Home, at the end of our street, gave me a ride to the hospital. A week later, they came back and took us home!"

"And?"

"So . . . . . your first car ride was in a hearse!!" my mother explained.

"No way! That's incredible, Mom!"

"Yep!"

My mother grinned widely and wiggled her nose.

"So, *I guess that means you're eternal, Ang!*" My mother laughed heartily, and, of course, so did I.

Suddenly after telling me this all-so-familiar story, my mother, sank into her new bed, and began sobbing.

"*I'm scared, Ang!*" she said, trembling. "*I am a widow now. I am so old; I am now 91 years old, Ang. I'm really scared.*"

I looked at her frail thin body, her trembling hands, her tears.

I showed her the twinkly lights high above around the edge of the ceiling in her new bedroom, and I ran her hand over the new quilt I had hand-stitched for her.

"Do you like your new room, Ma?"

"Yes, it's quite lovely," she said, wiping her tears.

"There's nothing to be afraid of," I told her, with a hug. "I will take good care of you."

————————••●●••————————

<u>Bless Me Father, for I Have Sinned</u>

In the living room, next to the Virgin Mary statue, was my father's vibrating, reclining chair. I loved the Virgin Mary, and Virgin Mary stood there as a constant reminder that I was to remain a virgin. Or as my father always put it, ***The noblest thing you could do, Ang, when you grow up is to become a nun.***

As a little girl, I certainly wanted to be that devout religious teacher one day, dressed in those long black robes, helping my pupils to learn the ABC's.

My favorite Sunday school Catechism nun was Sister Helen. I remember the day when she walked me into the darkened confessional booth for the first time and told me to stay inside there, kneeling, until the priest arrived behind the black, veiled curtain.

She had prepared me for what I was supposed to say~

Bless me father, for I have sinned . . .

This is my first confession.

At the age of six, there really wasn't a lot to confess, but my mother had also prepared me for what I was supposed to say.

"You tell the priest that you have been <u>mean</u> to your mother, and you ask God to forgive you!"

Down on my knees, my hands folded together in prayer, I heard the little door open in the confessional booth. The priest had arrived. I could only see a dark shadow as he made the sign of the cross over me from behind the curtain.

"In nomine Patris et Filii et Spiritus Sancti . . . Amen."

"And tell me, dear child. What are your sins?"

My lips quivered and tears ran down my cheeks as I tightly clutched my hands in prayer and mumbled a few words.

"What was that, dear child? Speak louder. I could not hear you."

I hesitated, then mustered up all of the courage I could find as I looked upward at the dark ceiling.

"I was mean to my mother."

There was a slight pause.

"How many times?" he asked me in a low, whispered voice.

I had to think quickly, because I really didn't know how many times I had pissed off my mother during my six years of life. She had often reviewed, during her screaming tangents, all of the horrible things I had done to her from the moment I was born.

But the exact number of times I had been mean to her escaped me.

"100 times?" I sheepishly replied. I figured a nice, round even number would sound best.

"All right," the priest replied. "Well, the Lord forgives you."

I felt so relieved.

"Now, as your penance, I want you to say six Hail Marys, six Our Fathers, and six Glory Bees, and now make a good Act of Contrition."

Sister Helen had already prepared me for this crucial moment, and I knew what memorized lines to repeat.

"Oh, my God, I am heartily sorry for having offended Thee. *And I detest all my sins because of Thy just punishments. But most of all because they offend Thee my God, who are all good and deserving of all of my love. I firmly resolve with the help of Thy grace to confess my sins, do penance, and amend my life. Amen*"

While I spoke these carefully memorized words, the priest once again, made the sign of the cross over me three times, as he spoke in Latin,

Indulgentiam, absolutionem et remissionem peccatorum tuorum tribuat tibi omnipotens et misericors Dominus. Amen.

My sins had been forgiven. I was so relieved to know that if I had died at that very moment, I would not be going to Hell.

I exited the confessional and wiped the little sweat beads from my forehead. Sister Helen was there to greet me. She embraced me clad in her black flowing robes. I was surrounded by black cloth and the warmth of her protection, as I burst into tears.

•••●●●•••

At Cleveland Elementary Public School, I was teased mercilessly by all of my classmates.

It was time for recess and the dreaded game of kickball out on the black, tarred playground. Donna Bailey, the tall, red-headed freckled daughter of the Mahoning County postmaster, and Paula Brody, the very mature-looking well developed daughter of a medical doctor, were usually the ones to form the two kickball teams.

Both teams had been selected with just one person—me—left over. That's when the two best friends, Donna and Paula, would engage in a little spat.

"Well, we don't want her on our team. We had her last time!"

"Well, we don't want her on our team, either! We picked first, so it's your turn. She belongs to you this time!"

"Nah. Huh! Not fair! She doesn't even know how to play kickball! Just look at her! She thinks she's a gypsy fortune teller! Look at all her jewelry

and 20 bracelets and ten necklaces and her long, ugly skirt and rings on all of her fingers. She's too weird! WE DON'T WANT TO PLAY WITH HER!"

"Well, just let her play this one stupid game," Vicky Carr chimed in, *"because I'm having a slumber party this weekend and everybody is invited -- except for her."*

The kids all laughed mockingly. The problem had been solved.

I ran off, crying. I went into the bathroom and gazed at my long, dark curly hair, my bangle bracelets, my colorful necklaces in the mirror. **They look pretty to me.** I liked my long, multi-colored skirt, my puffy sleeved blouse, my red sweater. My skirt looked like it had been made in Mexico. I thought it was beautiful. I sank inside a bathroom stall and talked with my special friends while sobbing. Large tear drops dropped down upon my fancy skirt.

"I think my outfit is beautiful, Virgin Mary. Don't you think so, too? Ask God and Jesus and Joseph if they think it's beautiful. Thank you for loving me. Thank you for adopting me."

[*IT'S SING ALONG TIME! "I WANNA THANK ALL THE KIDS!"*]

Soon, the school day was over and it was time to walk home with Freddie Williams. Freddie lived on the next block over in my neighborhood where the not-so-nice houses were located. He was one of six children. But it didn't matter to me that little Freddie

Williams was poor and wore tattered clothes and lived in a rickety house. Freddie liked me and he thought I was gorgeous!

We walked down Glenwood Avenue past the Foster Theatre and past the U.S. Post Office with our school books tucked under our arms and then we stopped inside our favorite candy store. I bought some tar babies and black licorice "records" -- black licorice strands wrapped in a circle with a red fire ball in the middle. Freddie purchased a Sugar Daddy candy pop and some clove gum. I still had ten cents left over, so I purchased some wax pop bottles with candy syrup inside and a couple of rolls of Life Savers.

We treasured our goodies and yakked about our favorite Popeye cartoons while skipping down the sidewalks, sharing our tasty, sweet treats.

Suddenly, some big kids, from out of nowhere, startled us and started to tease us. ***"What are you two, little kids doing with all that candy? You can't eat all that candy. Give it to us!"***

They started to kick and punch Freddie as one of them grabbed his Sugar Daddy candy pop.

"Run, Angie! Run! Just run home!" Freddie shouted to me.

I raised the hood on my coat and placed my hands back inside my furry hand muff. My skirt swooshed as I ran as fast as I could with my wool leggings tucked inside my galoshes. I ran, ran, ran as fast as I could and tried not to look back. Freddie was down on the ground and they were kicking him while laughing. I ran, ran, ran and tried not to fall on the slippery, icy sidewalks.

⋯•●•⋯

What a big, mansion house my mother took me to on Christmas Day. I had never been inside such a big house like this before with soft organ music playing in the background and flowers everywhere.

There were so many rooms. Everyone seemed so somber and quiet.

Ladies dressed in black wore their black pill box hats with the veils down.

It was Christmas Day, 1956, when I attended my first funeral. Little Freddie Williams was there; he looked asleep inside his white, satin lined casket, a Bible in his hands. He looked not real but perhaps just asleep; his puffy face and bloated arms made him look more like a mannequin. The mean kids had kicked him in the gut and busted his appendix. I stared at him inside the coffin. I *just knew* it wasn't real. If I stared at him long enough, it seemed like his chest was breathing.

"Freddie, wake up! I'm so sorry I left you! It's all my fault!"

My tear drops fell upon his perfect little pin striped suit. At last, Freddie was wearing such nice clothes.

⸺••●●●••⸺

You Are My Sunshine

Miss McGukken, our sixth grade teacher, always started the day with our class singing happy songs that she played on the big, old upright piano. Her favorite song was "My Sunshine" translated from an old, classic Italian folk song. My mother had taught me how to sing *"My Sunshine"* in Italian, *"O Solo Mio!"*

One day, while the kids were singing *"My Sunshine,"* I decided to sing it in Italian simultaneously. Miss McGukken stopped playing the piano and inquired, "Who is doing that?"

"It's me!" I said. "I know that song in Italian!

"Well, come on up to the front of the room and sing it for us!" she said.

The students, who relentlessly teased and tormented me for being the "weird girl," began to giggle.

And, so, there I was, "on stage," dressed up in my gypsy-style clothes, wailing out the lyrics to **"O Solo Mio"** with all of my heart!

Che bella cosa na jurnata 'e sole, n'aria serena doppo na tempesta!

The kids laughed hysterically, pointing at me, mocking me, as I belted out the lyrics.

Secretly, they were enjoying every minute of my performance. I realized that. And so I became a super star . . . in my own mind.

••●●●••

Back at home, my mother was preparing a second round of supper following our first large round of supper.

"Hun, heat up some leftovers!" my father shouted from his living room vibrating chair.

It didn't matter that the three of us had just finished a large meal that included mashed potatoes, pork roast, salad, and spaghetti.

The three of us enjoyed a pleasant evening of Lawrence Welk, salted peanuts, and warmed up leftovers.

"You want me to bring you a bowl of pistachio nuts, too?" my mother yelled from the kitchen.

"Yeah! And a bowl of ice cream!" my father relayed back. "Ang wants some butter pecan."

We sprawled out across the living room couch and watched TV with Dad. There was nothing tastier than leftovers, accompanied with plentiful slices of white bread and The Ed Sullivan show.

••●●●••

Down in the basement lived my paternal grandmother—not by choice, and not on the finished, knotty pine paneling side, that included real wine and my upright piano, a console TV, and a small vinyl record player.

No. Instead, "Nona" (my grandma) lived on the **real** cellar side with a damp cracked concrete floor and a coal furnace. She slept on a fold away cot between the wash tubs and the coal furnace. Clothes lines ran from east to west between the old Maytag washing machine and the big coal furnace.

How did this happen? How did my father's mother end up in the basement?

When I was six years old, my grandmother came to live with us. She had actually lived with us previously, up until I was three years old, but my grandmother and mother were jealous of each other. Each vied for my father's full attention. My mother, sick of the competition, had my grandmother declared "crazy" by her favorite doctor, and then my grandmother was transported to live in an insane asylum in southern Ohio called Massillon. Insane asylums were very wretched in those days. If you ever saw the movie **One Flew Over the CooCoo's Nest**, you'll have an idea.

Every time my parents went to Massillon to visit my grandmother, my mother felt guilty. She said the place was like a prison, with naked, crazy people roaming around behind bars in a large, damp cellar-like room. My grandmother begged to be freed from Massillon, so finally my father listened and brought her to live with us again when I was six years old.

For a few weeks, she shared my bedroom with me, but the two women battled every day. It really irritated my mother that my grandmother called her son "**Carina**," (my dear one, my beloved one), and so my mother banned my grandmother to the basement.

On Monday mornings, my mother would rise at 5 a.m. and go down into the basement to wash all of our clothes. She didn't believe in using a clothes dryer because she strongly felt that the modern day dryers of the 1960s tend to shrink and ruin the clothes. Instead, she would use a large sawed off broom handle to move the clothes through the wringers on her old, sturdy Maytag washer.

Next, the dripping wet clothes would be hung from one side of the basement to the other, from the wash tubs to the furnace.

Back upstairs, my mother would start preparing coffee in her percolator, scrambled eggs in her cast iron skillet, white toast with margarine, and, of course, fried bacon strips. Soon, I would awaken, but not from the smells or sounds in the kitchen. It was the sounds echoing from the heat register on my bedroom wall.

WHAT ARE YOU DOING!!!? WHAT ARE YOU DOING!!? WHAT HAVE YOU DONE!!? WHAT HAVE YOU DONE!!?

I could hear the sounds of items slamming and being pushed around in the basement. I would awaken with my heart racing.

"HOW MANY TIMES HAVE I TOLD YOU TO LEAVE THE CLOTHES ALONE!!!!?" How many times!!!? HOW MANY TIMES HAVE I TOLD YOU!!!?"

My mother enjoyed being repetitive to get her point across completely.

"Oh, Dio, oh, Dio! Leschme sta!" ("Oh, God, oh, God, leave me alone!") my grandmother would yell.

"I SWEAR TO GOD I'M GOING TO KILL YOU ONE OF THESE DAYS! WHY DO YOU ALWAYS DO THIS TO ME!!!?" my mother would retort.

The two of them would not stop screaming at each other until my father came downstairs to break up the predictable fight. He would order my mother back upstairs.

"What's going on here!? Louise, go upstairs!"

My grandmother had rearranged the clothes on the clothes lines once again, so that her flowered, cotton dresses would dry faster, next to the coal furnace. She always made sure that any clothes bordering her own belonged only to her beloved son, her **carina**.

"Louise, go upstairs!"

Each woman shouted her side of what had happened. It was the same story, every week, every Monday morning.

"I told her **not** to rearrange the clothes on the lines!"

Their voices were rather hysterical and my mother did not comply and return up the stairs until she had THE LAST WORD. The final word.

My mother *always* had the last word.

"You want to rearrange these clothes?? Then fine!!! Rearrange THIS!"

And with that one last sentence spoken, my mother would go over to my grandmother's little chest of drawers and fling out all of her clothes items, including her neatly folded house dresses, her bras, the rags she stuffed inside her bras, and even her underwear.

She flung her little wardrobe of tattered cotton dresses, underwear, and rags used for stuffing bras, and scattered them all over the soaking wet basement concrete floor.

It took several long hours for my grandmother, crippled by arthritis from years of living in a damp basement, to pick up, one by one, all of the clothes items, fold them, and put them neatly back into the little drawers.

••●●●••

It was my duty, as a child, to take a supper plate of food into the basement for my grandmother. I would oftentimes catch her writing on a piece of cardboard from the back of a used notebook with only her index finger.

I often wondered what the invisible words said on the piece of cardboard.

"Nona! Why are you writing with your finger on that cardboard?"

Startled that I had surreptitiously tip-toed down the basement stairs and was now behind her, my grandmother would reply, ***"Oh, Anja, I writa to God that he getta me outta thisa base – a - ment."***

Nona was my best friend. I used to go into the basement and tell her all about my adventures at school. Things I could never tell my parents, like my first kiss, my clandestine meeting with Jack McVey at the basketball court, the time we snuck off to see an Elvis Presley movie.

"That's a-nice, Ang."

It didn't matter that she didn't really understand most of what I was telling her.

She was my confidante, my friend. I'd pet my kitty cat, Bummy, in my lap as I watched her stitch by hand, square by square, all of the little pieces of leftover, unwanted fabric that my mother had thrown into the waste can. Square by little square, and soon there was another little blanket to put on top of her shivering, slender body on that little fold away cot in the basement.

•‑•●◉●•‑•

On Sundays, my mother would barge into my bedroom and announce, ***"Ang! Get up! It's time to get ready for Catholic mass!*** We'd sit near the front pew and my mother would always whisper in my ear, disparagingly commenting on other women's tacky outfits and their obesity.

"Ang, look at that fatty over there! Ha! Ha! Ha!!!! How do people let themselves get that fat? I bet she'd like to eat that whole cup of communion wafers. Ha! Ha! Ha!!!!!" My mother herself was a size 20.

I would clasp my hands over my mouth to keep from giggling too much. Mom was quite a comedienne at times.

When the communion boy would place the gold plate under people's chins at the communion rail, my mother would also crack up. It always gave her such a good belly laugh to watch people kneeling with their hands folded and their tongues hanging out. My mother and I would sometimes get on such a belly roll that my father would shoot us daggers and poke me in the side.

"Shhh! The Holy Father is watching you. You'd better shut up! Both of you!"

••●●●••

In 1962, my parents decided that it was best to send me to Catholic school. I had never attended Catholic school before – only Catholic Sunday school, Catechism.

During weekdays, there was that memorable, long dreaded ride to St. Dominic's Catholic school. We'd stop on Glenwood Avenue and watch the gasoline price wars on the two corners. "Yesterday, the gas was 24.9 cents a gallon at Gastown; today, it's back up to 25.9." my mother would lament, a tone of disgust in her voice.

"If gas gets any higher, Ang, I don't think we'll be able to afford Catholic school for you. You might have to go back to public school."

Some days, depending upon my mother's whimsical mood, the car ride was very long and tortuous; my mother might be on a tangent, reviewing, in screaming mode, all the "crimes" I had committed against her since the moment I had been born.

"I still remember the time when you were 10 years old and you locked yourself in your bedroom with your girlfriend, Geri, and the two of you were listening to music on your record player I had just bought you, and you wouldn't let me into the room!"

My mom reached over and pulled my long hair. **"How dare you! How dare you do that to me!!!"**

My "crime" of not allowing her into the bedroom had taken place more than five years earlier, but she spoke of it as if it had just happened.

"I feed you! I wash your clothes! I buy you beautiful clothes all the time, and you couldn't even (~WHACK~) allow me into the bedroom, you ungrateful little bitch!

She would rip a handful of hair out of my scalp and throw it out of the car window.

I actually felt nothing. I was used to having my hair pulled, and I had trained myself to feel nothing.

****

My Catholic School Crimes

According to an online dictionary, a **crime** is "an action or illegal activity that is considered to be evil, shameful, or wrong."

The first time I was accused of committing a "crime" I didn't actually commit was during my first week of Catholic school. Little did I know, it would become a recurrent theme in my life.

As an adult, I asked Bernard at the photocopy store where I frequently went to run off the latest batch of court papers. Bernard was just one of a dozen people I would share my exasperating litigious ongoings with.

"Why do weird things always happen to me?" I asked him.

"Because you're a freak magnet!" he quickly replied, with a chuckle.

Those five words probably explain the course of my life -- my twisted, amusing life -- best of all.

Anyways . . .

It was September 1962, and I had just been enrolled by my parents into Catholic school, after spending my first six years of education in public school.

My parents had decided to enroll me in Catholic school, hoping I'd grow up to be a nun, and to . . . protect my virginity. Unknown to me, I didn't even know I owned a vagina. My mother had told me that God plants a seed in your stomach when you fall sleep next to a man, and that's how babies develop and are born. I believed her. One time, at a basketball game with my father, I kept slapping myself awake. There was a man seated next to me, and I didn't want to end up pregnant.

During my first week in Catholic school, I was suddenly approached by a stern-looking nun who ushered me into a large, empty room.

"Come with me!" she ordered me, pushing me with one strong hand that seemed glued to my back.

She opened the door to a large room. Inside, there were several nuns clad in their penguin-style outfits, along with a few priests. They were all seated in hard wooden folding chairs around in a circle. I was ushered into the center and commanded to be seated. Was this the Inquisition?

Suddenly, one of the other nuns stepped forward and handed me some instant Polaroid photos.

"***Why did you do this***?!" she asked sternly, while pointing harshly at the photos. The rest of the sanctimonious onlookers glared at me with severe scowls.

I glanced down at the photos, scratched my head, shrugged my shoulders, and then looked back up at my accusers, confused.

Apparently, some mischievous kid (but not me) had sprayed painted in all capital letters the word "FUCK" on the side of St. Dominic's Catholic Church.

"We have questioned several of the children and they all say YOU, the new girl, are the one responsible for this obscene act!" Father O'Connolly declared.

"Well, I didn't do that!" I replied, pointing at the woeful photos.

White spray paint dripped down from every letter on huge stone blocks on the side of the holy church. F-U-C-K. "I wouldn't even know where to buy spray paint!"

"And I don't even know what that word means!" I added.

I looked at the word again.

"F-U-C-K."

"What does it mean?"

My pious prosecutors shifted uncomfortably in their wooden chairs. "Certainly, you must know that this is a very bad word. A very, very bad, bad word," one nun reiterated.

"Well, I don't! And I didn't do it!" I stated, tears flowing down my cheeks.

Welcome to Catholic school.

This wasn't the first incident in which I was chastised, falsely accused, and summoned to "court."

Just a few days earlier, when Sister Alberta, our homeroom teacher, had left the room to talk with another teacher, all of the kids started chatting. Her anger was apparent. In fact, she was furious. I had never before witnessed a teacher so apparently enraged over children talking.

She charged back into the classroom, her black headpiece flowing like wings on a large bat.

"How many times have I told all of you NOT to talk when I leave the room?!" she shouted, slamming the palm of her hand on the desk.

The class went instantly silent.

"Okay, that's it!" she said, exasperated. "Every one of you, take out 20 sheets of paper right now, and write 'I will not talk when Sister Alberta leaves the room -- **500 times!**"

There was a sudden loud groan from all of the students, but soon everyone was busy writing.

I sat there at my desk, not knowing exactly what to do.

I leaned to my right and whispered to the boy seated next to me. "What are we supposed to do?"

He held up his paper and showed me. "You have to write 500 times 'I will not talk when Sister Alberta leaves the room.'"

I had never seen such a punishment before. It seemed odd and tedious to me in my 12-year-old mind. I thought to myself. "Hmm. These Catholic school kids must have never learned how to do dittoes." And so, I took 20 sheets of loose notebook paper and wrote one time on the top line of each sheet, 'I will not talk when Sister Alberta leaves the room.' And then on the other 24 lines, I wrote dittoes.

Ditto.

Ditto.

Ditto.

Soon, I was proudly finished with the task, chuckling inside at my cleverness, and so I put the 20 pages aside and started working on my history homework.

The boy next to me glanced at me, and then looked curious.

"What are you doing?" he inquired.

"I'm doing my homework!" I proudly replied. "I'm all finished with that stupid task!" I held up the 20 sheets of papers, covered in dittoes, and showed him.

All of the other students were still writing, writing, their hands cramping up. They were flinging their hands in the air and twisting their wrists to relieve the aches. Certainly, I had no such aches!

The boy gazed at the dittoes and then openly laughed very heartily.

"What's going on back there?" Sister Alberta inquired in a stern voice.

He looked up at the Sister teacher, still chuckling, and replied, "The new girl wrote dittoes instead of doing the punishment!"

All of the amused children started laughing and peering in my direction.

Sister Alberta frowned boldly and crooked one finger at me. "Come up here right now with your papers. Let me see what you did."

I walked to the front of the room, clutching the papers to my chest, my heart beating rapidly. Sister Alberta grabbed the papers from me and quickly glanced at each page.

"Humph! So, you are mocking me!? You are mocking this assignment?"

"Oh, no!" I protested. "I thought I was saving time!" Large tears began rolling down my frightened, flushed cheeks.

"Well, you think you're so smart! When you go home tonight, I want you to write **one thousand times** 'I will not talk when Sister Alberta leaves the room!'

The children squealed in delight. Mortified, I slithered back to my desk without looking at anybody.*

[Footnote: *The Ditto Story is actually one of my fondest memories of my parents. The three of us sat on the living room that night. My parents each forged my signature repeatedly, as we each wrote "I will not talk when Sister Alberta leaves the room" hundreds of times. My parents saved me that night, and as they scribbled that monotonous sentence over and over, I was able to complete tons of Catholic homework until I finally hit the sack, exhausted, at about 1 a.m. We were all exhausted. Thank you, Mom and Dad.]

Just a few days previously, my mother had been phoned by Sister Mercedes, the school principal. "Mrs. Falvo, please come pick up your daughter and take her home!"

I sat in an office chair, waiting for my mother to come get me.

I didn't know what "crime" I had committed, but when my mother arrived, the nuns told her. "Your daughter is very talkative and is always befriending the boys, especially out on the playground. Today, she is wearing a red sweater with matching red socks!"

"Yes, I see that. But what is the problem?" my mother inquired.

"She is letting the boys know she has started her period!" the principal announced, with utmost certainty. This was news to me.

My mother looked at me in shock, and then slapped me hard across the face. "Get in the car!" she ordered me.

"Make sure she does not come back to school wearing a red sweater with red socks."

"I certainly will!" my mother curtly replied.

I tried to protest in the car, but my mother slapped me hard again and pulled my hair. "Shut up!"

"You little bitch! You whore!"

A swift blow to the head as my mother screeched to a stop at the traffic light.

I was frequently called a "bitch" and a "whore" by my mother throughout my entire childhood.

The following day, still curious from my original ordeal, I whispered to Sharon Grice, the Colored Girl who sat behind me (the only Colored Girl in Catholic school, and my only friend), "What does FUCK mean?"

"You don't know?" she whispered back, surprised.

I shook my head. "No."

"I'll draw you a picture," she whispered.

Soon, she snuck me a folded-up piece of paper. I surreptitiously unfolded it and took a look. She had drawn two childish stick figures – a naked boy, penis-less, with a very large curly smile on his face, lying prone on top of a naked girl who also had a very large curly smile on her face.

"**Now** do you understand?" Sharon whispered.

"Uh-huh!" I nodded.

And for many years thereafter, I thought that "fuck" meant two people get naked, and one lies on top of the other and they both smile.

———————— ••●●•• ————————

I had my own fantasy world inside my bedroom that kept me going during those tumultuous, sad childhood years. Despite my tormentors accusing me of crimes I did not even understand, despite my mother frequently beating me during her bouts of rage, I remained a jovial child who wrote jokes and poems and danced in the privacy of my bedroom with my best and only friend, my beloved cat, Bummy.

It didn't matter that I was singled out for crimes I hadn't committed because I knew that someday – I didn't know how or when or for what – I would become famous.

Bummy and I danced together and sang songs. We wrote poems and created a joke book. We read **MAD** Magazine. **MAD** Magazine was my daily inspiration for my own stories and poems, and I always laughed when I saw Alfred E. Newman with his dufus toothless smile asking, "What? Me worry?"

We drew pictures together. And when I was crying, Bummy would curl up in my lap on the bed and purr loudly. Bummy was my best friend in the whole world.

My other friends were Jesus, Mary, and Joseph. I frequently took long walks alone in Mill Creek Park near my home and would bring back wild flowers for my alter to the Virgin Mary. I talked to them. "Hello, Jesus, Mary, and Joseph! You are my *real* family, and I am having a happy day because of your love for me! Here are some fresh flowers for you, Virgin Mary!" A kiss on my fingertip and then I touched her statue that was placed in the cardboard box I used as her alter.

I petted Bummy and told him, "They can be mean to me, but I will be famous some day!"

I just *knew* that I was meant to be famous!

———————— ••❸ ❸•• ————————

Soon, it would be summertime and I would have the very best time of my life. My parents owned the pizza stand and the basketball stand at Idora Park, the summer amusement park in Youngstown, Ohio. I operated my parents' basketball stand starting at the age of nine.

My father handed me a basketball and said, "Ang, call in the crowds."

When I was nine years old, I didn't have to work all day long at the basketball stand. Ruthie Bugno, our employee, would relieve me—and that's when the fun would begin. All the rides, all the games, and all the junk food and cotton candy was mine for free. I was the little princess of the amusement park.

I'd approach a ride operator. "Can I ride the Merry-Go-Round? I don't have a ticket, but my parents own the pizza stand!"

The carnie, covered in tattoos with deep creases on his face, looked at me and replied, "Oh, yeah! You're the Falvo girl! Go ahead! Hop on! You don't need a ticket!"

There was a woman, Betty Pattison, who ran the cork gun game booth. One day, I was passing her game booth when she asked if I could pick up the corks from her game guns that had sprung off the targets and landed onto the midway. ***"Sure!"*** I stated. And that was the beginning of our splendid friendship.

There was a moving target with a rotating bull's eye. She'd load up the tip of the air rifle with a cork, and customers would shoot at the moving target in hopes of winning a souvenir.

Her get-up was quite flashy and very typical for the Sixties era. I thought she was absolutely gorgeous!

Every day, she wore a different, colorful paisley muumuu, and each day, she had a different color theme. On Mondays, she wore all blue – a blue bouffant wig, with matching blue nail polish, blue eye shadow, and a blue plastic cigarette holder that dangled from the corner of her mouth. On Tuesdays, everything was matching in pink. Pink wig, pink eye shadow, pink nail polish, pink cigarette holder. On Wednesdays, everything was chartreuse green, and so on.

On her lunch breaks, she'd walk her pet skunk with a rhinestone collar that she kept on a leash down the midway.

I told her, "I want to look like you when I grow up! I will be famous someday!"

She smiled and wrote in my joke book, "I will always be your friend, until the kitchen sinks and Niagara falls. Love, Betty."

At night, after Idora Park closed . . .

I remember spending many a hot summer's nights sitting down on the living room floor counting pennies, nickels, dimes, and quarters with my mother and father, rolling them into little spool-shaped paper bank wrappers.

"If you find an old Indian head nickel or a Liberty head dime, Ang, put 'em in this separate pile."

The electric fans would be cranked up full blast from both ends of the living room, but still it was hot. **HOT.** My mother would go into the bathroom and get wet wash rags for all of us to place on our arms and heads. All of the windows in the entire house were rolled open. I'd hear the sound of the crickets out in the front yard. We'd sit there on that living room floor for hours at a time, TV flickering in the background, counting those pennies and rolling them into the brown paper wrappers. One hundred pennies later, another dollar had been stacked into the dollar pile.

If my parents had been able to look into a crystal ball that read

"About 50 years from now, when you have amassed more than one million dollars, this money will all end up in the pockets of crooked Orlando-based attorneys within a few months. Your daughter, your sole heir, will never see a penny of it."

Would my parents have believed it?

My father greatly believed in **The American Way**.

My Father's Mottos

"Teachers are noble" was my father's first motto. Mr. Carl Falvo, junior high math teacher, was living proof. His photo had appeared many times in the ***Youngstown Vindicator*** with his students, first place winners of the Mahoning County math bees.

"Don't cheat the Internal Revenue Service." he used to tell me. I didn't even really understand what the Internal Revenue Service was.

But Dad knew this slogan better than anyone. He had worked as an auditor for the IRS in Cleveland, Ohio during the 1950s. He knew the tax laws, had also worked for H & R Block, and was good at keeping abreast of the legal tax loopholes. But don't commit fraud against the IRS. Take your legal deductions and then pay your fair share. That was his motto.

"The government cares about us."

My parents were staunch Democrats. They believed firmly that all politicians—from the time of Franklin Delano Roosevelt on – along with all police officers, and all judges were looking out for our welfare. If any scoundrel committed a misdeed, the courts would certainly bring about justice. If anyone ever stole their money, the courts would most certainly adjudicate the situation fairly and squarely.

"Attorneys look out for their clients."

That was another one of my father's true beliefs.

We sat there on the living room floor with our bowls of ice cream and our bags of pistachio nuts, nibbling on our treats as we rolled the pennies, nickels, and dimes, catching glimpses of performers on Ed Sullivan. The Great USA was providing a system that would carry us through for many decades to come. Between stock investments, money markets, CDs, and government bonds, these pennies, nickels, and dimes would someday add up to more than a million dollars.

••●⬤●••

My Mother's Secret/My Secret

No one knew our little secret. I could be down on the floor, my face twisted into the carpet, my back being punched and my hair being pulled, when suddenly the telephone would ring. My mother would pick herself up off of my slender, aching body and answer the phone in the sweetest, melodic tones.

"Oh, HI, Helen! How nice to hear from you!! Oh, no, you're not interrupting anything. I was just sitting here watching the Price is Right with Ang. So, what's new with you?"

I would pick myself up off the floor, my heart pounding, and carry myself into my bedroom, without shedding a tear.

"Where is Bummy? Oh, here he is on my bed, my sweet kitty cat."

I would place him on my lap and stroke his back as I rocked my body back and forth, listening to my mother on the telephone in the hallway.

"Have we ever vacationed in Washington, D.C.? Oh, yes, it's such a lovely place! So many nice things to see and do! Carl wants us to take another trip down there during the cherry blossom season. Ang loves it there! Have you ever been to Washington, D.C., Helen? You should go see the Smithsonian!"

I'd take my Fuller brush and run it through my long, knotted hair. Getting all of the tangles out took awhile, but it didn't matter. I had a purring kitty on my lap.

Soon Dad would be home, and when he'd ask, *"So, how was your day, Pudge?"* I'd tell him all about school and the new math I'd learned. Perhaps we'd solve math problems in our heads while eating supper.

"What's two minus six plus ten divided by two, take away seven . . . ."

I just loved playing those math games with my father.

"Ang, you want some more mashed potatoes?"

"Sure, Mom, thanks."

"Make sure you help your mother with the dishes tonight, Ang. She worked so hard to prepare this nice meal." my father would state. He had no idea that she had just been pummeling my back and pulling my hair in between mashing the potatoes.

"Your mother is too good to you."

My mother would suddenly approach me with a kiss on my cheek, and gently stroke my hair when my father was around. There was a small black and white TV perched on the corner of the dining room table. President Kennedy on the news.

"How good looking he is! If I wasn't already married, I'd go after that man!" my mother would say, and my parents would chuckle.

<hr>

Dr. Garritano

It was time for another dreaded visit to Dr. Garritano's office. As I sat in the waiting room, my mother who was seated next to me, stroked my forehead and clasped my hands. *"Oh, Ang, I'm so worried about you!"* she stated in tones loud enough for other waiting room visitors to peek over their magazines and glance at us. *"All of these expensive visits to the doctor! And nothing! They can't find anything wrong with you! Why are you <u>always</u> sick? Maybe it's because you've started having periods?"* she announced in a loud tone.

"Mom, <u>stop!</u>" I whispered in an irritated voice, shifting my body away from her and removing my hands from her hand.

For the entire summer of 1963, I was ravished with severe abdominal cramps that felt like razor blades piercing my lower stomach. The pains frequently appeared after eating a meal, but they were intermittent and unpredictable.

I *detested* being ill—not so much because of the sickness itself—illness can be overcome-- but primarily because my mother absolutely *adored* when I was ill and turned any infirmity—no matter how minor-- into a major catastrophe. Whenever I contracted even the slightest symptoms of a cold or even just something as minor as a paper cut to a finger, my mother would literally fall to pieces, frequently feigning tears and then spend hours on the phone with her friends, *"I'm sorry you haven't heard from me lately but Ang has been soooooo sick lately and I've had to drop everything that I was doing just to take care of her."*

"Oh, you are such a <u>wonderful</u> mother! You are so devoted to your child!" my mother's friends would say. Unlike me, a loner, and bullied at school, my mother was so popular.

She would frequently barge into my bedroom when I was forced to stay home from school for the smallest and most trivial of ailments. I was doted upon obsessively to the point of "ad nauseum."

I was served on a silver tray in my bedroom with warm tea with milk, accompanied with buttered rye toast and a peeled orange. A half hour later, my mother would be back in my bedroom with a glass thermometer to insert under my tongue, perhaps a cup of warm cocoa, a wet wash rag draped across my forehead, a heating pad under my back, Alka-Seltzer, a tablespoon of Pepto-Bismol, a bowl of tomato soup, a couple of St. Joseph baby aspirins, and each intrusion into my bedroom would be accompanied with the most dire tones in her voice, and a look upon her face as though at any moment I would be taking my last breath. There was always that furrowed brow, the quivering voice,

"Ang, are you okaaay? Do you think we should take you to the hospital?" Until finally, out of extreme exasperation I would yell, *"I will feel better when you stop bothering me! <u>Just get out of my room</u>! Leave me <u>alone</u>!!"*

Mother exited in tears and immediately dialed her friends sobbing to them about the rejection she just received for taking care of me.

"She just treated me like I was some type of criminal! And all I did was bring her a cup of tea!"

"That's AWFUL, Louise! You have such an ungrateful daughter! She should be spanked! Or take away some of her beautiful clothes. Teach her a lesson! Louise, you are such a saint!"

Now, here I was, back in Dr. Garritano's waiting room and not looking forward to seeing him. Every time we saw him, it was like Murphy's Law. The stabbing pains in my abdomen were not present. And he did not like me based upon what my mother had told him in the past.

"From what I see, she's just a spoiled brat, Louise. You should just take her home and spank her."

Dr. Garritano was agreeing with my mother's analysis. The pains were not real; I was just a rotten child.

"But I'm going to go ahead and schedule a week's worth of examinations at St. Elizabeth's hospital. We'll give your daughter every imaginable type of test there is and see if there is anything genuinely wrong."

During the week in which I was admitted to St. Elizabeth's hospital, I was given an EEG exam to determine if I suffer from Epileptic seizures (negative), a Barium colon test, in which I was forced to drink a chalk-like substance while my digestive track was x-rayed (negative), and I was even scheduled for a test in which water was supposed to be flushed through my bowels to determine if there was any type of obstruction. However, I did not wish to have a hose placed up my rectum and when the nurse tried to insert it, I dug my long nails into her hand.

Soon, I was back in Dr. Garritano's office and between his reading the nurse's notes about the nail digging incident and the aborted test, and his viewing the various lab results, he was more adamant in his negative opinion of me than ever before.

"As I stated previously, there is nothing, absolutely nothing, wrong with your daughter. As far as I can see, she is simply a very spoiled, ungrateful child. If I were you, I'd take her home and spank her until her bottom was very, very red."

A few days later, we had just finished eating a late meal at Scarsella's Restaurant on Midlothian Boulevard when, during the ride home, the lower abdominal pains came upon me in such a severe fashion that I thought I was going to die. I doubled up in the back seat of the car, writhing in pain and begged to be taken to the emergency room.

"Oh, don't even listen to her, Hun. The doctor said she's just a spoiled brat."

"Angie, stop faking that you're sick before I slap you!"

"But, Mom, I really AM sick! I'm in so much pain! Please take me to the hospital!"

My mother turned around and slapped me hard across the face, fire in her eyes.

Large tears rolled down upon my cheeks and I wept hysterically while still doubled up in pain. **"Make sure you give my cat, Bummy, to a good home when I die. And give all my pretty clothes to Gloria, okay? I'm dying, Mommy! I'M REALLY DYING!!"**

For some reason, my father tended to believe me and he decided to go ahead and drive to St. Elizabeth's emergency room, despite my mother's protests.

Soon, while I was still doubled up in excruciating pain, the doctor on call examined me. He pressed on my lower abdomen while inserting a hand inside. The examination took less than one minute.

"Your daughter's appendix is about to burst. We need to perform an emergency appendectomy ."

Within a few minutes, a gas mask was placed over my face and then I was unconscious. If not for my insistence that evening and my father believing me, I would have undoubtedly ended up like Freddie Williams.

⸺⸺⸺ ••●●•• ⸺⸺⸺

Grandma-In-The-Basement—The Last Day

In the summer of 1968, late one evening, my parents and I returned home after eating a midnight meal at a restaurant. We mostly always went out for supper after Idora Park closed at midnight.

Upon our return to our home on Dover Road, my mother went down into the basement to take a piece of meat out of the freezer so it could thaw overnight for the next day's meal.

We found my grandmother running around in circles, disoriented. There were large piles of loose fecal matter dropped all over the basement floor. My grandmother's face was twisted on the left side and her left arm seemed to dangle down, lifelessly.

My mother looked at the piles of fecal matter on the floor on the tiled side of the basement and became immediately enraged.

"WHAT HAVE YOU DONE TO ME!? WHY DID YOU SHIT ALL OVER THE FLOOR!!!? YOU DID THIS JUST TO GET EVEN WITH ME, YOU BITCH!"

She struck my grandmother across the head.

My grandmother wobbled a little, but managed to stay on her feet. She attempted to speak but no words could be uttered from her quivering lips.

My mother's tirade continued. **_"YOU'D BETTER CLEAN UP THIS SHIT RIGHT NOW. DO YOU UNDERSTAND ME!?"_**

My grandmother did her best to comply, even though she was wobbling and acting as if she were drunk. I was 17 and I had never witnessed such a thing before. I had no idea what it meant.

Despite her twisted face and inability to speak or move her left arm, my grandmother wobbled into the basement bathroom and unrolled several feet of toilet paper, then returned and did her best to painfully stoop down and clean up the mess, her hands quivering.

The next day, my grandmother, who had suffered a stroke, was removed to a nursing home where she died four years later. My grandmother's cardboard finger prayers had finally been answered.

⸺⸺⸺⸺•◦●◦•⸺⸺⸺⸺

CHAPTER TWO

Back in Time: My Mother's Twisted Childhood

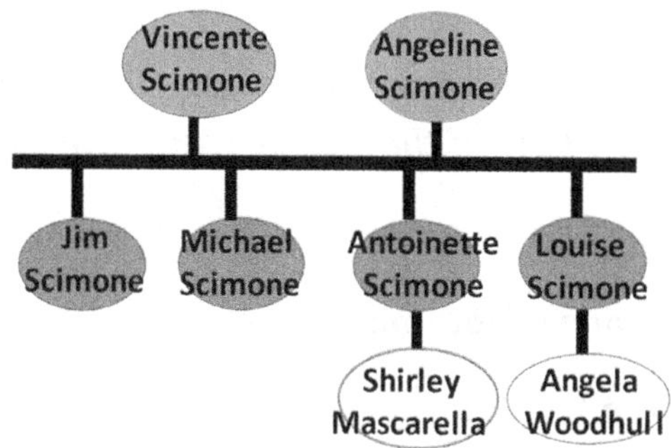

Snuggled in a lumpy cotton bed next to her sister, clutching her one and only doll . . . suddenly, it was time to leave again.

"Get up! Get up! Let's go! We have to get out of here right now!" her mother would whisper in loud, frantic tones.

"There's no time to gather anything. Your brothers are already inside the truck. We have to go!"

Two sleepy little girls rubbing their eyes in the middle of the night, barefoot, clad only in their cotton nightgowns. But Louise always clutched that one, special doll.

"Hurry! Hurry! Get into the back of the truck!"

Papa was there to lift them ever so high into the old, dilapidated pick- up truck. Mama hurriedly threw some blankets over the four of them, then quickly entered the front passenger seat. Vincent Scimone, with his family at his side, started the loud, diesel engine and away they sped in the middle of the chilly night, brothers on one side, and the two sisters on the other, not a word spoken as the noisy, old jalopy truck bumped down the back roads.

Louise looked up at the night sky and clutched her doll to her breast.

Time to move again. Time to move again. Move again.

A little tear drop rolled down her cheek. ***I wish we could have snuck the cat in the back of the pick-up truck with us this time.***

"Yeah, me too," her sister Antoinette said, squeezing her hand.

"I hope someone adopts him," Louise said.

"I hope so, too."

Louise closed her eyes and placed her head on her big sister's shoulder.

The boys, Jim and Mike, rested their heads together and closed their eyes. It was time for another long journey. Where would they end up this time? Kentucky? Pennsylvania? Indiana? West Virginia? Ohio?

They had never lived in Ohio before.

A large bump in the road jolted the children awake.

Michael sighed heavily and looked up at the stars.

"I wish Papa had never killed a man in Italy," Michael stated.

"Then we wouldn't have to be moving all of the time when the bad men find us."

"How do you know Papa really killed a man?" Antoinette inquired.

"Papa says he never did it!"

"I KNOW he did it!" Jim, the oldest, stated. *"Look what he does to us! Strappin' Mike and me in chairs up in the hot attic with no food or water! That son of a bitch should die. I hate him. You hate him, too, don't you?*

"Sometimes," Michael replied. *"But last week he bought us a new saw and that big, new hammer. Pop teaches us a lot of stuff."*

"God will take care of us," Antoinette said. *"And God says you're not supposed to hate your father."*

"There is no goddamn god!" Jim, the oldest, declared with utmost certainty, turning his head away and looking down the old road.

Mama, inside the truck, clutched her rosary beads and made the sign of the cross. Dawn was approaching and she squinted her eyes to read the sign just up ahead on the dusty, bumpy road.

"Welcome to Ohio."

THE HAMMER

High up on the hill on Mable Street overlooking the smoke stacks of the steel mills stood Vincente Scimone's house, a simple wooden bungalow with a plethora of fruit trees and a lush fresh garden in the back yard. Vincente and his two sons had built onto the back of the house to include an efficiency apartment. In the cellar, Vincente had built large tubs where he crushed grapes with his bare feet to produce his own moonshine. Life in Youngstown, Ohio had been pretty good. The steel mills provided thousands of jobs for the newly arrived immigrants so that plenty of people could hire Scimone and Sons to build cabinets, hang wall paper, and paint.

On Sundays, the family took a break from their business after Angeline prepared a nice Sunday dinner of fresh spaghetti with homemade tomato sauce with a side of chicken. Papa, on the piano, sang loudly while chugging down swigs of moonshine from a large wine bottle. The children and Angeline played along on their guitars, and as long as Papa didn't get too drunk, a good time was had by all.

But there were times when the music jams were cut short. Something caught Papa's attention out of the corner of his left eye. He abruptly stopped playing Italian tunes on the piano.

"Hey, woman, who are you looking at?"

"I'm not looking at anyone, Vincente!"

"Yes, you did! I saw you get up and look out that window!"

"I was just straightening the curtain!"

Vincente Scimone slammed down the piano lid, staggered to his feet, and slapped his wife hard across the face.

"Don't lie to me, woman! I saw the man out there. You gave him a signal, didn't you!?"

"What are you talking about?! You sound crazy!"

"You want him to know that I'll soon be asleep because I'm drunk!"

"Vincente, you sound crazy right now! You should lie down!"

Angeline began to usher the children out of the living room.

"Don't you leave this room when I'm talking to you, woman. Who's that man outside!? Who's the man of this house!? I'm the man of this house!"

He picked up a nearby hammer and hurled it at his wife, striking her in the back of her head. Down she went onto the floor and the children gasped and knelt down to assist her. She was not breathing.

Vincente, suddenly sober and horrified, fled the room and hurriedly departed in his pick-up truck.

"Antoinette and Louise! Hurry! Go down the street and get the neighbors! Tell them to come here fast!!" Jim declared.

The two little girls ran as fast as they could and knocked on the neighbor's door.

"Mama is hurt! She's down on the floor and not breathing! Papa hit her with a hammer in her head!"

Soon, an ambulance arrived. Angeline was rushed to the hospital and the four children spent the night in the Mabel Street house alone.

Jim lit kerosene lamps all over the house so that his brother and two sisters would not be afraid in the dark.

"I think we should pray!" Antoinette stated.

"There is no goddamn god!" Jim retorted. *"If there were a goddamn god, he wouldn't let this goddamn happen!"*

"Well, I'm going to pray for Mama anyway!" Antoinette cried.

Down on their knees in a circle, holding hands, on the living room floor, Mike, Antoinette, and Louise prayed.

"Dear Jesus, Joseph, and Mary, please make our mother stay alive!"

It was the summer of 1956 when Angeline Scimone passed away. She did not die from the blow of the hammer to the back of her head. No. She had survived more than fifty more years of beatings and bruisings, chokings, and being shoved to the floor. She had ironed his shirts, washed his clothes, and cooked thousands of meals for him and their four children. And now Vincente Scimone sat alone in his Mable Street home and could not stop weeping.

"She was my angel! My saint! Dear God, why did you take her away from me?!"

Vincente fell to the floor and wept the whole night long.

In the summer of 1961, Louise Falvo received a call from the Mahoning County sheriff's department in the middle of the night.

"Could you please come down to the morgue immediately? We need you to identify your father. One of the neighbors heard a disturbance at 1010 Mabel Street and called our department. Your father was found dead on arrival on his back steps with a severe gash to his head."

Louise quickly dialed her oldest brother, Jim, and together, the two of them proceeded to the morgue.

Down at the morgue, they lifted the white sheet off of the body.

"Yes, that is our father, Vincente Scimone," Louise stated, as Jim looked on, nonchalantly, apathetically.

"Well, Pa, it looks like they finally got you." Jim snickered.

Chapter THREE – 1950s & 1960s
A Tumultuous Marriage

It wasn't that Louise and Carl Falvo fought a lot. It was more that they had never learned how to get along. Both of them, hot tempered and opinionated, each wanted to be right. Louise learned that the best way to win an argument was to shout and scream until her opponent was worn out. As long as she could have **The Last Word**, she knew she had won the war.

But Carl had even a deadlier way of winning an argument.

Silence.

Silence is the deadliest of all weapons.

Carl, alone in his office in the spare bedroom, working on IRS tax forms, tabulating his earnings for the year, calculating his profits and losses. Alone in his bedroom office with the door locked. Classical music from WFMJ played in the background.

Two weeks passed.

"I can't take it any longer, Angie. Go into your father's office and ask your father if he'd like something to eat."

Little Angie dutifully knocked on the door.

"Dad, Mom wants to know if you want something to eat."

The door opened and Carl Falvo appeared, a pen and paper in his hand.

Louise, in the hallway, looked down at the floor, as though her husband was invisible.

And then my father walked into the living room where he resumed his position in his reclining, vibrating chair.

Louise propped herself directly across from him on the living room couch with me, "Little Angie," seated by her side.

Carl stared straight ahead, gazing at the television, and declared, ***"Well, ask your mother if she'd like to go out to eat."***

Little Angie turned ninety degrees and addressed her mother.

"Ma, Dad wants to know if you'd like to go out to eat."

Louise turned and addressed her daughter as though Carl was not present in the room.

"Well, tell your father that if he wants to go out to eat, I'll join him—as long as it's not Chinese food."

Little Angie turned back and addressed her father in the vibrating chair.

"Dad, Mom says she'll go out to eat with you as long as it's not Chinese food."

Carl turned his head and addressed his daughter, as though his wife was not present.

"Well, tell your mother that if she wants to go out to eat, we can go to Scarsella's. Ask her if she wants to go to Scarsella's."

"Mom, Dad wants to know if you'd like to eat at Scarsella's restaurant."

"Scarsella's will be fine."

As a child, I more or less enjoyed these Mexican standoffs between Carl and Louise. During these times, I received a lot of attention from both of my parents. Each one would want me to select him or her as my favorite parent. To accomplish this, Dad might take me out alone with him on an errand run to Wheeler's Potato Chip Factory to pick up boxes of fresh chips for our baseball concession stand businesses, while Mother might plan a special outing just for the two of us at the Boardman Plaza where I could select all the clothes I wanted from the discounted clothes racks. Then we'd go out to eat and then perhaps stop at Handel's Ice Cream for creamy dessert.

During these time periods, I was relieved of being the Black Sheep of the Family, a title I co-shared with Grandma-in-the-Basement. Instead, I was elevated to the position of the Family Counselor, the Confidante, the Court Jester, the Singer and Dancer, the Math Wizard, the Piano Performer, the Joke Teller, the Masseuse, and any other position my parents needed me to play during their long days of mutual silence. I was the Funny Girl, the Smart Child, the Math Genius, the Liberace, the Ballerina, the Princess, the Goddess, the Pampered Child. No longer did I need to descend into the cellar to have somebody to talk to. Both of my parents were vying for me and lavished me with attention. The gifts they bought me during these time periods were all the more reason to bask in the spotlight during their cold wars.

Then after a few chilly weeks, they would make up and were suddenly back in love, talking with each other in the sweetest of tones. At these times, I was The Outsider, The Undesirable, The Intruder.

Every dysfunctional family needs a Black Sheep and I became **_IT_** to help solidify my parents' camaraderie.

*"**Look at your daughter with all that make up on her,"** my father would announce in a disgusted tone at a restaurant table while the three of us would be eating. **"She looks like a putan."** [whore]*

"Well, she's no daughter of mine! I told you just the other day, the school called and said she had been wearing red socks with a matching red sweater and they had to send her home."

Carl shook his head and tsked, eyeballing me in disgust.

"What a loser she is! She's just boy crazy and she's not even gonna graduate from high school. I see it coming. Your daughter is going to end up pregnant any day now."

I stopped eating my meal, stared down at my plate, and twirled the pasta around and around on my fork.

"Look at that. Doesn't even finish a good meal. Always wasting her food.

Why did we even bother to bring her along? You should have left your daughter at home alone."

"Next time, we'll do that, Hun."

••● ●●••

In June 1968, a few days after my high school graduation, I packed my belongings and headed toward the front door with my boyfriend, Bob Bergagna.

"Where do you think you're going!?" my mother screamed.

"I'm leaving for good. I've run away many times before but this time I'm leaving FOREVER!" I yelled.

"You can't go anywhere!" my mother shouted. **"You're not yet eighteen!**

I'm going to call the cops on you!"

"Well, you just go right ahead and do that, Ma. But 'What will the neighbors think'? Huh? That's what you always say, Mom. 'What will the neighbors think!?"

Carl stood by and watched the scene without uttering a word.

Bob and I loaded a few bags of clothes and other belongings into his car and then I made one last trip back into the house to retrieve my beloved cat, Bummy.

"Oh, no you don't!" my mother shrieked! ***"That's MY cat!"***

"Oh, yes I will take him! He's MY cat, Mom! Hand him over to me!"

Mother clutched the cat tightly in both of her arms.

"Not over my dead body!!"

Not wanting to hurt the cat, the tug of war ceased.

"Okay, that's fine," I stated calmly, staring my mother down, my heart pounding. ***"I'll just wait 'til he's out in the yard."***

"I'm calling the cops."

"Yeah, Ma. Go ahead and call the cops."

And I slammed the front door shut behind me.

••● ● ●••

The spare bedroom at Mrs. Ennis' home was rather small and barren.

She had been using it as a storage area for many years but had agreed to let me stay there for $20 a month. I had hoped to move into my girlfriend Patricia's bedroom, since she was off at college living in the dormitories, but Mrs. Ennis, her mother, wanted to save that pretty room for Patty, for weekend visits, or just in case Patty's scholarship or plans changed.

I sat upon my new bed, with the door closed, looking at the barren walls, wondering what I might put on them. I had no pictures of anyone.

I looked at the nearby nearly empty closet with a few of my outfits now hanging neatly, and the chest of drawers sparsely filled. Most of my belongings had been left behind in the rush and madness of it all.

The barren room was now a reflection of my own new life. I had no plans to attend college because I had no money to do so, and, unlike Patty, I had not been offered a scholarship. I had no job. No skills. I didn't even know how to properly wash dishes, since Mother had always done everything for me. I did not even have the $20 to pay Mrs. Ennis, but Bob promised to pay it for me every month.

"What will become of me?" I wondered to myself, as I curled up under the blankets and stared at the barren ceiling.

But as the fear embraced me, so did the feelings of relief that washed over me, and I sighed heavily, for, alas, I was free. Was it merely a dream? Could it actually be? I was really free?

Free.

No longer could I be blamed everyday for all the things that had gone wrong in my mother's life. The marriage she had not wanted. The pregnancy she had tried to abort. No longer would I be shoved to the floor, pushed into the wall, my hair pulled, my back pummeled. There would be no more rides to and from school in which I was raged at for all the "crimes" I had committed since the moment I had been born.

A memory suddenly flashed upon me of a time when I was thirteen and I just couldn't take it anymore. I had exited the car, my mother still screaming at me, just a step behind me, and when I reached the back door, I put my fist through one of the little, glass panes. My arm began bleeding profusely and my mother screamed, **_"NOW LOOK WHAT YOU'VE DONE! YOU LITTLE BITCH! I'M GOING TO HAVE TO PAY TO HAVE THAT GLASS REPLACED!_**" and she slapped me hard across the face. I went into the bathroom and wrapped my arm in gauze and retreated into my bedroom. There was no checking in on me. There was no mention that I had been severely cut. Instead, my mother on the phone, out in the hallway pacing the floor, was livid about the cost of the replacement glass as she continued to rage at me in between phone calls to her friends.

No, there would be no more incidents like that. My body shivered as I recalled the traumatic images and I drew the blankets more tightly around my body.

At last, I was safe. There would be no more incidents like that.

It was difficult to absorb the reality of it all. Any minute, I kept thinking, my mother shall be here dragging me out of this bed, raging at me, pummeling me. But Mrs. Ennis assured me that she would not let her into her house. Mrs. Ennis was familiar with my story and at least offered me some little form of protection—a barren spare bedroom.

I turned off the overhead light and crawled back into my new bed.

At last, I was "safe," albeit plan-less, clueless, and destitute.

But I was free. I laid there in the dark and pined for my kitty cat, Bummy, tears streaming down my cheeks.

Alas, I was free.

••●•●•●••

CHAPTER FOUR – 1985

Decades passed . . .

Many years passed, and soon, decades passed. I had graduated from high school, graduated from Youngstown State University with a teaching degree, and now I was now living in Florida, after obtaining a Ph.D. I had a very glamorous, exciting job.

I worked as a seminar leader teaching business people the art of customer service, supervisory skills, and listening skills.

It was now 1985, and I was working for Dun and Bradstreet Business Education Services as a travelling seminar leader. Each day, I was in a different city giving another presentation. "Good morning, ladies and gentlemen! Welcome to a Dun and Bradstreet presentation on Customer Service Skills! My name is Dr. Angela Woodhull, and I will be your seminar leader for the day!"

But it wasn't the seminar business that brought me the inner satisfaction that I was seeking.

One day, while walking the streets in Miami, after completing a full day of a corporate seminar presentation, I moseyed into a Korean wig shop. It was November 1985, and Halloween had just passed. The owner of the wig shop had a barrel with a plentiful amount of ugly discount wigs in it. The sign on top of the barrel announced that all wigs in that barrel were only one dollar each.

Passing the time sorting through the barrel, I discovered a rather comical wig at the very bottom of the barrel. A big bouffant wig – blonde at the top, and two shades of brown in the back. The wig hair was coarse and wiry. I located a small mirror on one of the walls and tried on the wig.

It was perfect!

Soon, I set foot to find a cheap little musical instrument. Right down the street from the wig shop, I found a pawn shop. And there on the back shelf behind the counter, I saw a small beginner's accordion with only eight buttons on the squeeze box. It was perfect! It was compact and light, and easy to dance with.

I then purchased a pair of black lace fingerless gloves, a rhinestone necklace, and a puffy, old prom dress. I donned a tiara on top of the dollar wig, and, alas! I had now created my alter ego – **Angelina, the Polka Queen!**

Soon, I was a sensation at nursing homes across the nation! Alas! I had found my fame!

Activity directors created handmade posters and fliers announcing my arrival. **"This Thursday in our dining room! Immediately after lunch! Don't miss it, folks! Angelina, the Polka Queen will be here to entertain us!!"**

In Mississippi, the activity director had obviously never heard of "polka." In her best Southern drawl, she announced over the intercom, "Ladies and Gentlemen! Please welcome **Ann-joe-line-ah, the Poker Quine!"**

••●◉●••

"O Solo Mio!" -- My Sunshine: Way Down South in the Sunshine State . . .

Way down South, far from Youngstown, Ohio, another woman had also become keenly interested in the elderly. Her name was Rebecca Fierle.

I have never actually spoken to Rebecca Fierle face – to – face. We, in fact, have never spoken even a single word to each other.

Yet, while I was performing polka shows in Orlando nursing homes, Rebecca Fierle was also there – with a much more lucrative agenda.

Imagine you have the keys . . .

Imagine you have the keys to somebody's house. They are not home, and no one is going to call the cops on you.

You turn the key, step inside, and everything you see – yes everything – is yours for the taking. No one will ever call the authorities. You can remove anything that fancies you – expensive oil paintings, Persian rugs, coin collections, diamond rings, antique furniture, expensive China . . . and take it home, or, perhaps, slough it off to your brother-in-law, the auctioneer.

Notice that family album siting over in the corner? With decades of precious old irreplaceable photos in it? Just go ahead and dump it into the trash. No one will ever complain about it going missing. Perhaps the elderly person, who is now conveniently tucked away in a nursing home, might ask you, "Where are all of my priceless photos?" But you don't have to answer her.

If she claims that you stole the Persian rugs and other pricey valuables, you don't have to respond. Using your favorite corrupt judges and dirty attorneys, you had all of her civil rights removed.

*She cannot sue you.

*She cannot hire an attorney.

*She cannot call the police.

*She can't do anything at all.

And, besides, no one will believe her anyway. You had her declared "mentally incapacitated," right?

Utilizing the services of your favorite medical doctor friends (whom you always pay handsomely for their standard cookie cutter medical evaluations), she's now just a "crazy, old lady," imagining she once owned things.

So, instead of worrying about her claims that her coin collection and gold bars are missing, just give these items to your brother-in-law, the auctioneer, and split the profits with him.

Sounds like "fun," doesn't it?

How would you like to work your entire life, only to find yourself confined to a urine-smelling welfare nursing home, against your will, placed on psychotropic drugs to keep you sedate, while a professional guardian (and her attorneys) spend your lifetime of savings?

"Imagine a system of justice in this country that strips its citizens of their Constitutional rights, voids their existing legal documents, gives others the right to spend their money and sell their assets, isolates them, and has the ability to limit the time they can spend with their loved ones." ~Dr. Sam Sugar, author of Guardianship and the Elderly: The Perfect Crime.

She walks into court, so elegant and pristine. Tall and confident, she carries her

Gucci bag over her left shoulder and holds her black brief case in her right hand. Her long, flowing red hair partially covers one hazel eye. She sports an expensive gray pant suit, the finest that even a Kardashian would be proud to wear.

"All rise!" the Bailiff declares.

And she stands proudly next to her attorney, a short little unattractive middle- aged man, a bit unkempt, with a wry grin on his face.

"You may be seated," says the judge.

We actually have never spoken.

And as I sit down, a feeling of doom sweeps over me because I realize it's time to lose another $50,000.00 to Rebecca Fierle and her attorney, at the hands of a crooked judge.

Welcome to the world of a professional, predatory guardian.

CHAPTER FIVE -- 2023 --
MY SCRAPBOOK –

____

I'm sitting on my living floor inside my house assembling a scrapbook.

A friend of mine, Cheryl, a professional crafter, is sitting next to me on the carpet, onlooking.

"Who is that?" she inquires.

"Oh, that's Estranged Cousin Shirley."

"I don't know her and she doesn't know me."

"Then why are you putting her in your scrapbook?"

I looked at Cheryl soberly.

"This is no ordinary scrapbook," I tell her.

"This is a scrapbook that depicts all the thieves, liars, and crooks who stole, through "legal" court maneuvers, my inheritance money."

"How much money are we talking about?" Cheryl inquired. "Maybe fifty thousand?"

"No," I replied.

"Let me tell you the story."

Here is Estranged Cousin Shirley.

Her mother and my mother were sisters. The two sisters were very close when they were young.

Let's go back in time ...

Here are our mothers back in 1938.

They were inseparable, as young adults. They were also inseparable as children.

But they had a big fallout as adults in 1962.

I was 11 years old when they stopped speaking. The bitter battle took place in Attorney Solomon Malkoff's office during the reading of their deceased father's Will. I still remember that day, as though it was yesterday.

We were all sitting in Attorney Solomon Malkoff's office on the 7th floor of an old office building in downtown Youngstown, Ohio.

This was the office building. ^^^^

At the reading of his Last Will and Testament, only two of his four children were present — his two daughters, Louise and Antoinette. Grandpa's two older sons -- Michael and Jim – were absent.

Antoinette was eagerly awaiting (and silently praying for) her fair share of the inheritance.

With five kids and a poor steel-mill-worker husband, Antoinette keenly wanted her fair share of that little inheritance money from her father.

After all, she had done ***the most*** (cooking, cleaning, running errands, doctors' appointments, etc.) for their father during the last few years of his life, following his wife's death.

On the other hand ...

There was my mother, the middleclass housewife, who didn't really care about her father's little pittance of inheritance money. She lived in a nice bungalow house with her husband, a schoolteacher, and her only child (me). We maintained the outward appearance of normalcy and middle class economic comfort.

Desperate Antoinette crossed her fingers underneath her purse and held her breath as she awaited the reading of her father's Last Will and Testament.

It was time for Attorney Malkoff to unveil the decedent's final words.

"To my son Michael Scimone, I hereby leave _all_ of my worldly possessions . . . ."

ALL!!!???

A look of shock and utter horror came across Antoinette's beat red face.

Antoinette

Louise, on the other hand, her younger sister, openly laughed! Instantly! Openly! ***Uproarious*** laughter.

You see, Grandpa Scimone was famous for ***switching*** out his Will. Switch, switch. Switch, switch. One week, his youngest daughter was the sole beneficiary. Next week, his oldest son. The follow week, his youngest son would be the sole beneficiary, etc., etc.

Then back to his youngest daughter, etc., etc. Switch. Switch. Switch. It seems ***on <u>that</u> particular day that he unexpectedly died***, Grandpa Scimone had made out yet ***another*** Will to Michael Scimone, his alcoholic son.

Uncle Mike was a real ladies' man. He had been married nine times and had 27 children. He resembled Rhett Butler from "Gone

With the Wind" back in his good-looking younger years. But as far as doing anything for his dying father, he did nothing.

"What are you laughing about?" Antoinette yelled at her younger sister, with spittle flying out of her mouth.

Bitter tears flowed down her reddened cheeks.

"Well, the preposterous-ness of it all!" Louise replied, still chuckling.

"We both know that Mike did **nothing** for Pa," she added.

"Well, I think you'd better shut up before I come over there and knock you on the side of your head!" Antoinette shouted.

"Well, I think YOU'D better shut up before I pick you up and throw you out that open window!" Louise replied, her voice rising.

The reading of the Will took place on the 7th floor of a downtown office building in Youngstown, Ohio. It was **long** before the days of air conditioning, so the unscreened windows were rolled up, wide open.

Don't you just LOVE my dysfunctional Italian family so far? I asked Cheryl.

Cheryl chuckled. "They're pretty colorful!"

And thereafter, the two sisters did not speak for the next 23 years.

They made up just in time for Louise to learn that her sister, Antoinette, was dying from stomach cancer. At her sister's funeral, 23 years later, Louise openly wept and lamented that they had spent so many years foolishly apart.

****

"Well, that's a sad story," said Cheryl, "but what happened to your inheritance money? Let me guess. Did Cousin Shirley take it?"

"Well, you're close," I replied. "Cousin Shirley tried to take it, but the story is far more complex."

2007

Shortly after my father died, Estranged Cousin Shirley started phoning my histrionic mother every day. (Yes, my mother was professionally medically diagnosed as "histrionic" by a Florida psychiatrist. You might say that's a fancy psychiatric word for "Drama Queen.") Every day, multiple times a day, this Estranged Cousin Shirley suddenly started phoning her aunt (my mother) throughout the entire day – after 23 years of never speaking to her.

* She phoned my mother at breakfast time and asked her what she had eaten and whether or not she had taken her medications yet.

* She phoned her at lunchtime and asked her what she had eaten and whether or not she had taken more medications.

*She phoned her at suppertime and asked her the same questions.

Then there was that sweet daily bedtime phone call, in her sickening sweet fake voice.

"Aunt Lou! I'm just checking on you to see if you're all right and to tuck you in! I wish you were here with us! I love you! John sends you his love, too!"

Soon, Estranged Cousin Shirley became a daily, intricate part of my mother's life.

I should have suspected something, but I didn't.

At first, I didn't think much about these sudden **obsessive**, daily phone calls by Estranged Cousin Shirley to my mother. I just thought it was two lonely, older women passing the time. I was happy for my histrionic mother that she had someone else, besides me, for her obsessive needs for constant attention.

This is John Mascarella, Shirley Mascarella's creepy husband, who assisted Estranged Cousin Shirley, and masterminded the foiled plot to steal my $1 million inheritance money.

Out in the living room of her Tampa house, where my mother was eating her supper – prior to moving in with me . . . a lawsuit was brewing . . .

My mother's landline phone rang.

"Hello?"

It was estranged Cousin Shirley who was phoning my mother again for the **fifth time** that day.

"Aunt Lou! How are you doing today?" she asked in her sickening sweet fake voice.

"Oh, honey! How nice to hear from you!" my mother chirped.

"Did you eat your supper?"

"Oh, yes, honey! I'm eating it right now."

"And did you take your medicines tonight?"

"Not yet. I will take them after supper."

"Well, John and I just want you to know that we've been thinking about you all day long! We love you so much!"

"Oh, I love you too, sweetheart!"

Just a few weeks earlier, Shirley Mascerella had phoned the police on me and reported my mother as a **missing person**.

My histrionic mother was actually flattered and delighted when she heard that that she had been reported as "missing."

Here were six cop cars in her front yard when we pulled into her driveway that evening, their lights all ablaze.

"Mrs. Falvo! Are you all right?" an officer rushed toward my car and shined his flashlight in our eyes.

"Your niece reported you as a missing person! We were about ready to break into your house!"

"Oh! I'm **fine**!" my mother tittered, her eyes wide open and bright. She smiled widely. She was actually giggling.

"I was at the science museum with my daughter. We were looking at a traveling exhibit called "Dead Bodies!'"

So, here was a little old lady reported as potentially dead by her opportunist niece in Youngstown, Ohio while six cops surrounding her Tampa house, and listened as she explained she was looking at dead bodies.

The Tampa Police were on the verge of smashing out windows and breaking down doors in search of my mother's dead body if we had arrived only a minute later.

"Your niece reported that you were with your daughter. Is this your daughter, Mrs. Falvo?"

"Yes, this is my daughter."

This scene was the beginning of many, many similar scenes over the next three years in which police were asked to search for my mother's dead body. All of these searches initiated by an opportunist cousin and her coniving husband, John Mascarella.

"Why are they doing that, Mom? Why do they keep calling Elder Abuse on me?" I asked my mother.

"Oh, they're just trying to be **helpful**," my mother stated. "After all, you don't **actually** live with me. You live two blocks away. I'm sure if you moved in with me, the calls to Elder Abuse would cease."

My mother grinned widely and stared at me.

Not all calls to Elder Abuse or the police were initiated by Shirley and John Mascarella. Some were initiated by my histrionic mother herself.

For example . . .

There was the day when I was busy back at my little apartment, two blocks away grading papers for the online class I teach.

My mother called and claimed she was out of orange juice.

"Ang! You need to come over here RIGHT NOW!! I am out of orange juice and if you don't come over here RIGHT NOW and take me to the store to get orange juice immediately, I could **die**!"

In actuality, I knew as a fact that my mother was not out of orange juice. I had just purchased two gallons of orange juice for her the night before.

I was on the verge of losing my job if I didn't finish grading these overdue papers.

Next thing I know, the Gainesville, Florida police were calling me.

"Ms. Woodhull, the officer inquired, "why did you lock your mother out of the house?"

"What? I didn't lock my mother out of the house."

"Well, your mother is standing here outside in the hot sun and the door is locked. She said you purposely locked her out of the house."

And so, I turned off my computer and rushed over to my house where my mother was outside crying hysterically, while two police officers were comforting her.

"Why did you do this to your mother?" one officer inquired.

"I didn't do this!" I protested.

I unlocked the door, and the officers reassured my mother that they would be back pronto if anything else weird was done to her by me.

My mother smiled and thanked the two officers.

As soon as the two officers left, my mother looked at me, chuckled, and then reached under the dining room table and picked up her keys.

With her keys in hand, and still grinning widely while staring at me, she asked me in a low, calm voice, "And, so, now . . . are we going to get some orange juice????"

Indeed.

Soon, we were off in my car to go get her some more orange juice.

••●●••

MY SCRAPBOOK: REBECCA FIERLE – THE MAKING OF A PROFESSIONAL GUARDIAN (1993)

It started with a bankruptcy, a divorce, and perhaps the added responsibilities of having a handicapped child. Now living as a single mother with three children in a rundown trailer park, Rebecca Fierle put on her best black Wal*Mart blazer and headed down to Seniors First to fill out the job application.

Wanted – intake specialist to assist seniors in obtaining free services available to them in Orange County, Florida.

"Do you have any experience working with seniors?" the director asked her when she completed the form.

"I don't," Rebecca openly admitted.

"But I am very close to my grandmother," she quickly added. "And I understand that elderly people sometimes feel very lonely."

Lonely.

The director quickly looked over her application and said, "Well, I think you might be a good fit for this position. Your job will be to contact seniors who may need our services. You'll sign them up for state and federally-funded services – like free transportation, help with finding Medicare providers, and free food. Does this sound like a position that interests you?"

Rebecca smiled broadly, her long flowing auburn curls resting calmly against the padded shoulders of her Wal*Mart blazer.

"I think I would be a perfect fit," she replied.

••●●••

It wasn't long before Rebecca was wearing Prada, Dior, and Hermes for her daily outings to meet and greet the elderly in their homes.

She stepped out of her Black Mercedes-Benz wearing a sleek jet gray pantsuit. She walked gracefully to the front door of the elegant brick ranch-style home carrying her Satchel & Page black leather briefcase. She gently pushed the doorbell while removing her Dolce and Gabbana sunglasses.

An elderly woman clad in an elegant beige, ruffled full length bathrobe slightly opened the door and peered out at the stranger.

"Good morning, Florence! Are you Florence Barbour?"

"Yes, I am!" the elderly woman chirped.

"My name is Rebecca Fierle, and I am with Seniors First."

"Oh?! What is that?" Florence inquired.

"We help seniors find assistance with transportation, doctor's appointments, groceries . . . . just about anything imaginable! And all services are free! Here is a brochure about our many services! I'd love to tell you more!"

"Oh, certainly," Florence replied, opening the door widely. "I was just starting to prepare a little breakfast. Can I get you some coffee?"

Soon, the two women were chatting, as though they were old friends.

Within two weeks, after several more cozy visits to Florence's lovely home, Rebecca would secure a Power of Attorney over Barbour.

And this was the beginning of a most lucrative career of all. ***Caring*** for the elderly.

"I really don't have anyone else I can trust," Florence explained to Rebecca, as she signed the POA documents.

"You are such a sweet girl, and I know you will look out for my best interests," she added, with the stroke of her pen.

Rebecca grinned widely as she opened her briefcase and tucked away the legal documents, taking notice of the fine art and lavish collection of valuable antiques in Florence's home.

Within two weeks, Rebecca had Barbour legally removed from her home and placed into a nursing home against her will.

Within six months, Barbour was dead and Rebecca was the heiress to Barbour's estate.

------------------- ••●●•• -------------------

In the year 2000 ~

Down in Seminole County, Florida, professional guardian Nancy Alley was about to finish law school. Soon, she would specialize, as an attorney, in guardianship law. After all, it's much more lucrative to log in billable hours as a lawyer than as a professional guardian.

Within a few years, she would become a lofty judge in Seminole County – the probate division.

And now she could receive kickbacks from guardianship lawyers and their guardians. She had reached the top drawer, and Seminole County was the perfect place for guardianship players.

------------------- ••●●•• -------------------

Down in nearby Lake Mary, Florida, Attorney Ian Gilden, a guardianship attorney, was in the process of devising a great strategy for finding wealthy elderly folks.

"I'm holding a free meeting at Regions Bank on Tuesday," he told his wife, Attorney Ann Marie Giordano Gilden, his law firm partner at Gilden & Gilden. "It's called 'Seven Ways for Senior Citizens to Avoid Scammers."

"I *love* the title!" said Ann Marie, eyes wide open. "I betcha a lot of seniors will show up!"

"That's the ticket!" he replied, kissing his wife on the forehead.

••●●●••

The Free Public Meeting at Regions Bank.

"You can't really trust your relatives sometimes, folks!" Gilden told the audience of about twelve seniors. Several heads nodded in agreement.

"And that's why it's so important to create a living trust where your assets are completely protected. A living trust!" He held up a sample paper for the audience to see.

The amazed seniors leaned forward in their seats.

At the sign up sheet following the free meeting, seniors eagerly signed their names for a complimentary one hour follow-up consultation with Attorneys Ian Gilden and Ann Marrie Giordano Gilden.

••●●●••

Meanwhile, Ian Gilden and his former colleague, Nancy Alley (now a probate judge) authored a brochure, "Guide to Guardianships in Seminole County." The guidebook explained how professional, corporate guardians work with attorneys to "protect" the assets of seniors.

••●●●••

Rebecca Fierle now held the Powers of Attorney on at least twenty different seniors.

The job at Seniors First was certainly paying off handsomely, although her bosses probably didn't know about the POAs.

Upon their deaths, Rebecca would be entitled to any assets that remained in their trusts -- property, bank accounts, coin collections, automobiles, and any other valuables.

••●●••

Soon, Rebecca Fierle left Seniors First and decided to branch out on her own. For the fee of $65, she was able to incorporate in the State of Florida and become the owner of Geriatric Care Management, LLC.

40 hour course -- ready to rob

For an additional $150, she then took a 40-hour video-watching course in Volusia County, Daytona Beach, Florida. After 40 hours of viewing a dozen VCR tapes and then taking a short quiz, Rebecca Fierle was now ready to become a corporate, professional guardian. All she needed was an attorney to represent her.

••●●••

In Windermere, Florida, near Orlando, Rebecca Fierle visited the law office of Sawyer and Sawyer. Working in partnership with the Sawyers was Thomas Moss – an attorney specializing in estate planning and wealth management.

At her first meeting with Moss, Fierle learned that the Sawyers were also medical doctors. It was a cozy arrangement. The Sawyers, along with their partner Thomas Moss, had secured their own cozy team of medical doctors prepared to declare any senior "mentally incapacitated." Any wealthy senior could therefore be removed from their home, and then declared "mentally incapacitated" with the assistance of psychotropic drugs and Fierle's initiatives. While under the influence of these powerful drugs, the victim is typically asked questions like, "Who is the president of the United States? What is your address?" Nobody – repeat **nobody** – is able to answer these simple questions while under the influence of powerful psychotropic drugs.

One of the very first victims that Fierle secured as a new licensed guardian was Dorothy Wehrheim. Not only was she wealthy, but she was estranged from her three biological adult children. She seemed the perfect candidate for a corporate guardianship.

The three-part procedure is pretty simple and straight forward.

[1] Eminent Danger

The first step is to file an emergency petition with the court stating that the elderly person is in "eminent danger."

"I visited Dorothy Wehrheim at her home and she seems fine. Absolutely fine. So, what should we write as the 'eminent danger' that she faces?" Fierle inquired of Moss.

Moss replied, "Be creative! There are so many things you can write down as the reasons why an elderly person is in 'eminent danger.'"

"Perhaps she fell down in her house and was left lying there, unattended, for several days."

"That's a good one!" Moss said, with a wink and a smile.

"Or you could say that the house is filthy. That she has been living in utter filth for several months."

Fierle quickly scribbled the suggestions in her leather-bound notebook.

"But what if she is friends with the neighbors and they know she keeps her home pristine?"

"The neighbors will be forbidden to visit her at the nursing home. In fact, no one will be allowed to visit her except for you, me, and the medical team. We'll obtain an order from the judge that allows no visitation from outsiders."

Fierle sunk into the office chair, smiled and sighed.

Over the years, Rebecca became quite creative, and even a bit fruity, when it came to her claims for the emergency petitions.

- The (non-existent) neighbors were taking advantage of the elderly person and constantly asking for money.

- The inside of the house was covered in fleas and roaches.

- The elderly person had been sustaining herself on merely a single box of Velveeta cheese for more than a week.

- There were bats flying all over the house.

Paying the Right People. Keeping Everyone Happy.

After meeting with Dorothy at Golden Pond Assisted Living, Fierle had Thomas Moss draw up new legal documents that gave Fierle the Power of Attorney of Wehrheim's estate. With POAs executed, Fierle removed Dorothy's expensive antique wedding bands . . . .

"Don't worry, Dorothy. I'm taking these rings off for safe-keeping. One of the crazy, old people here could try to steal them from you."

. . . . and then Fierle strolled down to the nurse's station and plopped the rings on the head nurse's desk.

"Dorothy said she wants you to have these," Fierle whispered.

"What. Really? Why?" the head nurse inquired.

There were several beats of silence while Fierle was thinking.

"Because you pay so much attention to her."

The nurse scratched her head. "We've only spoken once, maybe twice."

Fierle leaned forward and whispered in the nurse's ear, pushing the rings toward her.

"Next time someone like Dorothy shows up here . . . call me." Fierle winked.

"I certainly will," the nurse replied, as she slipped on the antique diamonds.

Soon, Thomas Moss had drawn up all of the paperwork which declared that Dorothy Wehrheim wanted to leave all of her bank accounts to Golden Pond Assisted Living.

Fierle stepped inside the director's office and placed the legal documents on her desk with a wink and a smile.

"It's done!"

The director glanced down at the legal papers and smiled.

Both women locked eyes and grinned broadly.

The director added, "There's a woman worth about three million who's moving in here on Friday, Rebecca. I think she needs a good guardian, don't you agree?"

Both women laughed as they shared a high five.

About twenty minutes away from downtown Orlando is Longwood, Florida – home to approximately 15,000 residents and considered to be a safe and welcoming place for retirees.

Robert and Elsa Gallagher had recently purchased a townhome on a quiet cul-de-sac in Longwood and were happy to be away from the snow and freezing winter temperatures in their home state of Massachusetts.

Leaving their son, Kevin, with a Power of Attorney, they told him and his lovely wife, Lisa, "We'll miss you, too! But don't worry! We'll be back when the time is right. When we feel we can no longer take care of ourselves, we'll move back to Massachusetts – with your assistance."

"Don't worry, Dad," their son reassured them with a hug. "Lisa and I will do whatever you want when you come back some day. In the meantime, have fun in Florida!"

It had been a lifetime dream of the Gallaghers to one day retire in Florida. And now that day had come. Golfing, the nearby beaches, plenty of fine restaurants and antique shops. And, of course, Disney World and all of the other attractions. It was a dream come true.

A few years after settling into their lovely townhouse, something weird happened while the Gallaghers were driving back home from Sunday morning church services.

At the intersection where they normally turned left to get back to their neighborhood was a detour sign. They followed the detour and winding road and ended up back out on the highway. Confused, they made a U-turn and ended up back at the construction site on the original road. After more than an hour of driving around, panic-stricken, they finally reached their home.

It was a frightening and decisive moment.

Laying the car keys on their kitchen table, Robert sat down and looked up at his wife.

"Perhaps it's time," Robert stated in a soft voice.

"Perhaps. It's time," Elsa nodded, as she brushed away a tear.

Kevin, their son, agreed to start making all the arrangements for his parents to return to Cambridge.

Meanwhile, Kevin phoned his sister, Lori, who lived in Altamonte Springs, Florida – another suburb of Orlando.

"If you could just help Mom and Dad with some simple things – like buying their groceries," Kevin asked.

Lori, busy with her own career and three children, opened the Yellow Pages to "Senior Care," and there she found a business, "Geriatric Care Management."

She quickly dialed the number and spoke with a pleasant, soft-spoken woman.

"How much is their home in Longwood worth?" the woman inquired.

"Mmm. I'd say at least $350,000.00," Lori replied.

"And do they have a checking account or savings account?"

"Oh, yes. They have several," Lori quickly stated. "I think they have at least half a million in the banks."

Within 48 hours, Rebecca Fierle had all of the Emergency Petition legal papers filled out, with the help of Thomas Moss.

Both Elsa and Robert were declared 100% mentally incapacitated at the same exact moment, on the same day by Fierle and her legal and medical associates. The Gallaghers went from buying their own groceries, paying their own bills, and driving their own car to **completely incapacitated –simultaneously --** with the stroke of the Seminole County judge's pen, Nancy Alley.

"Your Honor," Thomas Moss explained at the Emergency Hearing, "They were driving so erratically through the streets that they nearly escaped death! They almost hit into a semi-truck. And then they landed in a ditch!"

The judge scribbled a few notes and nodded empathically.

"And besides, when Ms. Fierle found them, their house was covered in filth! There was a massive amount of roaches swarming all over the kitchen table while the Gallaghers were eating bologna sandwiches!"

Within an hour of the judge signing the Emergency Temporary Order, Rebecca Fierle arrived at the Gallagher's townhouse, armed with two deputy sheriffs.

The Gallaghers opened their front door and peered at the unexpected visitors.

Fierle flashed the paperwork. "We're here to help you!"

The Gallaghers started to close the door. Robert said, "Let me call my son."

But before Robert could close the door all the way, the two deputies were inside the home and escorting the Gallaghers against their will into the squad car.

Upon arriving at the run down nursing home facility, Elsa Gallagher cried out. "Help! Help! Somebody help us, please! I don't want to be here! Take me back to my home!!"

A doctor approached and jabbed Elsa in the arm. Soon, she was extremely calm and slumped over in the wheelchair.

"I think it's best that we separate them," Rebecca said to the staff.

"You're the boss, Ms. Fierle," a staff member replied. And the two wheelchairs with the Gallaghers were taken to different wings of the nursing facility.

Step Two.

Soon, three medical professionals arrived.

Elsa was still slumped in her chair, a rope tied around her torso to make sure she did not fall to the floor.

"What's your name? Do you know your address?"

Elsa stared at them blankly, as the three professionals scribbled their notes.

Back in court, Rebecca Fierle proudly opened her leather briefcase and handed the three medical reports to Thomas Moss, who handed them to the bailiff, who, in turn, handed them to the judge.

The judge quickly shuffled through the three papers and then signed and stamped her own paper.

"Ms. Fierle, I'm sure you will take good care of the Gallaghers. Your petitions are granted."

Fierle stood up, and softly clapped her hands. "Thank you, Your Honor!"

Outside in the parking lot, with Thomas Moss in step at her side, Rebecca squealed in delight, as Moss grinned and patted her on the back.

⸻ ••●●•• ⸻

CHAPTER SIX

It's Raining Lawsuits in My Life,

. . . and I Just Wanna Be Angelina, the Polka Queen!

It's Raining Lawsuit, and . . .

It's not easy being a polka queen.

Donning my rhinestone tiara, purple wig, lace gloves, and sparkly pink prom dresss – while toting my accordion on the front passager seat –I suddenly heard the sounds of screaming police sirens and flashing lights behind me.

"Driver! Pull over!" the officer shouted in loud, somber tones from his megaphone.

"Driver! Pull over immediately!"

"What had I done?" I wondered. "Certainly, I hadn't been speeding."

Lawtey, Florida is known as a speed trap town.

With this knowledge in the forefront of my mind, I am always extra cautious when driving through Lawtey, Florida. I always drive through Lawtey at a snail pace.

The officer swaggered up to me.

"Ma'am, do you know why I stopped you?" he inquired.

"I have no idea," I replied.

"Well, you were swerving in and out of traffic," he responded.

"That's totally not true," I protested.

"Have you been drinking?"

"No. Never."

"Are you taking any kind of medications?"

"No. Not at all."

We were now keenly eyeballing each other – eyeball to eyeball.. Yes, we were eyeball to eyeball, and he was about to **get to the _real_ point**.

He cocked his head and looked up at my purple wig and tiara.

"Ma'am, is there a reason why you are wearing a purple wig and a tiara?"

Aha. **_Profiling. We are finally arriving at the _real_ reason for the traffic stop._**

"Well, yes there is," I curtly replied, pointing to my accordion.

"I'm on my way to your public library to do an educational music show for children."

His face suddenly turned a bright shade of MD 20/20 red. You see, it's not every day that a boneheaded small town traffic cop is embarrassed by a Polka Queen.

He quickly snatched my driver's license and huffed off.

Several minutes passed.

He soon returned, empty handed, with nothing more than my driver's license in his hand. Having run every possible background check upon me, he had been unable to find any damning evidence against me. He had been unable to find any outstanding warrants for my arrest. And I had not (and never had) been drinking. His face was now an even brighter shade of Florida cracker red.

"Ma'am, I don't know why you were weaving . . ." he said, in an attempt to cover his ass.

"I wasn't weaving," I stated sarcastically, and he knew I was right, but he continued.

"I'll just give you a warning this time, ma'am," he bellowed.

I scoffed.

"But whatever it was that was causing you to weave in and out traffic, I hope you get your mind straight."

"Yeah, sure," I replied, chuckling under my breath, while patting my accordion.

Being profiled in Lawtey, Florida for wearing a purple wig was just the beginning of my weird day.

Back at my home just a few hours later, I was in my side yard jumping on my trampoline when I spotted Attorney Tom Daniel again -- spying on me through the dense trees that separate my side yard from the adjacent street. With binoculars in hand, he peered at me from his little black pickup truck. Daniel is no ordinary attorney. First of all, he is a dead ringer for Ted Bundy (minus the charm), especially the frightening eyes, the smirky "gotcha" smile.

His windowless Gainesville office looks more like an illegal abortion clinic than a law office.

After I had reported Tom Daniel to the Florida Bar for writing rules and regulations that exceed the HOA covenants, Daniel suddenly became **keenly** interested in my jumping on my trampoline – a trampoline I had been leaping on for more than 14 years, unhindered, in the same location, in my side yard.

I was used to Daniel spying on me while I jumped on my trampoline, so I flipped him the double bird and went inside my house.

I went inside and turned on my computer.

My computer, after all, was my safehaven. It was the one place where I was always lawsuit-free.

Or, so I thought.

It was time to for me to complete the simple task of grading papers for the online psychology class I was teaching.

But just for the heck of it, I decided to Google my name that particular day. I was wondering what would come up in a Google search of me.

I was about to make a discovery that was going to turn my world upside down.

Suddenly, to my shock and horror, at the top of the list in a Google search of my name, I discovered that an unknown woman to me – a complete stranger to me – who lives in Sandia Park, New Mexico -- Carolyn P. Meinel, a fundamentalist Christian who hacks into people's websites and computers in the name of Jesus, was claiming that I perform accordion polka music shows at nursing homes with "dancing penises."

The claim read, under the first choice under my name:

"Angela V. Woodhull, Ph.D., also known as Angelina, the Polka Queen" stages shows with dancing penises."

It was a jaw-dropping moment.

"Dancing penises?" I wondered. "What even is a "dancing penis"?

I quickly conducted a furious internet search to see if I could discover what are "Dancing Penises."

Lo and behold -- there they were – all chorographed in a row – a chorus line of muscle-bound naked men all gyrating their erections together. A show that travels to nightclubs in Europe.

And now, the claim that Angela V. Woodhull, Ph.D., also stages "dancing penises shows" – for the whole world to see.

I toggled back to my name search.

I read it over and over and over again on Carolyn P. Meinel's Happy Hacker website: "Angela V. Woodhull, Ph.D., also known as Angelina, the Polka Queen" stages shows with dancing penises."

Dancing penises. It was a jaw-dropping, horrifying moment. I stared at the computer screen for more than one hour, motionless.

--------------●--------------

It was time to go tuck my mother into her new bed at my castle home. I had obtained a small apartment, a mere two blocks away from my mother, so that I could have some privacy and some sense of self. Also, if my mother was in a wound-up screaming mode, I could retreat to my safe haven and then return back when she was calm.

--------------●--------------

Following The Big Car Wreck (I broke my right leg in eight places, 2004—You'll read more about this later.), and my return to my home in Gainesville (after the production of Remember Idora!), I was confined to a wheelchair, and I was terribly depressed. Not only had I lost my mobility, but I had also lost my husband of 10 years, and the majority of my so-called friends, who simply stopped coming around when all the parties and free food ended.

To snap myself out of my blue funk, I decided to turn my house into a castle. After all, I was Angelina, the Polka Queen. Shouldn't a queen live in a castle? I started drawing big splashy flowers in a collage on one bedroom wall. Soon the wall was filled with yellow daisies and purple pansies, bright, colorful tulips, mums, and lilies. I looked at the flowers and my mood lifted. Soon, I bought about 100 rolls of cheap wallpaper that had these adorable purple pansies on them. I didn't want the wallpaper as is, so I sat on my bed, my cast still on, and I took tiny scissors and cut out each and every small pansy. Then, with the help of a bottle of Elmer's glue, I began gluing the elegant purple pansies in a collage all over the bedroom and bathroom doors. Alas, the large hole that Kurt (an ex boyfriend) had punched into my bathroom door in his final fit of rage was now obscured by adorable purple pansies. Soon, I hired two guys off of Craiglist. "I want you to tear down this hideous wall that separates the dining room from the living room."

"But what if it's a supporting wall?" they stammered. "We think it's a supporting wall and your roof will fall down."

"I don't believe it is," I told them. "Just tear it down."

Soon, they were taking large mallets and there was drywall dust everywhere on everything. Meanwhile, I had bought some fabric, and using thread and needle, I handstitched elegant hand-made curtains for the castle with lace trim from my wheelchair.

Artists arrived. "Use your imagination!" I told them.

One artist drew criss-cross lines across the far right living room wall and then painted fleur-de-lis inside each diamond. Another went into the hallway bathroom. I directed her to paint the New York skyline.

And then, on the wall above the bathroom door, another artist painted three jovial-looking dinosaurs playing their accordions.

Soon, my artist friend, Ed Pressley, came over. I had ordered a fiberglass castle backdrop which we placed on the back wall of what was now a huge open double room. Ed painted windows with a floral view. A stage was built and stage lights were added. And, of course, I bought a wooden door that became the Castle Table. On the castle table is a painting similar to the last supper. But the guests are the Polka Queen and King, their court, and Nini cat!

In the master bedroom, there is a mural of St. Basil's Cathedral. On the wall across from it are real wooden pipes from an 1800s pipe organ in descending order. On the two short walls, there are church windows with Latin wooden words high above them that read Dominius Vobiscum (God Bless you). I had tiny shelves built on the cathedral wall which contains hundreds of tall glass bottles filled with candles. And on the front door, a picture of the Cinderella Castle with the words on top, "Welcome to Angelina's Castle." Last of all, I added twinkly lights to the stage and in both bedrooms and bathrooms. Alas, I was living and healing my leg inside an enchanted castle!

••●●••

And now my mother had come to live in the enchanted castle – a castle she did not appreciate. The first thing she did was put a large, portable plastic toilet up on the stage next to my real wooden throne.

On top of the castle table, she kept all of her medicines – hundreds of bottles of prescription drugs, along with her latest batch of honey buns, white bread, rolls of toilet paper, and cleaning fluids.

She had populated the bathroom sink with an array of Dollar Tree toiletries in their cheap plastic bottles. And in her bedroom lay stacks of mail from her various banks and insurance policies.

The once vibrant castle now appeared battered and depressed.

On this particular evening, she seemed a bit agitated, but I didn't know why.

My mother looked up at the twinkly lights in her bedroom.

I tucked my mother into the bed and pulled the hand-stitched quilt I had specially made for her up to her chin.

"Do you want me to leave the twinkle lights on or off, Mom?"

"Leave them on, Ang," she stated, while dozing off. Then suddenly, she opened her eyes wide.

"Ang, we need to go to the banks tomorrow."

"Okay, Mom. Whatever you want to do. We will go to your banks tomorrow."

I knew it would be just one of many tasks the following day, and I didn't think much about it. After all, I had always been told by my parents that they were "broke."

As I exited my mother's new bedroom, I had a flashback of what that bedroom used to be.

That bedroom used to be our recording studio. It was the room where my husband of ten years, King Ira, and I recorded hundreds of songs over hundreds of hours. Most of all, it was where we created a two-and-a-half hour musical about Idora Park that we eventually staged in Youngstown, Ohio.

CHAPTER SEVEN:

(1993 – 2003) THE DECADE I DIVORCED MY PARENTS

My parents continued to use me as their pawn, even during my adult years. One day, something snapped inside of me. I had had enough. I had had enough of my own life being completely disrupted by my dysfunctional, "destitute" parents. I had had enough of the name calling. I had had enough of the verbal and emotional abuse. After all, I was now 43 years old.

Here were the incidents that led up to my divorcing my parents.

During my adult years, my mother would periodically call me on the phone (collect) and sob, "Ang! I can't take it anymore! Your father is always ignoring me! I am sooo lonely! I get in my car and walk around the mall, all alone. I watch other elderly couples at the mall, holding hands. But not your father! No! He never comes with me!!" (Breaks down into hysterical tears.)

"Ang, please, please come and get me! I'm very serious this time! I am all packed up and ready to go! I want to leave him! I want to come live with you in Gainesville!"

My relationship was basically only with my mother when I was an adult. My father never really spoke to me. I had had several long-term relationships with various men over the years, and was therefore a "putan," and Carl Falvo didn't bother to speak with "putans."

I didn't really take it personally most of the time that Carl didn't speak with me. I was, after all, the youngest of four children my father had brought into the world. He didn't have a relationship with **any** of his children. So, it was "equal opportunity" for all four of us.

It was very odd how I had even found out that I have a half-brother. I didn't even know he existed until I was 17 years old. One day, while I was working at the basketball game booth at Idora Park, I saw my father approaching my basketball stand with a man who looked so much like him. As they were approaching, the younger version of my father was beaming at me, with an excited twinkle in his eye. The resemblance was so striking that I said, "Wow. You two look like father and son!"

But my father shook his head "no" and the man remained quiet.

"Ang," my father said, when they arrived at my stand. "This is a distant cousin of yourself, John Romeo, who lives in Columbus, Ohio."

The man shook my hand and then gave me a long embrace. He was in the process of moving to Youngstown with his wife and two children, so he could attend college at Youngstown State University.

It was about a year later that his wife confided in me one day. It was a shocking moment. "John is not your cousin. He's really your half-brother," she confessed. "Your father doesn't want anyone to know that he's been twice divorced before marrying your mother."

I replied, "I always suspected I was adopted," but Joann explained further. "No. Your father was married to John's mother a long time ago."

Soon, my mother and John's wife had heated argument, and that was the end of the "friendship." I didn't see John any more after that. His family soon moved out of state.

Three decades later, I looked up my estranged half-brother, John Romeo, who was living with his second wife in Atlanta, Georgia. "John, do you want to speak with Carl and Louise before they pass away? They are getting so old."

My half-brother replied, "It's too late. Your father had decades to contact me, but never did. And he sold me for a car. Were you aware of that?"

Indeed, I was not aware of that, but John Romeo explained. "Carl did not want to sign the adoption papers when my mother remarried. Carl said he would not sign the adoption papers unless he got paid. My adoptive father and my mother were very poor. All they owned was an old car. Carl took the car in exchange for signing the adoption papers. Yep. He sold me for a Studebaker. So, do you actually think I really want to meet them?"!

Back in Tampa, Florida, my mother was on the phone begging me, once again, to come rescue her.

"Ang! I am sooooooo lonely! Please come get me! I want to come live with you!"

I could hear my father in the background, during my mother's pleadings.

"I don't care! Go live with your putan daughter! Get out of my house!"

And so, I dutifully got in my car and drove to Tampa. I spent the next two and half hours driving to Tampa to fetch my mother and bring her back to my home in Gainesville, Florida.

I then took all of my mother's belongings out of my car and unpacked them and then organized all of her belongings in the spare bedroom.

But, within a few hours of arriving at my house, my mother said, in her most pathetic-sounding voice . . .

"Ang, can you just phone your father and see if he is okay? I'm worried about him. After all, he can't walk very well, and he never learned how to use the washer and dryer."

And so, at my mother's request, I dialed my father.

"Hello."

"Hi, Dad, Mom is here. She wants to know if you're okay."

[my dad sobbing into the receiver]

"Ang! Put your mother on the phone."

[now both of them crying]

"Hun! I miss you soo much! I am sooo sorry! Please come back home, Honey! I can't live without you!!!"

[more hysterical sobbing from both of them]

"Okay, Hun! I'll be right there!"

My mother hung up the phone and looked at me with pathetic eyes.

"Ang, can you take me back to Tampa right now?"

I looked at her in disbelief.

"But, Mom! We just got here! I just drove for two and a half hours to get you, loaded up my car with all of your belongings, dragged them into my house, and unpacked them. Can we at least wait until the morning? Mom, I'm so tired."

My mother's voice started to rise and became very stern.

"No. I can't wait 'til the morning. I want to go **right now**! Right now!! Your father needs me. NOW! Why don't you understand that!?"

Two hours later, we were back in Tampa.

When I stepped inside their home, escorting my mother, my father looked at me with fire in his eyes.

"So, you like hanging out with putans, do you?" he asked my mother.

"No, I don't!" my mother replied to him. I was a virgin when you married me. You remember that, Hun?"

"I do, sweetheart. How did we end up with such a piece of shit daughter?"

I quickly left their house, started up my car, and headed back up the highway. There were no emotions to be felt. I had heard these caustic comments since I was 11 years old.

•••●•••

Two weeks later, my parents were having another Mexican Stand-off. I had resolved that I would not comply with any more requests made by my mother of me the next time she called. My mother must have sensed that . . . .

The phone rang.

"This is AT&T calling. May I speak to Angela Woodhull?"

"This is Angela Woodhull."

"I have a collect call from Louise Falvo. Do you accept the charges?"

Even though I was flat broke, I replied "Yes."

"Mom. What is going on?"

My mother sobbed loudly into the receiver.

"Oh, Ang! I'm all packed and ready to go! I am divorcing your father.

Please come and get me."

After about half an hour of manipulating me, I got into my little Volkswagen bug, and off I dutifully drove to Tampa.

When I arrived at my parents' home in Tampa, my father was busy inside the garage, as usual. In his old age, he had taken a keen interest in rickety, old, non-functioning computers. He spent most of his time in the garage with the garage double door rolled up, surrounded by a graveyard of worthless, ancient computers that were piled high to the ceiling. There was only a small pathway for walking through the garage. Armed with a screw driver and a pair of pliers, and wearing his bifocals and baseball cap, my father carefully disassembled each dinosaur computer down to its finite, miniscule parts. Little plastic containers and empty, huge glass empty pickle jars from Publix supermarket were amassed in rows on large folding tables. My father's self-mandated daily task was to place each computer part into a jar, box, or plastic container. He had a container with just plastic letter A's, and another with just B's, and so on. There were large boxes just for computer wires. There was an area with plastic parts. Then, on the weekend my mother dutifully would load up the van for him and they would drive to a local flea market where my father would sell these miniscule computer pieces to the public. To my amazement, there was a customer who bought a letter L that had come off of his computer. For this, my father earned 50 cents.

On Mondays, my father went to Salvation Army auctions where he purchased even more old computers. And now, when I arrived at their home, there were so many junk computers strewn about everywhere that he could no longer fit them inside the double garage. The computers were scattered all over the long driveway.

And now, his old computers had taken over the dining room, too, inside their house – all over the large walnut dining room table, the chairs, the floor.

My mother was enraged by the sight of all of these tattered, rusty useless computers strewn all over the driveway, the dining room, the garage. My father was also heaping them in the spare bedroom. My mother screamed daily about the junk computers, but my father simply retreated into the garage, wearing headphones, listening to Rush Limbaugh, and blocking out my mother's screaming utterances.

My mother was used to winning. She had often told me, "Ang, you are too easy-going. If you want to win a fight, do like I do. Just scream and shout down the other person until they give up."

But my father had learned to block her out with talk radio and headphones. Tinkering away at the old computers, while living mostly in the garage, he appeared quite content.

The computer graveyard had also brought with it another problem – cockroaches.

Late that evening, my father had finally come inside from the garage to watch Jeopardy and a football game. My mother dutifully brought him a plate of Kentucky fried chicken and mashed potatoes, which he ate in silence, while watching the TV. As soon as she put down the plate, I noticed little German cockroaches swarming around his plate on the TV tray. My father simply took a can of Raid that was on the floor next to his vibrating chair and sprayed them dead.

"Dad! You and mom need to hire an exterminator!" I was aghast by the site of cockroaches in my parents' home.

"No! That's too expensive!" my father declared. "It's unnecessary. I just spray them, and your mother cleans up the dead ones. You are stupid, Ang! You never think of saving money!"

I was horrified.

Then, my mother ushered me into the back bedroom and asked me to sit on her bed. She had moved out of their mutual bedroom and was now sleeping in a small bedroom alone.

She reached into the back of the closet, and she took out an old plastic yellow purse from the 1960s and handed it to me.

"Shh!" she said. "Don't tell your father. He would kill me. Open the purse," she whispered.

I opened up the purse, and there inside of it was approximately $3,000.00. My mother had never bestowed such a present upon me before. My parents had not even paid for my college tuition. I was shocked, amazed, and deeply touched by this random, unexpected act of generosity. The money was neatly stacked in little piles of twenty dollar bills, ten dollar bills, fives, and ones, and a few two dollar bills.

"Ang, I want you to know that I have been saving up this money to give you for many years. It represents money from all of the years I've sold used sewing machines at the flea market."

While my father sold the used computer parts at the flea market, my mother sold used sewing machines and knick knacks. She had been a sewing machine mechanic during WWII and had learned how to repair commercial sewing machines.

Overwhelmed, I burst into tears. After all, this was the same mother and father who had refused to pay for my college education, or even buy me a bag of groceries when I started a new job and my boss called them and told them I had no food in my home.

"Can you help her out a little until she receives her first pay check?"

"Charity begins at home," my father told my new boss, "and my wife and I can barely make ends meet ourselves." My father slammed down the receiver.

I had asked my boss for an advance on my first cheque because I had been living on a bag of potatoes for more than a week. She felt confident that a phone call to my parents would certainly solve my dilemma. She shook her head in disbelief after hearing my father's words, and then offered me a twenty dollar bill out of her own pocketbook. "Don't worry about it. Consider it a gift," my new boss had said.

⸻ ••●●••• ⸻

Now here I was, sitting next to my mother on her bed, an old plastic yellow purse with $3,000 in it between us. Yellow was her favorite color. I hugged my mother.

"Oh, Mom. Are you sure you want to give me all of this money?"

"I am certain," she replied.

"Hurry up and put this purse in your car before your father sees it. He would kill me if he knew about this."

I hesitated.

"Mom, I'm going to use this money to pay for an exterminator for you and dad."

"No, ***please don't do that***, Ang! Your father will kill me. In fact, he'll kill both of us."

Having in the meantime changed her mind about divorcing my father, my mother stayed behind in Tampa, and I drove back to Gainesville with a yellow purse filled with $3,000 in cash.

⸻ ••●●•• ⸻

Back in Gainesville, Florida, I was somehow reluctant to put that $3,000.00 in the bank. I just had a ***bad feeling***. So, I left the purse sitting on the floor of the passenger door, the car locked.

Sure enough. A few days later, my parents called me. They were a united voice. My mother was on the phone in her bedroom. My father was on the phone in the living room of their Tampa home.

"You little bitch! Calling the authorities on us!"

"What?"

Someone (probably a neighbor) had called the city of Tampa and reported that my parents had computers strewn all over their driveway and that it was a ghastly site. My parents were fined and told by city officials that they had two weeks to clean up the mess or face further fines. Social workers were also then contacted by city officials to conduct a wellness check and inspect the inside of their home. Pest control was mandated. My parents concluded that it had been me who had made the initial phone call.

"I want you to drive down here right now and give back that $3,000.00 to your mother or we're going to call the police and press charges against you for theft," my father sternly stated, in hostile tones. "You are a worthless daughter," he yelled. "Just leave us alone. You are not welcome in our house."

I dutifully got into my car instantly and drove the next two and half hours to Tampa. When I arrived, my parents glared at me with hatred as they sat together on their front porch holding hands. I tossed the yellow purse out of my car window and onto their front lawn, and drove back up the highway.

A few weeks passed.

My phone rang.

"Ang," my mother began in a tearful pathetic voice. "Can you come and get me?"

"Come and get you?"

"Yes! I want to divorce your father, and I want to come live with you!"

I laughed heartily.

"It's not funny, Ang! I'm really, really, really, really, **really** serious this time. I have already packed my suitcases. I want to come live with you."

"Why, Mom. Why is that . . . that you suddenly want to come live with me after 55 years of marriage?"

"I just can't take it any more! Your father always ignores me! I am sooo lonely! He spends weeks at a time in the garage and doesn't speak to me." Suddenly, my mother was crying hysterically.

"Please! Please, Ang! Please come get me!"

There were many beats of silence, as my mother continued to sob so pathetically.

"Okay, Mom. When do you want me to come and get you?"

"Right now! Right now!!" The sobs grew louder again.

"But, Ma, it's already 7 p.m."

"I know! Just please come and get me!"

"Have you informed Dad that you wish to leave him?"

"Yes! He can hear me right now! He knows I am serious!"

(turning to my father) "I am divorcing you, you son of a bitch!"

(father replying in the background) "Get the hell out of house, you son of a bitch! Have your worthless daughter come and get you right now!!"

"She's on her way, you son of a bitch!"

"Good! You son of a bitch! Have her take a plane so she can get here sooner, so I can change the locks!"

(back to me on the phone) "Ang, did you hear that? He is sooo cruel to me! After all that I do for him!"

(father in the background) "Yeah. Yeah. All I have to do is hire a maid. Now, get the hell out of here!!"

(sound of my father hitting my mother with his cane)

"Ow! You stop that, you son of a bitch! Or I'll call the cops on you!"

"GET THE HELL OUT OF MY HOUSE RIGHT NOW!!" my father roared.

"Mom! Mom! Can you hear me?"

(sobbing hysterically) "Yes, Ang! I can hear you!"

"Mom! I'm on my way!"

Crying on my way to Tampa, I started envisioning how I would have to spruce up the spare bedroom in preparation for my mother's arrival.

Speeding, down Interstate-75, it took me less than two hours to arrive at my parents' house in Tampa.

And there was my mother, waiting on a chair on the front porch with three suitcases by her side.

I exited my vehicle and began loading up the suitcases.

My father, noticing I had arrived, slammed shut the front door and locked it tightly.

Soon, my mother was inside my car, and off we went back to Gainesville. It was about 11 p.m. when we arrived back at my house. I was exhausted.

With the sound of the crickets chirping on the front lawn, I unloaded my van and brought my mother's three suitcases into the house.

"Mom, can I get you something to eat?"

"No, I'm not hungry. I'm too upset to eat."

"Do you want something to drink?"

"Just a little water, Ang."

"Here, Mom. Have a seat."

She sat down, took a few sips of the water, then started sobbing hysterically.

"Mom! It will be all right! I'll take care of you!" I said, rubbing her back, and caressing her.

Suddenly, she pulled away, and looked up at me. The tears had stopped, and now there was just a pathetic look in her eyes, and a pathetic tone in her voice.

"Ang, could you do me a little favor right now?"

"Could you phone your father for me?"

•••●●●•••

CHAPTER EIGHT –

THE LOVE OF MY LIFE (1993)

Thereafter, I took about a six-year hiatus from my parents. You see, I had found the love of my life.

He was 23 years younger than me, and his name was Jud. "Jud, like Mud," he said to me during our first conversation. "That's how you'll remember my name."

He was 19 years old.

He was 19 and I was 42 when we first met.

His mother was certainly the new mother in my life, but not much of an improvement over my own blood mother.

Cathy was just two years older than me, but she looked about 20 years older.

Whenever we were together, people would ask her, "Is that your daughter?" Cathy was a sweet, Tammy Faye-style Southern belle. She would reply, with a big fake smile, "Oh! Bless your heart! How I wish she was my natural-born daughter! She is my son's wife!"

The first time we met, I could see the tension and disapproval in her smiling face. "Let's go for a walk," she said, the anger dripping from her smile. Cathy then told me that she and her sisters just happen to practice witchcraft. "And we didn't like my other son's girlfriend. So, we all got together and had a ceremony. Within a week," she snapped her fingers, "they were broken up."

It was pretty obvious why Cathy was telling me this information, but I stayed quiet. We walked to her house, not far away from my house, and there she showed me her Coca-Cola memorabilia room, her collection of Barbie Dolls in the spare bedroom, and her mannequins. At the front entrance of her foyer stood a mannequin of a young boy with bright, red hair. "It looks just like Jud, doesn't it?" she asked me. "He was such an adorable little boy. I just want to always remember him that way."

My friends comically referred to my mother-in-law as "The Coca-Cola Witch." I guess it was a befitting title. Even the license plate on her Merecedes proudly announced "WITCHY" in all capital letters.

Back at my house, Cathy asked me, "Have you put salt all around your house?"

"No, why should I put salt all around my house?"

"It keeps away curses," she stated.

****

For ten years, I was married to Ira Judson Philpot.

We had met at a wedding. He was friends and a high school buddy with the son of the bride. I was friends with the bride and groom. After talking about our mutual interests in music, at the wedding, and exchanging phone numbers, Jud began phoning me multiple times on a daily basis. I thought nothing about these phone calls. It was a little flattering to have a young guy who had recently graduated from high school and was now working as a stock boy at a local grocery store phone me daily, but Jud was never on my horizon as a potential lover. He was a scrawny kid, 5'7" with bright red hair, freckles, and he loved to skateboard. He was quite good on the skateboard.

I actually was involved in a relationship with a very dull man when I first met Jud. I was very bored with my lover, who suffered from a chronic sinus infection. Additionally, Kurt sported an elongated Hitler-style mustache, which was not sexy at all.

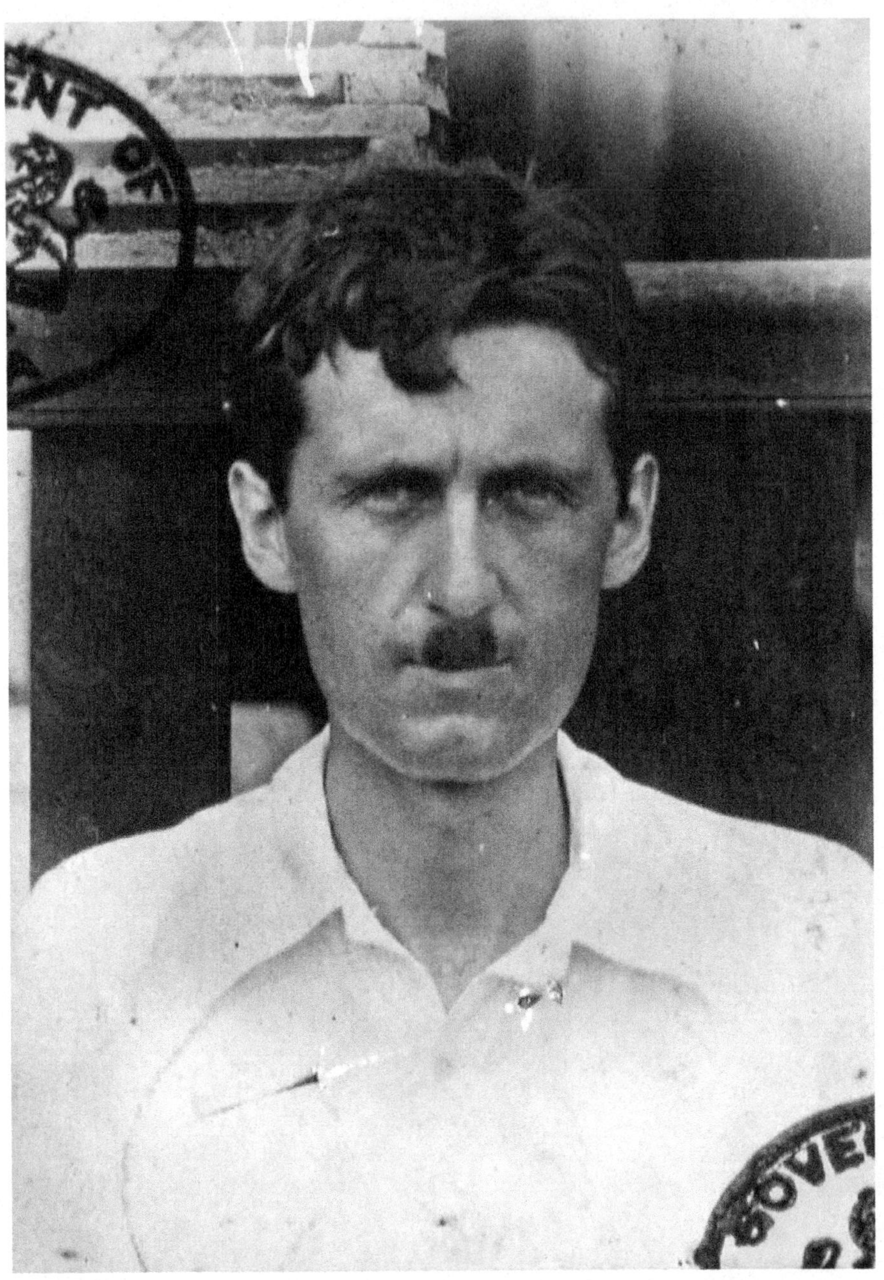

I was baffled that anyone would want to sport a mustache that reminds people of the world's most infamous tyrant. Kurt would come visit me on the weekends, mow my grass, putter around my house, and run errands for me. At night, he would sit in a chair and watch TV and constantly blow his nose and leave all these little wads of snot-infested toilet paper balls all over my coffee table. Kissing his lips with a patch of Hitler on top became increasingly repulsive, as time passed. Yet Kurt was extremely attached to me, and the longer our relationship went on, the more "in love" and insecure he became.

One weekend when he came to visit me, I could not sleep. Rather than wasting time tossing and turning in bed, I got up and decided to wash the dishes and take out the trash.

Now here, suddenly, was Kurt outside where I was throwing away the trash on the south side of my house, clad in his boxer shorts, and shining a flashlight in my face.

"Where is he!?" Kurt interrogated me.

"Where is **who**?" I replied, startled by his presence at 2 a.m., while I was outside taking out the trash.

"Where is your **lover**?" he stammered.

"My lover??? And, who, pray tell, is my lover?" I inquired.

"I don't know 'who' your lover is!" Kurt raged. "All I know is that it's not normal to be taking out the trash at 3 a.m.! Now, where is he?" Kurt began aiming his flash light at the trees, at the trampoline, at the bushes. But no lover could be found.

Later that day, I decided to attend a Pentecostal church service with a friend of mine. I had never attended a Pentecostal church service before, and the organist of the church, whom I had met in a local music store, had invited me. Out of curiosity, I had decided to attend. Little did we know that a Pentecostal church service is an **all day ordeal.**

We watched in fascination as African American true believers ran around the room with hands up, screaming out the name of Jesus and praising the Lord, dropping to the floor and shaking like a cockroach that is in the process of dying. The entertaining religious service commenced at 11 a.m. and did not finish until about 6 p.m. And then there was a meal we enjoyed after the long service.

Back at my house, a very agitated Kurt was again convinced that I was cheating on him. When I finally came home from the long Pentecostal service, Kurt had gone out jogging after tearing up my house in a fit of rage.

I entered my home to find my computer screen smashed out, shattered glass all over the floor, the bathroom door had a fist hole punch in it. A large hanging picture on the wall of the "Mona Lisa Cat" had also been smashed and there were shattered glass pieces all over the floor.

Upon his return from jogging, Kurt entered his car and drove off in a huff. That was the last time I ever saw him.

I was quite startled by the disarray of my demolished home, and wondered whom I should call. The first person who came to my mind was my little buddy, Jud, who lived about two blocks away.

"Jud, could you come over here right now?"

Jud came right over.

Jud was silent and stunned as he walked through the rooms of my house and took notice of the smashed items and the fist-sized hole punched through the bathroom door.

"You don't need this," he concluded. "You are a nice lady. You need a real man, like me."

I looked at this 19- year-old boy standing tall before me, and giggled. Jud reached down and gave me his first kiss.

Our First Date

Our relationship commenced with a date in an old 1800's cemetery. I had these five friends from Canada – nerdy Kanuck biker guys who used to come visit me once a year, every year, for Bike Week in Daytona Beach. Every year, they would arrive at my house from Gulph, Ontario, spend a few days with me in Gainesville, and then whisk me off to Daytona Beach with them on the back of one of their Harleys.

I always planned something special and comical for their arrival. During the time period when I had just met Jud, I asked him if he'd be willing to dress up as a skeleton and hide behind a tombstone inside a spooky old cemetery.

Sure enough, when the Canadian guys arrived, I drove them to the cemetery where they could hear the sound of a bass guitar twanging a single spooky note repeatedly from behind a tall, old tomb stone.

And there was Jud, dressed as a skeleton with his bass guitar strapped on. He jumped out from behind the tombstone and began to wail out a Grateful Dead tune on his guitar.

The drunken Canadians laughed, and then we all went back to my house and spent the evening talking and drinking beer.

That evening, Jud went back to his condo, packed up his belongings, and moved into my home.

It was to be the beginning of the most happy, creative, productive, and adventuresome 10 years of life, performing as Angelina, the Polka Queen and King Ira. We appeared on "To Tell the Truth." We sang on The Howard Stern Show. We were interviewed by the BBC. We were featured on international news during the Gore/Bush election mess. Jud was my rock. We were the Sonny and Cher of Polka.

Remember Idora!

In 2003, the last year of our ten-year marriage, Jud and I produced a Broadway-style theatrical production with $96,000.00 and a cast of 186 volunteers.

Here's the unusual story of how we produced a spectacular show for my hometown called **Remember Idora!**

RECAP

Idora Park was a charming amusement park in Youngstown, Ohio. It was first built in 1899 and it burned down in 1984. The people of Youngstown were devastated. They tried many times to get the funding to rebuild Idora Park, but it never happened.

I have a very unique connection to Idora Park. My parents owned the basketball stand and the pizza stand within the park. From the ages of 9 to 17, I operated my parents' basketball stand. I also had the freedom to roam the midway as a kid, ride all of the rides for free, and eat all the cotton candy, etc., that I wanted – for free. I loved

Idora Park and it saved me from a very dysfunctional and abusive childhood.

There was a woman named Betty Pattison who operated the cork gun game booth.

She wore a big, blue bouffant wig, with matching blue nails, blue eye shadow, and she toted a blue cigarette holder. She also kept her pet skunk, that wore a pink rhinestone collar, inside her cork gun game booth at the amusement park where I grew up. By far, she was the most memorable and influential person of my childhood.

I'll never forget the day I met her.

"Pssst! Little girl, could you pick up all those corks off the midway? I'll pay you ten cents!"

Wow! I had a job! I was nine years old.

Every day, I picked up those fly-away corks. And every day, she paid me that ten cents.

But more importantly, she *listened* to me!

"You are soooo *fascinating*!" she would say to me.

I went around the park with a notebook and collected jokes and poems from the ride operators and the other carnies. All the rides were mine to ride for free, absolutely free, since my parents owned a food concession booth (the pizza stand) and a game booth (the basketball stand).

"I don't have a joke or a poem for you," Betty stated, but how 'bout this?

Betty wrote, **"I'll always be your friend until the kitchen sinks and Niagara Falls. Love, Betty."**

I was a friendless kid alone in a big amusement park, free to roam the midway, unattended. **But now I had a friend!** — a very, very special friend with a big, bouffant wig! — who listened to me!

Which leads me to this story I want to share with you.

In the year 2000, the most unusual thing happened to me. I had never had an experience like this before.

I woke up in the middle of the night, and there were songs – original songs – complete with all of the lyrics playing in my head. Night after night, this continued to happen. I quickly found out that I had to turn on the light, grab a pen, and scribble down the lyrics that would be pouring out of my head, or they would be lost forever.

Night after night, this experience, that I must call *spiritual,* happened to me. In all, 32 songs poured out of my head in this manner in honor of the extinct and beloved Idora Park.

I truly felt this was a gift from the Divine, as I had not consciously planned to write a musical that honors Idora Park.

My husband at that time, Jud, a.k.a. "King Ira," took the project quite seriously. He was always quick to learn new things, a very talented guy. Soon, we had set up a music recording studio in our home. The two of us took this project quite seriously. For the next two years, we spent thousands of dollars and thousands of hours producing a CD, a complete musical titled "Remember Idora!" Now that I had all of the songs, it was just a matter of writing comedy vignettes that would transport audience members from one part of the park to another.

Hundreds of amateur singers and speakers came to our house and performed so that we would have the variety of voices to make it sound like an actual adventure at Idora Park. We included midway ambiance. We even took a camcorder with us and rode a wooden roller coaster in Tampa, Florida so that we could add the sounds of a real wooden roller coaster descending, with the riders gleefully screaming, during that first big descent.

At the end of two long years of working multiple hours a day on the script and CD, we were ready to tell Youngstown, Ohio that we had something they could cherish. I remember there were tears in my eyes, and King Ira and I hugged and cried tears of joy at the completion of this long, tedious, expensive project.

"Oh, honey!" I told him. "We are going to bring so much joy to the people of Youngstown!" Through theatrical illusion, we would soon be bringing the beloved and well-missed Idora Park back to life.

Then there was that fateful day when I phoned the Youngstown Playhouse and asked to speak with the managing director, Robert Vargo.

"You don't know me, but my name is Angela Woodhull. I grew up in Youngstown. I literally grew up in Idora Park. My parents owned the pizza stand and the basketball stand during the Sixties. I have written a 2 ½ hour musical about Idora Park."

"You're kidding me!" he replied.

I could tell by the enthusiasm in his voice that he was quite intrigued, quite interested. Yes, he wanted me to send him the script and the CD immediately.

Soon, a contract arrived in the mail. I was living in Gainesville, Florida – far from my hometown of Youngstown, Ohio.

But there seemed to be something very odd, very weird about the contract. I didn't know exactly what it was, but my gut told me that something was not right.

I went to see the managing director of the Hippodrome State Theatre in downtown Gainesville and he looked over the contract with me. He looked absolutely floored. It was jaw dropping for him as he read the contract.

"You don't want to sign this," he told me. "You **really** don't want to sign this!" he said.

"Why?"

"Well, it gives the Youngstown Playhouse permission to write a derivative of your musical. They can take your ideas, switch things out, and create their own musical about the amusement park. Do you want that?"

I was so disheartened. I went home and cried. For a week or two, I simply did nothing. I went home and I cried. And cried.

Meanwhile, without my signature, and without my permission, the Youngstown Playhouse was casting for an Idora Park musical! When I found this out from old friends I still had in Youngstown who had read about the auditions in the **Youngstown Vindicator**, I was absolutely floored.

A friend of mine went to the auditions and verified that my script had been altered. My songs had been used to create derivative songs, which is copyright infringement.

I didn't know what to do.

I called the **Youngstown Vindicator** to tell them what happened.

They wrote up a story about the controversy, pretty much stating that some unknown "woman from Florida," as though I had no connections to Youngstown, had allegedly written some musical about Idora Park, and Bob Vargo was now suddenly claiming to the newspaper that he had originally written his own version of an Idora Park musical waaaaay back in the 1980s and was now finally staging it!!!

I contacted several attorneys in Youngstown. Some had been former board members of the Youngstown Playhouse over the years and were reluctant to do anything to assist me. This was a true case of copyright infringement, and yes, my materials had already been copyrighted by me.

One day, I received the weirdest phone call from some guy who claimed he was calling me from Chicago. He said his name was Bentley Lenhoff.

"You don't know me, but I used to be the managing director of the Youngstown Playhouse. I hate that Playhouse! Let's sue them! I have a free attorney for you!"

Apparently, the word had gotten out in this small cliquish town of Youngstown that I was attempting to find an attorney and have an injunction placed upon the Youngstown Playhouse for copyright infringement.

The "free" attorney that Lenhoff directed me to go see just happened to be his son-in-law, Attorney Marc Dann. (I didn't realize that at the time.)

Dann, I noticed, was not taking any notes when I spoke to him about what had transpired so far, and he did not seem to be really listening. I decided to not use his "free services," which was a wise intuitive move, since it turned out that Bentley Lenhoff was actually coming back to Youngstown to, once again, becoming the managing director of the theatre he told me he allegedly "hated."

I was inundated by emails from young people who told me, "Don't sue the Playhouse. It's all we have here in Youngstown."

The next day, armed with about 1,000 copies of my CDs and scripts, and a back seat filled with clothes, a few pots and pans, and my two cats, I drove to Youngstown. I decided that somehow, some way, I was simply going to put on my own show, my own way.

You see, I had hired a private investigator who had videotaped one of the rehearsals at the Playhouse. It was uncanny how they had taken my content and reworked it, twisted it, and made it worse. I mean, if you're going to take my original work and steal it, please make it better, not worse.

My musical showed actual people from back in the day walking around, talking, riding the rides, etc. It also included a special little girl who ran around the park collecting jokes and poems from the ride operators and game booth carneys. This little girl is then a teenager who attends the sock hop during the second half of the show. Yes, this little girl was me.

Instead of making the musical a whirlwind experience about real Idora Park patrons from back in the day, The Youngstown Playhouse took my song concepts and had midway barkers relate the history of Idora Park. For instance, they mentioned that Ethyl's French Fry Stand burned down during the Fifties and had to be rebuilt. So, their version was a history lesson and then songs about the park, derived from my songs. For instance, my musical shows a couple with the man proposing to his girlfriend on the top of the Ferris wheel. The song is sung by a barbershop quartet. Their version also showed a barbershop quartet singing to a couple sitting in a Ferris wheel car.

I wrote a song about Big Band Night at Idora Park.

They too, had a song that ended with the same, ***"Ole!"***

When I arrived in Youngstown after decades of being away, everything looked pretty bleak. Youngstown had become the Detroit of Ohio. All of the steel mills had closed. There had been "white flight" out of Youngstown, and all that remained now were boarded up buildings and pot holes in the roads. Scary Youngstown.

I rented an old warehouse above an ambulance station (that had used to be a Cadillac dealership back in the day), and there I lived, in one of the dusty office rooms, with only a mattress upon the floor, a space heater, and my two cats.

Every day, I would get up and face the snow. I had thousands upon thousands of fliers printed.

Every day, I would accost strangers – in parking lots, in bank lines, at the supermarkets, in the mall, and tell them, "I am Angela Woodhull. I wrote the *real* version of the Idora Park musical. I will be holding a meeting at Leonardo's Restaurant on Saturday. I would like you to be in my show. Can you make it? I'll be playing my songs at that time. Please come!"

The first meeting I held, six people showed up. Three of them, I had known from my childhood. They listened to my CD. There were tears in everybody's eyes. "Oh, my gawd," Darlene said. "We have to put this show on."

"Well, there are six of you here today. Now, each of you, come back with six more next Saturday."

And they did. I continued to accost people in parking lots.

I also started contacting local dance studios. I thought, "If each dance studio in Youngstown could take two or three of the songs, we'll have a spectacular musical."

The first dance studio to come on board was Sandy Bee's in Struthers Ohio, a suburb of Youngstown. Her teenage dancers were excited to be in an upcoming show about Idora Park. Momentum was growing.

Soon, I had a kiosk inside the Southern Park Mall in Boardman, Ohio (another suburb of Youngstown). I dressed up as a cup of French fries, in memory of Ethyl's French fries, and passed out fliers, selling tickets in advance. I desperately needed advanced ticket sales in order to fund this huge theatrical project.

As the momentum gained, so did the tension between me and the Youngstown Playhouse clique. One day, a group of about 12 older men all came by my kiosk in the Southern Park Mall, where I was clad in the French Fry costume, and took my fliers, announcing my show, **Remember Idora**, which was going to be performed at Powers Auditorium in Youngstown, Ohio (the biggest, baddest theatrical venue in Youngstown), had been cancelled. Soon, the rumor spread, all over town that my show had been cancelled. (It was not true.) People were advised NOT to buy an advanced sale ticket to my show, **Remember Idora**. They were told that I was just a flim-flam con artist who would take their money and head back to Florida; and that there would be no **Remember Idora** show.

Members of the Playhouse also vandalized my car. I had bought an old convertible from the Sixties and had paid to have it painted "Remember Idora" with the dates of the show also listed on the car. Cast members, clad in Sixties getup, would drive around town, waving at passersby. Twice, members of the Playhouse spray painted and vandalized my car.

But in the end, the Judi Conti Dance Studios came on board. In the end, I had a cast of 186 volunteer cast members, which was no easy feat, and my show was a sellout. There, up on the stage, when the curtains opened, was Idora Park, rebuilt for the stage! In one scene, there were 25 cups of tap-dancing French Fries in honor of Ethyl's French Fry Stand. We also had dancing bumping cars and ballerinas performing the Merry-Go-Round song. About 6,000 people saw my show Memorial Weekend, 2003, at Powers Auditorium.

**And there was "Betty" up on the stage, clad in her blue
bouffant wig, toting a live skunk wearing a rhinestone collar!
Yes, we even obtained a live skunk for show. Betty sang to Little
Angie, as they danced together . . . .**

I'll always be your friend
I'll always be your friend
Until the kitchen sinks and Niagara Falls
I'll always be your friend
I'll always be right here
Come every Spring, you'll see!
That all the clowns will dance and the bands will play
They'll always be right here . . .

At the end of the 2 ½ hour musical, I received a standing ovation
from the people of Youngstown. It was my moment of moments. It
was truly the biggest moment of my entire life.

The Playhouse then decided to put on their crappy derivative
version of my show for a **second** time after seeing that my show was
a sellout. At that point, I did obtain an attorney, Bruce Wilson, Akron,
Ohio, and we sued the Youngstown Playhouse in federal court. We
prevailed in an out-of-court settlement in federal court. The
Playhouse was given a permanent injunction. It wasn't yet raining
lawsuits in my life. But it was a start. Lawsuits take a lot of time and
energy and distract from creative pursuits.

Staging "**Remember Idora**" was the biggest moment of my life. It
also brought so much joy to my hometown, and an opportunity for
people of different ethnic and racial backgrounds and sexual
orientations to interact with each other and understand each other in
a theatrical setting. There is often a real division in Youngstown, and
my show, my cast members, succeeded in moving beyond that.

Perhaps, in the future, my musical about Idora Park will be re-
staged and will bring life back to Idora Park, through theatrical
illusion.

IDORA PARK

CHAPTER NINE --

2004 A TEARFUL PHONE CALL FROM

MY DAD

"Ang, could you come down here to Tampa?" my father sobbed into the receiver of his phone. It had been more than six years since I had last spoken to my parents. ***"Your mother had quadruple open heart surgery more than a week ago, and she is still in a coma. I think she is going to die. Can you please come, Honey? I am here all alone, and your mother would like to see you."***

My father burst into uncontrollable wailing.

Like a scene from ***"Stuart Smally Saves His Family,"*** I dutifully got into my car and headed to Tampa, wiping away tears from my cheeks.

The hospital staff led me into a large private hospital room where my mother was hooked up to many monitoring machines. She laid there under the oxygen tent, oblivious to everything.

"She's been that way for several days," the nurse told me. "It is not looking hopeful. When a patient remains in a coma for that long, it is unlikely they are going to snap out of it."

I went over to my mother and held her hand. I rubbed her arms as I brushed away tears.

"Mom, can you hear me? Mom."

I burst into bigger tears.

"Mom," I whispered into her ear, "you have been in a coma for four days, following surgery. It's time to wake up, Mom. Come on, Mom. Wake up. You can do it."

Her eyelids suddenly seemed to move a little.

"Mom," I said, stroking her hair. "If you can hear me, then squeeze my hand."

I felt a little tugging on my hand.

"Good! Mom, open your eyes."

She started to take large gasps of breath. And then her eyelids fluttered. And then she opened her eyes. It was an amazing moment. I called the nurses so they could see what had just happened. They rushed to my mother in disbelief.

"Mom! Where were you?" I asked her. "You have been in a coma for several days following your heart surgery!"

"I don't know, but I'm happy to be back!" she said, her throat hoarse.

The nurses offered her some water. Within a few weeks, my mother was back at home. I had brought with me a video tape of the **Remember Idora!** show. "***Alas, my parents would be so proud of me!***" I thought.

I had also purchased a VCR for them so that they could watch the video. Together, we sat in the living room, watching my recreation of the beloved amusement park, the dancing French fries, their pizza stand.

Upon the completion of watching the video, I was in joyful tears. I turned to my mother,

"Well, how did you like the show, Mom?"

My mother frowned.

"Why did you have someone **so fat** play my part? I was NEVER that fat! I feel so embarrassed!! I hope none of my friends from Youngstown saw that stupid show!"

My father, silent, got up on his three-wheeler and rolled back into his computer-ridden garage.

••●●●••

The next time I saw my father was three days before his death. After suffering a stroke, he seemed to be making a miraculous recovery. My mother had summoned me to drive down to Tampa and sit with her as members of Hospice entered and exited their home. My father had a sudden burst of energy. He began riding around the house in his scooter at high speed. He had lost his ability to speak English. He was only speaking in Italian.

He came over with his scooter and stared at me while I was seated at the kitchen table.

"Chi è questa bella donna?" he asked my mother. ("Who is this beautiful woman?")

My mother replied, **"Lei è tua figlia."** ("It is your daughter.")

My father deepened his stare of me. Then he said, **"Non ho una figlia. Lei è una puttana."** ("I have no daughter. She is a whore.")

And with that, he began to ram his scooter multiple times into my shins.

"Dad! Stop!" I screamed, and I moved my legs underneath the table, as I cried.

"Don't pay any attention to him, Ang. He doens't mean it. He's lost his mind."

Three days later, my father was in a coma. He breathed rapidly, while all of the lights in house flickered for several hours.

I held his hand and whispered in his ear.

"Dad, will you please give me your blessing? Dad, I do so many creative things. I am a song writer. And I believe in my creative projects. I want my creative projects to succeed. I want children all over the world to sing my songs, Dad. Will you give my creative projects your blessing?" I whispered into his ear.

I felt a slight movement in his hand, in his quivering hand. He was trying to squeeze my hand as he breathed so rapidly, as though he was running his final marathon.

And then he squeezed my hand twice.

And then he took his last breath.

••●●●●••

AT MY MOTHER'S BANKS -- 2007

But I was now at the bank with my mother. My mother had moved into my Gainesville, Florida home, and I had obtained a small apartment, two blocks away, to have some semblance of peace and sanity in my life in case she got into one of her "moods."
My ten-year relationship with King Ira was over. There were no more Broadway-style shows. There were no more dancing French fries. What had happened?

I had found King Ira in bed at La Quinta Hotel, Room 325, with my "best" girlfriend, Anita Dolak. For one year, during the rehearsals of *Remember Idora* in Youngstown, Ohio, they had sworn to me, repeatedly, that I was "crazy" to think they were having an affair.

"Ang! Look me in the eyes!" Anita would say to me very dramatically, repeatedly, when I'd take her out for supper every

140

Friday at my expense. She was part of the cast of *Remember Idora* and featured in a scene where she and my husband danced the polka together while singing a love song to each other that I had written.

"I am NOT interested romantically in your husband! He is **_NOT MY TYPE!_**"

And there I found them, in La Quinta Hotel, Room 325. I had posed as the maid, and they had – to their surprise -- opened the door. There was my husband, in the bed, butt naked, eating red licorice and sushi and watching cartoons. Anita came to the door with a towel wrapped around her head, and another big, white hotel towel wrapped around her body. She stared at me for a long time. I stared at her for a long time. We were both silent. Finally, Anita spoke.

<u>Well, at least now it's out in the open</u>," she stated, as she cocked her head to one side and adjusted the chintzy motel towel over her nipples.

That was her <u>*exact quote*</u>, and I shall never forget it. It marked the end of my 10-year marriage to King Ira, Ira Judson Philpot.

[IT'S SING ALONG TIME! "BEST FRIENDS FOREVER!

"Break a Leg!"

Alone in my SUV, heading back to Florida after picking up my clothes and some furniture from Youngstown, Ohio, I happen-chanced upon an accident scene that was in progress on the interstate, approaching Columbus, Ohio. A light sleet snow was falling across the highway as I entered the accident scene. I pressed on my brakes, and there was nothing. No response. My SUV continued to roll forward, gaining momentum with every inch.

Two Ohio State troopers made large X's with their flash lights, advising me to stop. Panicked, I continued to press on the brake pedal as hard as I could. But the brakes did not engage as my car moved full speed ahead. And soon there was that fateful second when my SUV, while towing a 8 X 12 U-haul trailer, crashed into car number six, shattering my right leg – breaking it in eight places. Even my right femur bone snapped in half. State troopers and paramedics already on the scene rushed over to my driver's side window. I tried to remain calm, as I felt my leg expanding to the size of an elephant's leg.

"Are you all right?" they inquired, shining their lights into my face.

"I believe my right leg is broken," I calmly replied. It was best not to think about it. I actually felt no pain.

Soon, a helicopter arrived and I was air lifted to Ohio State University Medical Center for six hours of intensive surgery to repair multiple fractures in my right leg. I remember my last thoughts before the anesthesia kicked in. "Well, I have been always told in show business to 'Break a Leg,' so I guess this is meant to be some type of good luck."

While in the hospital, recovering, I realized I had a big problem. I wondered how, in my incapacitated state, I was going to get back to Florida. I was now confined to a wheelchair. And, so, I placed a "Help Wanted" ad in the **Columbus Dispatch** advertising for a ride back to

Florida. "Wanted: Someone with a van, preferably with a bed in it. I am recovering from major surgery and need a ride back to Florida. You will also need a hitch on the back of your van for pulling a 8 X 12 U-Haul trailer." After all, my SUV had been completely totaled, and I still had an 8 X 12 U-Haul trailer waiting in a junk yard for me to claim. I was still being charged daily by U-Haul.

As a variety of strangers came to my hospital room to be interviewed for the driving gig, the hospital social worker appeared.

"Ms. Woodhull. Why are all of these strangers coming into your hospital room? We can't have this!"

"I'm advertising for a ride back to Florida," I explained.

"Well, don't you have any friends or relatives down in Florida who can come and get you?"

"I do not," I stated. "My friends work. I have no relatives."

"Why were you up here in Ohio in the first place?" the social worker inquired.

"Because I just finished producing a $96,000 Broadway-style musical with a cast of 186 individuals."

The social worker smiled widely, gave me an open stare, opened her notebook while clicking on a pen, and began writing. "Tell me more about this Broadway production you produced up in Youngstown," she stated.

"Well, we had 50 cups of tap-dancing French fries up on the stage," I said proudly. "We had 30 dancing bumping cars," I continued. "And the Merry-Go-Round scene was so amazing, with elegant ballerina dancers simulating a carousel in honor of Idora Park," I explained.

"Well, that's quite interesting," she replied, and she snapped shut her notebook and departed.

Next thing I know, about half an hour later, four psychiatrists with clip boards appeared in my hospital room.

"Why are you here?" I asked them.

"The social worker reported that you were delusional. Talking about being the producer of a Broadway Show with dancing French fries" they replied.

I suddenly felt terrified. I realized I was on the verge of being Baker Acted in the State of Ohio. What would this lead to? Would I end up in Grandma-in-the-Basement's Massillon with no escape?

I sat up straight in my hospital bed and grabbed my cell phone. "Hold on," I replied. "I am calling a medical doctor."

Luckily for me, one of my cast members from *Remember Idora*!, Anne Harmon, is also a licensed osteopathic doctor. I hastily dialed Dr. Anne on my cell phone.

Luckily, Annie answered the phone. She already knew I was in the hospital recovering from major surgery.

"Annie! There are four psychiatrists facing me at the moment here in my hospital room. Can you please verify to them that there really was a Broadway-style production in Youngstown, Ohio of Remember Idora, and I was the producer? They were told by a social worker that I am delusional."

Anne verified that, indeed, there had been 50 cups of tap dancing French fries, and dancing bumping cars etc., in the musical I had recently produced in Youngstown, Ohio, *Remember Idora*!

The four psychiatrists took their clipboards and left, as I eyeballed them with a hostile stare as they sheepishly departed from my hospital room, my heart pounding in fright.

****

Finally, a retired Marine with a large van, with a bed in the back, and a trailer hitch, answered my ad. He was the perfect person to take me back to Florida, and a perfect gentleman.

Soon, I was back at my house in Florida. And then I was being summoned to Tampa by my mother.

There were no more polka shows. There was no more traveling or nursing home gigs. There were no more parties at my house, music jams, or celebrations.

There was only mom and me, me and mom, and her daily phone conversations with Estranged Cousin Shirley and Shirley's conniving husband, John Mascarella.

CHAPTER TEN:

AND NOW, WE WERE AT MY MOTHER'S BANKS

On a Monday morning in the month of October 2007, I rolled my mother in her wheelchair into Wachovia Bank, at her request. (My mother could walk, but she enjoyed being pushed in a wheelchair by me.) I assumed it was just an ordinary day of running errands for my mother, and one of those errands just happened to be depositing her modest social security cheque into the bank.

Customers entered and exited the bank, as I rolled my mother in. A tall woman wearing a business suit stood at the front entrance of the bank.

"Good morning, Mrs. Falvo. How may I assist you today?"

"Yes, I would like to see your bank manager," my mother replied. "My husband has died, and I want to remove his name from all of our CDs and money markets," my mother explained.

"Certainly," the tall woman replied. "Please be seated in our waiting area, and I'll have Ms. Freeman come and get you as soon as she is available."

While we were waiting on Ms. Freeman, I had flashbacks of all of the times during my adult life that my parents reassured me that they were broke and almost penniless. I believed them. I had always believed them. After all, when I was a college student, struggling just to have enough money to buy a bag of potatoes, my parents would require me to pick up the tab if we went out to eat. I also paid for all the long distance phone calls when I would phone them on a weekly basis. After all, they were old, and they were broke.

"We only have our social security cheques now," my mother used to tell me in a sad voice.

Ms. Freeman suddenly appeared and invited us back inside her office and closed the door behind her.

"Mrs. Falvo, how may I assist you today?"

My mother grinned widely, then replied, "I want to remove my husband's name from all of my CDs and money market accounts and add my daughter's name instead. Make all of the accounts POD to her, "Payable on Death."

"All right, we can do that, Mrs. Falvo," the bank manager stated, as she opened a new computer screen.

"And please let me know the balances on each account," my mother stated.

"Okay, we can do that, too."

It was a shocking, dumb-founding moment, as the bank manager read off the current value of each of my mother's CDs and money market accounts -- $250,000 in one account. $179,000 in another. $220,000 in a third account, $154,000 in a fourth account, and $138,000 in a fifth account.

Words can't describe how I felt at that moment. To suddenly realize that my "broke" mother had more than half a million dollars in Wachovia Bank was a complete and total shock to me. How could my parents have kept such a secret from me my entire life? Why did I never suspect that my parents were actually quite wealthy?

Well, to answer that question, let me describe the inside of my parents' modest three-bedroom home in Tampa, Florida. Their house was covered in tattered 1970s orange shag carpet that appeared to have never been shampooed. Both of my parents drove old station wagons, a little bent and rusted out here and there. Their furniture was also shabby and slightly ripped. My mother's dishes were mismatched and had been purchased in the 1960s and never replaced. My mother always dressed in cheap tennis shoes, unattractive t-shirts and baggy shorts. My mother never visited a beauty salon or a nail salon in her entire life. Her stringy gray hair was cut short in a page boy, combed to the side, with a single bobby pin holding her hair back from her face. She carried an old plastic purse with a metal button on top – a purse she had purchased from the five and dime store many years before.

I looked at the bank computer screen, and then I looked at my mother.

I had to suddenly come to terms with the fact that my mother, sitting there in her wheelchair, looking like a little old ragamuffin, while clutching her tattered plastic purse was actually a millionaire.

Next, my mother asked me to chauffer her to Bank of America. It was a repeat of what had just transpired at Wachovia Bank. Only, instead of naming accounts as "Payable on Death" to me, the accounts were titled "ITF" or "In Trust For."

Together, between the accounts in Wachovia Bank and Bank of America, I was now suddenly aware that I was the heiress to a millionaire mother who had always appeared to be, and proclaimed to everyone, that she was a **pauper.**

My Mother's Mandate

A few weeks after my father's death (and prior to the trip to the banks), my mother sent me a letter announcing that she was selling her Tampa home and moving in with me. There had never been any discussion about this. It was simply my mother's mandate, sent to me in a two-sentence letter.

"I've decided to sell the Tampa house and move in with you. You need to start taking my belongings in your van to Gainesville."

My mother, who claimed she was too broke to afford a U-Haul truck, mandated that I use my minivan to start gathering her tattered belongings and delivering them to my home in Gainesville. A dozen or so round trips later, my home was populated with stacks of old towels with holes in them, shoe boxes full of sneakers my mother had never worn (some of which she had purchased in the 1960s), old tee-shirts, baggy pants, and lots of boxes of honey buns from Dollar General. My garage soon looked like a hoarder's garage.

"Mom! We're running out of space in my garage! This is my tenth trip! There is no more room, Mom!"

"Then I'll buy a storage shed!" she announced.

And she did.

She bought not one, but two expensive storage sheds.

Soon, a semi-truck with a flat bed arrived at my home to deliver and anchor the two storage sheds to my side yard -- the same side yard where I always was jumping on my trampoline.

Back in Tampa, I was packing up old photos of my mom and dad, old worn out bed sheets (enough old, holey sheets to cover all of the beds in a small motel) my mother's tattered, ugly flannel night gowns, and loading them and other junk into my car. My mother, in the living room of her Tampa home, was watching **The Price is Right** while eating her lunch. Never mind asking her why she needs 100 sets of old mismatched sheets. She had her reasons, and her mind could not be changed.

Back and forth to my car from the back bedroom . . .

Suddenly, I noticed that my mother had slumped over in her living room chair, her mouth agape, her eyes rolled back in her head looking up at the ceiling.

I chuckled softly, and then kept moving boxes from the back bedroom and into my car.

Every time I passed my mother, she remained in this comatose-looking state, now with drool running out of the corner of her mouth for a more dramatic effect.

I chuckled under my breath and kept loading up all of the boxes of my mother's junk.

After about 20 minutes of this, my mother suddenly sat up straight in her chair, and stared at me with wide, angry eyes.

"I can't believe you did that to me!" she shouted.

"Oh, Mom!" I said, giggling. "I knew you were not dead!"

"Yeah, but what if I really WAS dead? You didn't even come over and check on me!!!"

"Well, if you were **really** dead, I guess I would have stopped moving all of these worthless boxes into my car!" I laughed heartily.

"I can't believe it!" my mother cried. "You didn't even care if I were dead!"

This was not the first time my mother had faked being dead. Throughout my childhood, she had gasped for breath and faked heart attacks, so I was used to these antics.

The Problem of Fluffy

During the multiple trips to and from Tampa to pick up my mother's junk, my mother always asked me repeatedly, "Ang, what are we going to do with my old cat, Fluffy?"

"Well, we are simply going to load up Fluffy and take her with us to Gainesville," I replied.

My mother scowled.

"But you already have a cat. And I don't think your cat is going to get along with my cat."

"The cats will adjust to each other," I assured her.

But my mother continued to nag me. She frequently called me on the phone when I was Gainesville, asking me repeatedly what she should do about Fluffy.

My answer remained the same, but my mother insisted that it was going to be a disaster.

If my mother believes something strongly, then that belief becomes <u>the fact</u>, and there is nothing other than her fact.

During the final week of moving my mother's tattered belongings from Tampa to Gainesville, my mother suddenly announced that her cat was "missing."

"Missing?"

"Yep. I haven't seen my cat in several days now," my mother said.

"I wonder what happened to my cat," my mother asked sheepishly.

"Well, did you call the pound? Did you contact the shelter?"

"I did. They do not have Fluffy."

My mother went over to her chair and sighed. "I think somebody poisoned Fluffy," she said in a low voice.

"What makes you think that, Mom?" I asked her. "Fluffy is 12 years old. Why would somebody suddenly want to poison your cat?"

"I dunno," my mother replied softly, looking away.

It was finally my last trip of dragging my mother's ridiculous belongings from her Tampa home to my home in Gainesville. On this particular day, I was supposed to be removing her things from the garage. My mother had already emptied out most of the garage and cleared out my father's old computers. Now, it was bags of old shoes, table cloths, and other worthless stuff that my mother wanted me to place in my car.

When I entered the garage on this occasion, I immediately smelled the most putrid smell coming from inside the garage. My mother was in the kitchen preparing lunch for us. I opened up the door from the garage that leads into the kitchen and asked my mother, "Mom, what is that horrible smell in your garage?"

My mother turned around from the kitchen sink and gave me a blank stare and then shrugged.

"I dunno."

"Oh, come on, Mom. You've got to be able to smell that." I stated.

"Come," I said, grabbing her hand.

She then moseyed into the garage with me.

"Do you smell it?"

"No," she replied. "I don't smell a thing," as she took a breath and so innocently shrugged again.

"Mom, **really!?** You don't smell that putrid smell? It's **overwhelming**!"

"Nope, I don't smell a thing," she replied, nonchalantly, and she walked back into the kitchen.

I then began using my sense of smell to track where the hideous odor was coming from.

And suddenly, there in the corner, behind some old boxes was cat fur flattened on top of the skeleton of a cat. It was the decomposed Fluffy.

I walked back into the kitchen, where my mother was rinsing dirty pots and pans.

"Mom. I found your cat."

"Oh!?"

"That smell, Mom. It's Fluffy."

I escorted her over to the spot behind the boxes so she could view the remains of her cat.

My mother looked on nonchalantly, and then after a long pause, she looked at me, and then suddenly burst into hysterics, feigning tears.

"Oh!" She wailed! "Poor Fluffy! Poor Fluffy! Somebody poisoned Fluffy!! One of my neighbors poisoned Fluffy!!!"

My mother faked tears and screamed hysterics.

"How did Fluffy get back inside the garage if somebody poisoned her?" I asked her.

"How am I supposed to know?! I'm so sad right now, Ang, and you're asking me stupid questions! Aren't you sad for me?!!"

My mother then went inside the house and phoned one of her neighbors while still boo-hooing.

Still sobbing, she told the neighbor, "Ang found Fluffy! Somebody poisoned Fluffy!"

She wailed into the receiver, as the neighbor spoke words of comfort to her.

Alas, the problem of Fluffy had been solved.

•••●••

CHAPTER ELEVEN:

THE LAWSUITS UNFOLD

Out in New Mexico, a Lawsuit was Brewing . . .

After the trips to Wachovia Bank and Bank of America, it dawned on me that my lifetime dream would be able to come true when I inherited a million dollars.

Just imagine. All of my songs – all of my beautiful children's songs that teach literacy – would have a chance to be known. Children all over the world would be able to sing my songs. There would be books of my songs! There would be websites! There would be electronic versions of my songs and books!

Meanwhile, I was happy to spend time with my mother and plan unique outings for her on an almost daily basis.

We were about to enter the car and go out shopping for the day, when the phone rang. It was an attorney from Albuquerque, New Mexico.

"Ms. Woodhull, at your request, I spoke with Carolyn P. Meinel, the owner of the Happy Hacker website, who lives here in New Mexico."

"And what did she say?" I inquired. "Is she willing to take down the claim on her website that I stage 'dancing penis' shows?" I asked him.

"No, she is not," the lawyer responded.

"Why?!" I replied. "She doesn't even know me! Why would she want to do this to me, a complete stranger to her?"

"She wants you to repent to Jehovah God," he replied, "for having 'dancing penis' shows."

I collapsed in my office chair, and my heart was pounding. I was on the verge of fainting.

"Please, could you talk with her again?" I begged him. "Within the next ten years, I am going to have a lot of money. I plan to market my children's music shows. If this false claim keeps coming up on the internet – first place under my name, this will certainly destroy my chances of performing kids' music shows!" I declared.

"I'm sorry. But I have already given you about three hours of my time for free," the attorney responded. "Why don't you just file an injunction yourself?" he suggested. "They're easy to file, and the Albuquerque courthouse has a free paralegal service. They can help you fill out the form for free. I'm certain the judge will grant the injunction."

Meanwhile, my mother, on her walker, was calling me from the living room.

"Ang!!! Why are you on the phone!? You said we were going shopping, and now, you're on the phone!!"

"Okay, thanks for the advice," I told him. "I've got to go."

My mother wanted an explanation of "why" I had wasted her time while I was on the phone.

"Mom," I said, knowing she would probably not understand the situation, "there is a crazy lady in New Mexico claiming I have 'dancing penises' in my accordion polka music shows."

My mother got it. She actually looked quite concerned.

"And this is posted on the internet for the whole world to see and read about you?"

"Yes, Mom."

"Oh, Ang! You've got to do something about that! Sue her, Ang!"

"I'd like to, Mom, but I can't afford an attorney!"

"How did she come up with this bullshit?" my mother inquired.

"Let me show you," I replied.

And then I went inside the garage and dragged out the furry phallic costume that Jud had worn in one, just one of our college shows titled "Her Majesty's X-travaganza." Trying to appeal to the college crowd, we assumed that Jud hopping around in a furry phallic would hit the mark and produce a lot of laughter. Indeed, it did.

I slipped inside the furry phallic and then emerged from the garage and showed it to my mother.

"Mom," I said, while peeking out from the top of the furry phallic, "this is why she says my shows have 'dancing penises' in them.

"But that's not a real penis," my mother stammered. "It has no balls!"

"Exactly, Mom! Exactly!!!" I replied. "And penises are not furry, either!" I added.

My mother agreed.

"I don't think any judge will view this Halloween costume as 'dancing penises,'" she added.

Then my mother sat down as she was still staring at me dressed in the furry phallic.

"Oh, Ang!!! Just deny it! You've got to deny it! Throw that damn costume away!!!"

"I don't want to throw it away!" I said. "I think we should show it to the judge!"

Soon, I would be flying out to Albuquerque, New Mexico, with my mother, to file an injunction against Carolyn P. Meinel, the Happy Hacker.

•••●•●•••

Meanwhile, it was time to grade papers back in my little apartment, two blocks away from Mom.

Mom was pissed. She was in a bad mood, to say the least. Despite having spent the last three full days with her, in which I had taken her to the St. Augustine Beach to feed the seagulls, and out to dinner where we fed fish (the restaurant is literally in the river and there's little boxes on the window sills that open and you throw your scraps into the water below to the hungry snapping catfish), and to a snake store where my mother reluctantly petted a snake for the first time in her life, and to the local museum where we sat among hundreds of live butterflies.

But now it was time to grade papers.

"Mom, did you have a good time the last three days?"

"Yes, Ang. Wonderful! Wonderful!"

Then don't forget this when I'm off grading papers!" I told her.

"I won't."

But soon, she was on the phone with Shirley Mascarella.

"Shirley!" she lamented. "I am here all alone! All alone!!! I haven't seen Ang in about a week! She leaves me here all alone!! I am soooo lonely!!!"

Next thing I know, my phone was ringing.

"Hello."

"Ms. Woodhull?"

"Yes."

"This is Richard Shiner. I am an investigator with Elder Abuse. Could you please come over here to your mother's house? I need to speak with you."

I turned off the computer and rushed over to my house.

"Do you realize that you are about the 10th investigator to come here?!" I said, in a heated voice, when I arrived a few minutes later. "I do NOT abuse my mother!" I protested. "In fact, the last investigator, prior to you, said that my mother is so independent – she washes herself, cooks for herself, mops her own floors, and takes public transportation for the elderly to her doctor's appointments – he said I don't even need to see her every day!"

"Yes, I have read that report," Investigator Shiner stated.

"But this latest report states the neighbors heard you shouting at your mother. They said you were screaming at your mother in a very loud voice."

"Oh, **really**!?" I replied.

"Well, I suggest we go over and talk to those neighbors!" I stated.

And then the two of us walked outside. I then pointed to the very conspicuous **FOR RENT** sign on the empty house immediately next door.

"No one has lived there for at least three months," I told him, my arms folded across my chest.

And then we looked at the house immediately across the street.

"It's vacant, too," I said. There was a large FOR SALE sign on the house.

Behind us, a vacant lot.

"Ms. Woodhull," he replied, "I hope you have a nice day," and Richard Shiner began heading toward his car.

"You know 'who' is doing this, right?" I said to him, following him. "It's my cousin Shirley, from Youngstown, Ohio!"

"I can't verify who made the report," he replied. "It was anonymous."

"Well, it's her and her husband!" I responded.

Richard Shiner was about to enter his car. He turned and gave me a long look.

"Ms. Woodhull," he stated, "just between you and me . . . I feel sorry for you. I can see what is going on here. Have a nice day."

And he pulled away.

I walked back into the house, fuming.

"Mom! You've got to call your friends Shirley and John Mascarella, and tell them to STOP these insane calls to Elder Abuse!!"

"Well, I'm sure that if you would just simply **move in here with me and give up that stupid little apartment of yours**, Shirley and John would stop phoning Elder Abuse!" my mother chuckled.

****

THE HAPPY HACKER HALL OF SHAME

Back in New Mexico, I was required to find a process server to deliver the original civil complaint to Carolyn P. Meinel. It was actually a snowy night in 2007 when we climbed the hills via his jeep in search of Meinel's ranch home in Sandia Park, New Mexico.

"I think she intentionally put down the wrong address on her website," the process server stated.

And then the process server came up with an ingenious idea.

"Instead of going to the east part of this long dirt road, I believe her ranch might be on the **west** side of the road."

This little error would cause us to drive clear across the other side of the mountains.

Sure enough, the process server was correct in his hunch. When we arrived at her mobile home on a large ranch, the snow was tumbling down that evening very heavily. The process server left his engine running. I was safe inside his warm and toasty car, with his toddler child asleep in her baby car seat in his back seat. The process server had the summons and civil complaint rolled up in the back pocket of his jeans as he approached Carolyn P. Meinel's front door. He lightly knocked on the door. Soon, the porch light turned on, and there she was – the Happy Hacker, opening the door to her upscale trailer home. After verifying that it was, indeed, her, he whisked the rolled up court papers out of his back pocket and handed them to her, then briskly walked back to his car. I watched as Carolyn P. Meinel began reading the court papers. But rather than looking horrified, she simply smiled widely and appeared absolutely delighted that she was being sued. I was about to enter a 10- year lawsuit with an absolute nutcase who hacks into websites in the name of Jesus. The Happy Hacker was about to become an everyday part of my life.

The HOA & The Illegal Grass Fines! [Cha-Ching!] ~or~

"The Grass is Always Greener – and Finer!"

Back in Gainesville, Florida, the days were as sunny as the HOA's zealous Attorney, Thomas A. Daniel fervently creating additional rules and regulations that exceeded the HOA covenants -- putting a new spin on the phrase, 'above and beyond.' He piled rule upon rule on top of the existing HOA covenants like a shifty Jenga tower of bureaucracy.

"This is quite illegal," announced Sandy, my intoxicated alcoholic law school dropout neighbor. She bore an uncanny resemblance to a disheveled, vodka-fueled Sherlock Holmes, her home a scene from a detective novel with an unhealthy overdose of 'Hoarders.'

Strewn from one side of her living room to another were papers about the Tower Oaks Homeowners' Association, its origins, the illegal fines that were being collected, and everything possible you wanted to know about the sniveling Ted Bundy-resembling Thomas A. Daniel, Esquire.

Daniel, with his uncanny resemblance to Ted Bundy, but without the charm, had a particular talent for stirring up the absurd. It was as though he'd made a hobby of crafting rules so ridiculously stringent that one would think they were competing in an extreme version of The Sims, where even the color of your mailbox could become a point of contention.

Sandy was convinced she was going to get justice. In her dogged pursuit of justice, Sandy amassed a mountain of complaints and appeals meant for state agencies and the Attorney General. Sandy was always in the process of sending off her detailed mass of paperwork to any government agency that she thought might listen to her.

The only thing is, the paperwork never got sent. After a full day of carefully analyzing all of the homeowner association documents, Sandy would then hit the bottle. Sadly, her ambition, much like the paperwork, was always lost to a haze of evening alcohol.

Her house and yard were a disaster. A dozen cats ran in and out of her tattered front screen door. There were roaches, mosquitoes, and flies everywhere inside her townhouse.

But distressed neighbors believed in her and trusted her. She kept one bedroom quite clean and clutter free. She used this room as her office, and when frustrated neighbors, about to be foreclosed upon for some petty, illegal grass fine would come to visit her, they would leave her all of their paperwork, and threatening letters from the homeowners' association with her. Sandy dedicated herself to trying to help the neighbors every day.

Sandy was in her early seventies when I met her. She wore her messy gray hair in an upswept bun. There was a lit cigarette dangling from her hand at all times when she was talking with you. Her smoky gesticulations were as animated as her rants about the oppressive TOHA and rat-like Tom Daniel. "I'm swear I'm going to get him disbarred!" she would frequently declare, as trails of smoke drifted throughout the darkened room.

Outside of her townhouse was the Tower Oaks neighborhood – in shambles. Back in the 1980s when the townhouses had been built, they had been quite cute and lovely. Most of the townhouses back in those early days were occupied by University of Florida college students. But over the years, landlords had accepted payments from Section 8 HUD. The neighborhood was now a disaster. Many front yards had no grass whatsoever. There was debris everywhere, pot holes in the roads, rotten wood on the buildings. Low-income individuals walked the streets in gangs. The local sheriffs frequently patrolled the neighborhood and were an ever-constant presence. There had been shootings, break-ins, drugs, lots of reports of domestic violence, and a few murders.

Two blocks away from this ghetto side of Tower Oaks was Peppermill, a neighborhood consisting of about 100 single family homes. These homes were kept up well. My yard and my house were one of the most pristine of all.

So, while the ghetto side remained unattended, trashy, dangerous, and filled with drug dealers and crime, Thomas A. Daniel,

Esq. and his comrades on the TOHA board decided they should sue me. They suddenly aimed their legal crosshairs at me, over a trampoline that had experienced 14 years of innocent jumps and giggles. After all, who needs to worry about actual crimes when the real neighborhood threat is a middle-aged woman finding joy in trampoline-leaping?

I was mid-leap on my trampoline one sunny afternoon when I noticed Attorney Thomas A. Daniel, peering through binoculars, tucked behind a veil of Spanish moss. His camera was in hand, clicking away as if I were some kind of elusive wildlife discovered in suburban Gainesville. He was creepily snapping photos of me once again. Why? Yeah, I wondered why, too.

"Mom, why is an attorney snapping pictures of me jumping on my trampoline?" My mother immediately replied with her theory – a theory she instantly declared as fact.

"He wants this property so he can demolish our house and build a McDonald's!" my mother stated with utmost certainty. My mother was absolutely convinced that the Golden Arches would soon replace my bouncing regimen.

She painted a vivid picture: Our cozy home would soon be replaced with the gleaming Golden Arches, the aroma of fresh fries replacing the scent of her rose garden. My trampoline, a source of so much joy, replaced by a bustling drive-thru. In her mind, our house wasn't just under attack, it was under the threat of fast-food conversion.

My mother was adamant, her convictions unshakeable. No amount of reassurances from me could change her mind. Every time I looked out of the window to see Thomas skulking about, I soon expected to see Ronald McDonald waving back at me.

I smiled and scoffed as my mother frequently pronounced this preposterous conclusion. But when you're 91 years old and you've never heard of a homeowners' association before, I guess hamburgers and French fries replacing your home is a fair conclusion.

"Mom, he can't do that," I replied. Our home is not zoned commercial.

"Oh, he'll find a way!" my mother replied, with utmost certainty. She was convinced.

Meanwhile, naïve homeowners were suddenly having to pay various hefty illegal fines for things like . . . letting their grass grow taller than six inches. ~or~ Having their house painted the wrong color (There was nothing in the original covenants about house colors or grass length – and by law, that cannot be changed.)

As my mother and I were dealing with our peculiar McNightmare, Thomas was busy transforming the neighborhood into his own personal fiefdom, seemingly adding a new law every time he took a breath.

With each passing week, he filled his coffers with fines levied for the most ridiculous offenses - blades of grass that dared to grow beyond six inches, houses daring to wear the 'wrong' colors. It seemed he had taken the phrase 'nipping it in the bud' quite literally.

Thomas' obsession with nitpicking the minute details was legendary, leading one to believe he owned a magnifying glass specifically to inspect every blade of grass in the neighborhood. Was it too long? Was it too green? Was it too...grass-like? He probably held nightly vigils, praying to the god of turf for the power to measure each homeowner's lawn down to the millimeter.

Every time he brandished his fine book, it was like he was engaging in a strange game of neighborhood bingo where he derived inexplicable joy from matching the numbers on his fines sheet with the addresses in the community. "Bingo!" he'd cry out in his office, another 'unruly' grass blade brought to justice.

Homeowners would witness the snickering, arrogant Thomas A. Daniel, attorney-at-law, running around in our neighborhood, exiting his little black Mazda pickup truck with a ruler in one hand, and a camera in the other, measuring the grass in our yards.

Folks who didn't pay these bogus fines were suddenly being foreclosed upon.

And then, Attorney Thomas A. Daniel just happened to be buying up these foreclosed properties at way below market value! Soon, my neighborhood was quickly becoming The Thomas A. Daniel, Esq. Kingdom.

And so, it was time for me to write a formal complaint letter to the Florida Bar and actually mail it off.

A few weeks later . . .

To my complete astonishment and surprise, the Florida Bar actually acted upon my complaint! The Bar recommended that Attorney Thomas A. Daniel, at the very least, step down as treasurer. He was also told that he could no longer be the attorney of record for the HOA. They called it a "conflict of interest." Daniel was mandated by the Florida Bar to give up his conflicting positions on the TOHA board.

Suddenly, all those little profitable grass fines came to an end.

My neighbors were elated.

But Tom Daniel was **not** elated.

Soon, after Thomas A. Daniel was severely reprimanded by the Florida Bar, I was to learn yet another life lesson -- in the form of a big, brown envelope that arrived via a deputy sheriff at my front door.

There were no bulldozers ready to build the Golden Arches, as my mother had predicted, but now, Thomas A. Daniel was suing my mother and me for my jumping on a trampoline!

****

"Off to Albuquerque: A Phallic Adventure"

In the Spring of 2007, my mother and I loaded up my car and headed to the Gainesville Regional Airport with her wheelchair, her diapers, her medicines, and ... a furry phallic.

My mother had never been on an airplane before in her entire life, and she and the phallic were somehow selected for special treatment when we arrived at security at the Gainesville Regional Airport. It had been rolled up like a sleeping bag, with a spring cord wrapped around it. But after it went through the X-ray machine, the guards decided to subject my mother for further treatment. My mother's wheelchair, luggage, and the phallic were all examined in detail by airport security. Her two suitcases were completely opened and rummaged through. And the furry phallic was examined internally via two airport police and their flashlights, while my mother, a first-time flyer, looked on, somewhat irritated, somewhat amused. Flashlights plunged into the innards of the phallic, probing its plush mysteries.

My mother was made to stand up from the wheelchair and patted down. I'm not quite sure why a little old lady in a wheelchair with a furry phallic was of such dire interest to the Gainesville, Florida Airport security police, but the ordeal took more than an hour, and we almost missed our plane to Atlanta, (which would then take us to a connecting flight to Albuquerque).

Albuquerque is a large, high desert metropolis near the center of New Mexico.

The highways are wide and open. You can see the sky and mountains for miles and miles. Or as my new Albuquerque friend, Jerry, the Native American, said, "I don't know how people can stand living in the East. All those trees in the way. Blocks the sky. Blocks the view. Gives me claustrophobia."

I had never thought of it that way, but driving across the interstate in our rental car, my mother in the passenger seat, decked out in her Dollar Tree sunglasses, puff paint tee-shirt that read "I Love Bingo" (even though she never plays Bingo), and wearing her baggy trousers, we were embarking on a once-in- a-lifetime adventure. Meanwhile, the furry phallic, our unsolicited trip mascot, lounged in the back seat.

Since it was early in the day, I had planned a special event for my mother and me prior to our checking into our efficiency apartment at the Route 66 Hostel.

My mother sipped on her can of V-8 and took notice of the exquisite sunrise peering over the mountains.

"Ma! You see that mountain over there? That's where we are going today! Are you excited?!"

My mother turned her head to look at the ominous mountains.

"How are we getting up that mountain?" she inquired.

My mother stared at the steep mountain with its rugged peaks as though it was about to engulf the surrounding land and our rental car.

"You'll see! Wait until you see, Mom!! It's a surprise for you!!!!"

In Sandia Park, New Mexico, there is a tramway that glides across the mountains and delivers the passengers to a snow- covered restaurant – even in the middle of summer – at the top of the mountain.

I had taken what little money I had out of my savings to pay for this lavish trip.

Soon, we were inside the tram car.

Inside the tramway, my mother looked out over the mountains and down inside the valley in the mountains as the cable car glided across the sky.

Mom looked out the windows from her wheelchair and was truly amazed by the sights. As we ascended one of America's most stunning urban peaks, reaching upwards of more than 10,000 feet, my mother closed her eyes after quickly glimpsing the panoramic view.

"Ooo, Ang! It's making me feel queasy!"

"Yeah, me too, Mom!"

I was so excited to be doing something positive with my mother.

When we arrived at the mountaintop, I pushed my mother's wheelchair across the snow- covered trails, and soon we were inside the cozy, elegant restaurant atop the mountain. My mother, now 92, had never had such an experience in her whole life.

"Oh, Ang! This place is gorgeous!" she stated. We marveled at the classic natural wood walls, the dimly lit flameless candles, the soft jazz music in the background. It was a very romantic moment for a middle-aged woman and her geriatric mom, clad in a bingo jersey shirt!

We enjoyed a lovely lunch, laden with luxurious ingredients, while watching the snow tumbling down outside the restaurant's windows. It was a day of many firsts, unexpected detours, and the beginning of an unforgettable vacation.

Back in our efficiency apartment, inside the Route 66 Hostel, my mother and I watched the local Albuquerque news with fascination. As evening fell, the Route 66 Hostel became a microcosm of the world.

Out in the living room common area, we chatted with other travelers who were visiting from around the world, and then played a few rounds of Scrabble with them. There were visitors from Spain, from Belgium, from other parts of the United States, and a couple of travelers from Japan.

Later that slightly chilly Spring evening, we all sat on the large porch outside which faces the old Route 66. Musicians brought along their guitars, and I joined in the jam sessions, playing my accordion. Mom clapped her hands in delight, "This is wonderful! Wonderful!"

Then back inside our efficiency room, my mother took notice of the furry phallic that was haphazardly draped over a chair.

"Why on earth did we take that stupid costume with us?" my mother inquired.

"I'm going to show it to the judge tomorrow," I replied.

"Ang," she suddenly said, her mood abruptly changing, once again. "Put that thing on. I want to see you dance in it."

I looked at her with comical eyes. It was a request I could not resist, given our splendid day at the mountain.

"Sing me a song, Ang," my mother added.

"What song should I sing?" I asked her, as I slipped into the costume.

"Oh, I don't know, Ang! Your choice!"

"Hm!" I had to think about it. "Okay. How 'bout this one! This song is called 'No Beer on Sunday.' Come on, Mom! Sing along!"

I strapped on my accordion, and began wailing out the lyrics.

We were riding in our car on a Sunday afternoon! All we had left was a dollar! We went into a tavern to get a little drink, then we heard the bar tender holler!

"Okay, Mom! You have to ask me 'What did he say?' That's part of the song."

"Okay. 'What did he say?'" my mother replied.

No beer today! No beer today! You can't have beer on Sunday. No Beer today! No beer today! You gotta come back on Monday!

The top of the furry phallic wobbled as I shuffled across the room with my accordion strapped on, my mother clapping and laughing.

"Your turn, Mom! Now let's sing the Mexican version, since we're here in New Mexico!"

I went out into the living room of the hostel and borrowed a Mexican sombrero from off of a shelf and then put it on top of the furry phallic, as my mother and I sang together~

"Come on, Mom! *You* put the costume on now!"

My mother stopped clapping and her smile evaporated.

"Oh, no!" she replied, obviously reluctant.

But I approached her and carefully slipped the long cylinder over her head, and now, she peered out of the top of the furry phallic, giggling.

I took her over to the mirror on the back of the door and showed her what she looked like. My mother laughed so hard that she was brushing away tears. The whimsical costume was a big hit. The sight of her giggling through the top of the costume, a Mexican sombrero perched on its head, was ludicrously endearing.

And now there was my mother, dressed up as a furry phallic, singing the Mexican version of "No Beer On Sunday" with me.

No cerveza today! No cerveza today! You can't have cerveza on Sunday! No cerveza today! No cerveza today! You gotta come back on Monday!

This bizarre, uproarious moment of absurdity, thanks to Carolyn P. Meinel, would be forever fondly etched in our hearts.

•◦●◦•

The following morning, however, I was in court facing my stalker, Carolyn P. Meinel, a hacker who claimed on her website, The Happy Hacker, ***for the whole world to see***, that I, Angela V. Woodhull, Ph.D., stage "dancing penis" shows. In my haste to leave the Route 66 Hostel that morning, after getting my mother dressed and fed for the day, I accidentally forgot to load up the furry phallic. (which then mysteriously disappeared from my room at the hostel and was never to be seen ever again).

When I arrived in court, I found my tormentor, Carolyn P. Meinel, was armed with (not one) but TWO attorneys!

Let me repeat that.

Meinel, a total stranger to me, had decided to hire (not one) but TWO attorneys from the largest law firm in the state of New Mexico -- the Rodey Law Firm. She looked absolutely delighted – smug! Her smile to me was body language that said, "You don't stand a chance! Look what I have!" Truly, this was a shocking moment. Attorneys had told me that getting an injunction would be a very simple matter. But who knew this New Mexican crackpot would show up double armed with two attorneys?

First, I was allowed to speak, and I started by showing Judge Huling (who very much resembled Condaleeza Rice) the photos of The European Travelling Stage Show -- naked men gyrating their perfectly choreographed erections on bold display.

The courtroom was suddenly thick with an awkward, near palpable silence, save for the rustle of photo papers as I handed one set to the judge, and another set to Meinel's two attorneys.

But that was merely the first act.

Then I was ready to lay more evidence on the table—literally. From my bag, I retrieved a small wind-up toy, an item so ridiculous in its design that it could only be described as an actual "dancing penis." In fact, it is labeled and sold as a "dancing penis." Just days before leaving for Albuquerque, I had gone to an XXX Adult store in Gainesville and had shyly asked the clerk if he had any dancing penises for sale. And there, under his glass counter, on display, was a small plastic wind-up toy, shaped as a penis, with plastic feet on the bottom, that hopped along when wound up. I gave it a few twists, and set it on the judge's table.

The toy hopped across the smooth surface, creating a bizarre spectacle that was as mortifying as it was amusing.

The two attorneys from Rodey, along with my accuser, Carolyn P. Meinel - infamously known as "The Happy Hacker" - watched, their eyes wide and mouths agape, as the dancing penis made its merry journey across Huling's table.

"Your Honor, you can clearly see that this toy, from a porn shop, is what is sold as a 'dancing penis.' I showed her the label from the package which read "dancing penis." I have nothing pornographic in my comedy shows. Ms. Meinel is attempting to mislead the public into thinking I have pornography shows.

Judge Huling observed the wind-up spectacle with a somber, poker-faced expression that betrayed no emotion. Her gaze followed the little plastic performer's every move until it ran out of steam and wobbled to a standstill.

The courtroom fell silent once more. Then, Judge Huling, without commentary, turned her gaze back to me and asked, "Would you like to question Ms. Meinel?"

"I certainly would!" I exclaimed, ready for the next round.

It was my first time in a courtroom acting as Perry Mason.

The Happy Hacker approached the stand, clad in double-arm metal canes, and hobbled up to the witness box. She could barely keep her balance while raising her right hand, and posing as a pathetic cripple, as she swore to tell the whole truth, and nothing but the truth. And then she slowly sat down, making groaning noises while wobbling into the witness seat. (I later found recent photos and videos of her posted to Facebook, riding horses at high speed – no arms canes -- not a thing wrong with her.)

First, I simply stared at her, as she smiled nervously through her Coke bottle eye glasses. Her appearance matched the bizarreness of her actions. She had hired not one, but two attorneys at $450 an hour. (I know. I called the Rodey Law Firm and pretended to be a potential client, inquiring about prices.) This enormous expense to her, so she could continue blasting to the world that I stage "dancing penis" shows was as bizarre as her appearance. I looked at her long, stringy hair, her nerdy, librarian-style get up. After several beats of silence, I asked her, ***"Why are you doing this to me?"***

Meinel replied that a news reporter from the ***Independent Florida Alligator*** (Gainesville, Florida, University of Florida student newspaper) had sent her an e-mail verifying that I have dancing penis shows.

"***Really***?" I stated in disbelief. "And what is the name of this show?" I inquired of her.

"The show, as I recall, was performed in Youngstown, Ohio. It was called '***Remember Idora***!'"

I turned and looked at the judge, stunned.

"Your Honor," I stammered. "That show that Ms. Meinel refers to was a heart-warming ode to an ***amusement park*** in Youngstown, Ohio. That show was about Ferris Wheels, roller coasters, and ballroom dancing at the amusement park. Certainly, there were no 'dancing genitalia' in such a show!" I proclaimed.

"What about the ballroom dancers?" Meinel interrupted. "They have jumping genitalia while dancing!"

"Ms. Meinel, please do not interrupt," Judge Huling interjected.

Then the two attorneys from the Rodey Law Firm explained to the judge that Carolyn Meinel is immune for publishing the e-mail words from the 19-year old kid from the ***Independent Florida Alligator*** newspaper because of a federal law called 42 CDA.

The mumbo jumbo from the two attorneys being explained to the judge really confused me. I sat there at my table staring at the un-hopping, sedate plastic penis wind-up toy and the photos of European erections.

The judge then asked me, "Do you understand, Ms. Woodhull?"

"Not really," I admitted. "Does it mean that the defendant is allowed to keep her claim on the internet for the whole world to see?

"Exactly," the judge stated.

I put my head down on the table and began weeping.

The judge looked on, nonchalantly. The defendant was smiling widely, looking absolutely delighted to see my sudden burst of tears.

Perry Mason was now a blundering faucet.

"Your Honor," Attorney Bryan Davis stated. "If Ms. Woodhull wants to write up a response on Ms. Meinel's website, The Happy Hacker, we will allow her to do that."

"I am not interested in doing that," I sobbed. "I want this whole thing to end – not grow larger!" (no pun intended!) I stated.

Judge Huling then said she would not be granting my injunction, but she would allow my lawsuit to proceed.

"You can prove your truth, Ms. Woodhull, in subsequent hearings. I will allow this lawsuit to continue."

In hindsight, I now understand why the judge did that. Meinel had **two** attorneys. Those two hungry attorneys would not have chalked up any further billable hours if the simple injunction had been granted to me.

Judges help attorneys get billable hours.

And so, it was now up to me to prove that my polka music shows do not contain "dancing penises" and to save my reputation on the internet so I could someday realize my dream of staging kids' music concerts. This litigious task took up more than a decade of my life, thousands of dollars, and more than two dozen additional trips to Albuquerque, New Mexico over the years.

****

Back in Gainesville, Florida

My mother and I had just spent a lovely (and costly) week in Albuquerque, New Mexico. We'd traversed ancient Catholic churches, indulged in gastronomical delights across the city, and even gambled away a few nickels at the Sandia Park Casino. From sampling homemade ice cream to taking a tram up the mountain, our journey was a collage of joyful memories. But memories, like a sand castle against an oncoming wave, can be fragile.

"I won't be able to see you tomorrow, Mom," I told her, as I tucked her in her bed that evening we arrived back in Gainesville. "So, don't forget this lovely week we just spent in Albuquerque. All right? Okay?" I was very much behind on my online tasks, which I had ignored during my vacation in Albuquerque. I was in fear of losing my little online job.

"I won't forget," she proclaimed. "It was a lovely week! You are the best daughter in the whole world!" she said, with a hug.

But come Monday, as I sat in my computer chair, carefully grading an endless amounts of overdue papers, it seems she was not pleased that I was not at her/my house to entertain her.

She began incessantly phoning me.

Submerged in a sea of overdue papers, I was startled by a sudden flurry of phone calls from Mom.

I picked up the first time she called and told her I was truly busy grading papers. "Remember, Mom? I told you I'd be grading papers today. You gave me your word. I've got to go."

"Yeah, I remember, but you left a light on in the back room, and the door to that room is locked."

The dire issue? An errant light bulb.

"Well, don't worry about it, Mom," I replied.

"Yes, I'm worried about it!" she snapped. "It's a complete waste of electricity!"

"Mom, it's just a light bulb! I **_REALLY_** have to grade these papers, or I could lose my job," I pleaded, before diving back into my sea of work. "Tomorrow, I will give you $20 for that stupid lightbulb that is on. Okay?"

And I hung up.

My mother then called me right back, but I didn't pick up.

She then proceeded to phone me **17 times in a row**. (I counted.) Each time, she let my phone ring long enough until a busy signal came on.

She was relentless.

Finally, after a staggering 17 phone calls to me, I picked up on the 18th call.

"Mom. What. What is it?"

"Somebody is here to see you," she chirped in an overly-friendly voice.

"Who, Mom? Who is there to see me?"

"Guess!" she said.

"I don't know, Mom. Just tell me!"

"No, guess!" she said, chuckling.

"I don't know! One of my ex-boyfriends?"

"No."

"One of the neighbors?"

"Nope. No. Guess again. One more guess!"

"Ugh. I don't know. An old friend of mine? Someone from Youngstown?"

"Nooo!"

"Then who?"

"A man from Elder Abuse! He's here and he wants to talk to you. Here. Let me put him on the phone."

"Good morning, Miss Woodhull," a man declared in a low-pitched, flat voice. "My name is Corey Preston and I work for the State of Florida Department of Elder Affairs. I would like to speak with you."

"Okay, I'll be right over," I stated. My heart thudded a frantic beat against my ribcage as I rushed over to The Castle.

When I pulled into the driveway, there stood a man wearing a light blue shirt and black tie, and black trousers with a clipboard in his hands.

"Good morning, Miss Woodhull," he said, shaking my hand. "May I talk with you in private, please?"

My mother, standing on the walkway behind us, appeared quite amused and pleased.

Preston and I walked around to the trampoline side of the yard, where we leaned up against the rim of the trampoline and he rested his clipboard and pen on the edge of the trampoline.

"There's been a report that came in to our hotline regarding neglect of an elder, and I have been assigned to this case," he stated.

"And how, exactly, have I been neglecting my mother?" I asked him defensively.

"The report stated that you allow your mother to live in filth and that you ignore her, leave her without food in the house for several days at a time."

"That is complete bullshit!" I told him. I was extremely upset. "Who made this false report?"

"I am not at liberty to say," he stated. "The reports are anonymous."

"I know who made this outrageous report," I told him. "It's Shirley and John Mascarella, my mother's estranged niece and her husband from Youngstown, Ohio."

"How would they know your mother's living conditions?" he inquired.

"Exactly!" I stated. "They have already called the police on several occasions when I took my mother to the beach. "Fire and Rescue broke into the house recently when my mother and I were at the beach. Fire and Rescue left a note on the dining room table stating they had broken in. We had to phone Fire and Rescue when we came back from the beach and assure them that my mother was all right."

Preston then did a walk-through of my house, looking for evidence of neglect, or dirty dishes, or filth, etc. He found no evidence.

We walked down the hallway, and there at the end of the hallway, my mother had plastered a hand-written sign, in all capital letters, onto the locked bedroom door. It read, **"THIS IS AN EXAMPLE OF ELDER ABUSE BY A DAUGHTER UPON A MOTHER."** And she had added a child-like drawing of a lightbulb at the bottom of the paper. [IT'S SING-ALONG TIME:

Preston snapped a photo of the sign with his phone's camera, as I explained, "My mother is unhappy that I left the light on."

"Why is the door locked?" he inquired.

"Because I have more than $50,000 worth of musical and video equipment inside this room, and I'm afraid my mother will harm it. She has threatened to take a baseball bat and smash my equipment."

I opened the door and showed him the expensive cameras, lighting equipment, microphones, speakers, etc.

"Mrs. Falvo," Corey asked, "do you need access to this back room?"

"Not really," my mother replied, sheepishly.

I then turned off the light and relocked the door.

Preston then asked my mother to step outside, so that he could continue talking with me in private.

"What makes you believe that your mother would harm your professional equipment?" he inquired.

"Well, when I was a child, my parents owned an Italian restaurant in Youngtown, Ohio. My mother did most of the work at the restaurant. She hated that restaurant. She asked my father to sell the restaurant on many occasions, but he refused to sell it. Finally, she simply burned down the restaurant."

Preston, caught off guard, managed to utter, "She set the restaurant on fire?"

"Indeed, she did," I stated. "I always suspected it was her who had set the fire, and recently she confessed to me."

"I see," he responded.

Preston walked into the kitchen. "Well, there seems to be plenty of groceries inside the refrigerator and cupboards."

"Yep."

And the house is clean.

"Yep."

"Truthfully, I feel sorry for you," Preston said. "I can see what's going on here."

I gave him an appreciative nod.

"I will periodically check back to see how things are going," Preston said, and he closed up his clipboard and started to leave. Then, as he was approaching his car, he turned back and added, "Truthfully, your mother is so independent right now, you don't even need to see her everyday at this point," he stated. It was a shocking and liberating statement for me to hear.

My mother appeared as soon as Preston was out of sight, but I was wordless toward her. I silently got back inside my car. As I was walking away, still processing the unexpected morning, her voice echoed behind me,

"You know, if you would simply move into this house with me, I'm sure Shirley and John would stop making silly phone calls to elder abuse and the police!"

THE HBO MOVIE STAR! (2007)

Back at my little apartment, while grading papers, I checked my e-mails.

There was a curious e-mail in my inbox that stated, "Hello, we are a talent agency located in Miami, Florida. We have been searching for Angelina, the Polka Queen to be cast in an upcoming HBO movie, **Recount**. If this is Angela Woodhull, could you please contact us at your earliest convenience?"

I read the e-mail over and over again. Was it for real? Or was it some kind of spam? Was it from somebody in Nigeria? It just didn't sound real.

Curious, I decided to give a call.

"Yes, this is Angela Woodhull, also known as Angelina, the Polka Queen. I received an e-mail from your talent agency?"

The receptionist sounded very excited.

"Oh, my!" she proclaimed. "We have finally found her! I have Angelina, the Polka Queen on the line!"

Soon, the owner of the talent agency was on the phone with me.

"Miss Woodhull! We're so pleased to finally hear from you! We have been searching for you for nearly three months! HBO is in the process of producing a movie called "**Recount**!" about the Gore-Bush election controversy. As I understand from actual news footage, you were there at the actual event, singing a song."

"Yes, that's true!" I told her, excitedly.

"Well, would you like to audition to play the part of yourself? We originally cast a movie star to play the part of you, but the producers did not like her style, and told me to find the real Angelina, the Polka Queen."

I laughed. "What if I don't pass the audition?"

She laughed, too. "I'm sure you'll pass the audition."

****

Back at my real house (the castle) (where my mother was living), I was so eager to share the exciting news with my mother.

"Mom!!!! Sit down for this one. I have some very unusual news to share with you!"

I just knew my mother would be so excited.

As she seated herself, I continued, "I'm going to be in a movie, Mom! A real movie!!!"

My mother scratched her head and adjusted her glasses.

"A talent agency from Miami has contacted me!!! I'm going to be cast in a real HBO movie!!!"

My mother scowled.

"And how many days will you be gone for this movie shooting?"

"Just two days, Mom. Two short days."

My mother looked at me fuming, like a volcano ready to erupt.

"And what is supposed to happen to ME?" my mother declared, her voice rising in rage.

"Oh, Mom!" I said, hugging her. "You have enough money in the bank to hire a whole army of people!" I stated.

She was terribly upset, and she walked with her cane over to the front door, where there was a painting of the Cinderella Castle on my front door that I had commissioned an artist to create a few years previously.

"Why do you have this ridiculous painting on your front door?" she snarled.

"Because I'm the Polka Queen!" I chuckled. "This is my castle!"

My mother could not understand this. Nor did she care about my alter ego, **The Polka Queen**.

"Oh, you're **nothing**!" she snapped. "**Shirley** could paint a much better painting than **this** stupid one!" pointing her cane at my front door. "After all, **Shirley** is a REAL artist!"

Shirley this. And Shirley that. I was constantly hearing about Shirley.

"Well, I paid a **real** artist two hundred dollars to paint that castle!" I declared.

As you can imagine, that answer did not settle well with my mother.

"Well, you wasted two hundred dollars!" she shouted. "You are stupid and ridiculous."

"One of these days, I'm going to take a can of white paint and cover up this ugly painting!" she proclaimed.

A few hours later, inside a Mexican restaurant, my mother continued expressing her list of miseries.

As we sat there, enjoying our Mexican dishes, my mother suddenly declared in a loud voice, loud enough for all of the other restaurant patrons to hear, "Look at these Mexican paintings on the wall. You know, your cousin **Shirley** is a professional artist, and

Shirley can make paintings much, much, much better than these ones!"

I sat quietly, and didn't bother to respond. I continued eating my quesadillas and refried beans.

My mother then continued her verbal assault, elevating the volume of her voice even louder.

"Which reminds of how much I hate that ugly painting of a stupid castle on your front door! You actually PAID someone to create that hideous castle on your front door? The stupid things you do! You wasted two hundred dollars – **two hundred dollars** – on that ridiculous, moronic painting? You do the stupidest, silly things with your money! How did you get to be like that? I swear to God they must have given me the wrong baby at the hospital because no child of mine . . ."

As she continued her verbal tirade, I could feel my heart pounding, my face flushed, as all eyes in the restaurant were upon us.

I got up from the restaurant table and quickly made my way into the bathroom.

I sat there inside the bathroom stall, feeling my heart pounding, but now I felt safe, confined to the little four walls inside the bathroom stall.

A good twenty minutes passed, and I did not budge.

Finally, one of the waitresses from the restaurant entered the bathroom.

"Angela? Is there someone in here named Angela?"

"Yes, I'm in here," I replied softly, from inside the bathroom stall.

"Are you okay?"

"Yes, I'm okay," I responded, in a dejected tone of voice.

"Well, your mother has been waiting for you. She's all finished with her lunch, and she wants to go home."

"Okay. Thank you," I replied, quietly. "I'll be right out."

I waited a few more minutes inside the bathroom stall, then took a deep breath and arose from my refuge, the toilet seat.

I slowly walked back to the table where my mother was seated, but I didn't sit down.

"Mom, are you finished with your verbal tirade?"

She did not reply. She simply stared at me, with fire in her eyes.

I leaned over and whispered, "Because if you start in on me again, I will go back inside that bathroom. I swear to God, I'll go back inside that bathroom stall and sit in there **all day long**."

"Just take me home," my mother replied, shooting me dragon daggers.

"I don't want to talk to you anyway," she snarled.

"Okay, but you'd better stay quiet in my car," I told her.

My mother arose from the table and began making her way to the exit door of the restaurant.

We rode in silence back to the castle house, and then I drove to my little apartment that was just two blocks away.

It was my own little escape place – a small little apartment I had rented, just two blocks away, my safehaven, where I could retreat to when my mother was in one of these wound-up moods.

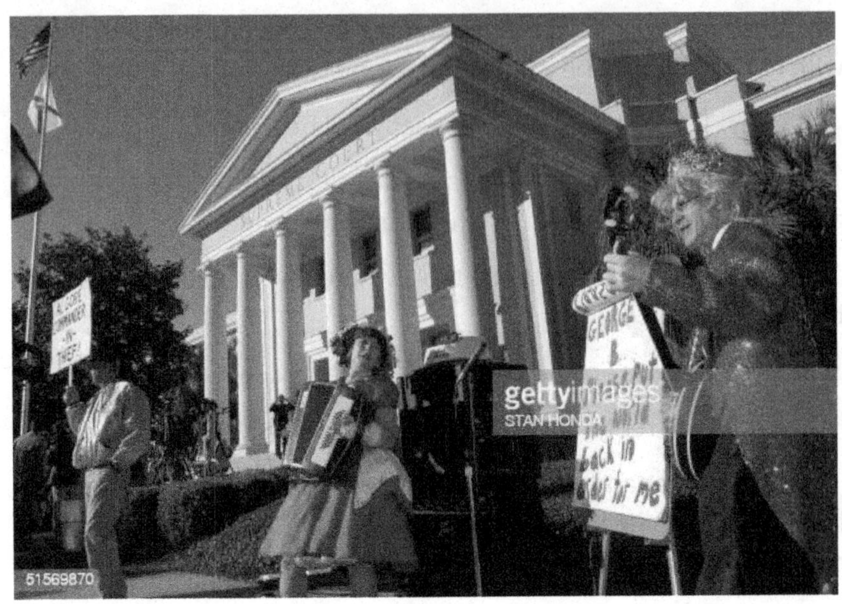

[*Making History: Angelina, the Polka Queen and King Ira made international news while singing one of Angelina's original songs about the Gore-Bush election mess, while demonstrators on either side of the stance, held up signs.*]

[*Angelina, the Polka Queen on set for the HBO filming of "Recount"*]

A few days later, I was in Tallahassee being followed around by my own make up crew, waiting for the next shoot as I sat inside my own personal trailer on set that HBO had provided just for me.

Stepping onto a film set is a bit like walking into a different world, one that operates on its own unique rhythms and rules. In Tallahassee, on the set of the Gore-Bush recount film, this otherworldliness was amplified by the significance of the story we were telling.

As soon as my feet hit the ground, I was quickly ushered away by my personal makeup crew. These artists were my guardian angels, primping and preening me, making sure that every hair was in place, that my makeup was flawless. Every wrinkle in my clothing was attacked with a steamer, every smudge on my face addressed with a makeup brush or sponge. They would fuss over me, their attentiveness a reassuring presence in the swirling chaos of the film set.

I was then escorted back inside my personal trailer, a cocoon of calm in the frenzied world of the film set. Stepping inside was like crossing a threshold into a different universe. The trailer was surprisingly spacious, filled with comfortable furnishings and a warm, inviting ambience. It felt like a home away from home, a place to retreat and recharge between takes.

In the corner, a compact, well-stocked refrigerator held a variety of snacks and beverages. Along the wall, a small makeup station was set up, complete with a lit mirror and a full assortment of beauty products, ready for last-minute touch-ups. A cozy seating area provided a spot to relax or run lines, and a private restroom offered an extra dash of luxury.

Outside, the film set hummed with its own peculiar energy. Crew members moved with focused intention, adjusting lights, moving props, checking sound equipment. They buzzed around like bees, each person with their own task, contributing to the hive of creativity.

The director's voice boomed out, calling for quiet on the set, and everyone would still, the air filled with the potent mix of anticipation and focused concentration.

Then the call came: "Action!" And for a few minutes, the world stopped spinning as everyone held their breath, eyes fixed on the action unfolding before the cameras. In these moments, it felt like we were doing more than just making a movie—we were creating a piece of history, capturing a moment in time that had reverberated across the world.

Once the scene was over, the whirlwind of activity resumed, everyone moving to strike the set and prepare for the next shot. Amid the pandemonium, I retreated back to my trailer, to the serene sanctuary that was my refuge from the chaos. There, waiting for the next shoot, I found myself reflecting on the surreal nature of it all. I was a part of something bigger, something meaningful, contributing to a narrative that had captured the attention of the entire world.

It was exhilarating, exhausting, and utterly unforgettable. The experience of being on that film set was unlike anything else, a whirlwind of creativity, chaos, and profound connection. It was a reminder of the power of storytelling, and of the countless people and pieces that come together to tell a tale. And I was a part of it. A cog in the vast machine of movie magic, and it was an experience I would treasure forever.

Little Did I Know, However . . . .

Meanwhile, at the same time that I was filming "Recount" in Tallahassee, back in Gainesville, Florida, Shirley and John Mascarella (I was to later find out) had arrived by airplane, and were escorting my mother to all of her banks. Shirley and John Mascarella, like twin serpents, had wound their way into my mother's life after 23 years of never speaking with her. As I was caught up in the spectacle and excitement of Tallahassee, they used that opportunity to escort my mother to her banks, greasing the wheels of their nefarious plot.

In the air-conditioned sterility of the Bank of America, Shirley's grip tightened on the wheelchair's handles, pressing my mother forward toward the bank manager.

"I'm changing this account so that my niece will have money to pay my bills while I'm visiting up in Youngstown, Ohio."

"Oh, you're moving to Ohio, Mrs. Falvo?" the branch manager curiously inquired, her eyebrows raising in surprise.

John Mascarella, standing behind the wheelchair, allowed a satisfied, shark-like smile to play on his lips, nearly invisible to anyone who wasn't looking directly at him.

"Well, just for a little while," my mother confessed. "I really hate the snow."

•◦•●•◦•

When I returned to Gainesville after my two short days in Tallahassee as a "movie star," I went immediately to my castle house to let my mother know I was back.

It was some time in the afternoon, and my house was eerily dark.

I walked up the walkway, and the castle painting was gone. My mother was sincere. She had taken a bucket of flat white paint and crudely whisked over the stunning castle drawing on my front door. "Welcome to Angelina's Castle." These words had also been hastily painted over with sloppy, crude flat white paint.

I walked in and turned on the living room light switch, but no lights turned on.

I walked over to the dining room table, where the large array of my mother's daily medications were always kept. But the medicine bottles were all mysteriously gone.

"Mom? Are you here?"

There was no reply.

There, on the dining room table was a note that had been hastily hand-written by my mother.

"You want your own life? Okay. Go ahead and have your own life! I have gone with Shirley and John to live with them in their house in Youngstown. Have a nice life."

I used my cell phone to contact the electric company. Indeed, my mother had cut off all of the utilities.

I read the little note several times, and then I chuckled. I read it again and again, and then I laughed out loud. And then I phoned one of my friends – a friend who had started a support group called "Daughters who have overbearing, unreasonable mothers."

"Iris," I told her, "my mother is gone. She was taken up to Ohio by the Mascarellas."

"Oh. How do you feel?"

"Well, a bit relieved," I confessed.

I had just started a new relationship with the new love of my life, David Newman – a harmonica player. I really didn't want to add mother drama to a brand new relationship.

"But I know my mother will be back shortly. She has no intentions of living up in Youngstown, Ohio in the snow and in the cold. She's just hoping I'll give up my apartment and move back into the house with her, and then when she returns, I'll be here with her every minute of every second."

That was the last conversation I ever had with Iris.

Her Jewish mother, who was even more overbearing and unreasonable than my mother, suddenly entered hospice and soon passed away. Iris' mother had a complete stranglehold on her daughter. On the day that her mother died, so did Iris.

Butt Prints at the Art Opening

With my new-found freedom, I started phoning some of my old friends that I hadn't seen in over two years, since my mother had first moved into my castle. One of the first people I called was my old friend, Floyd, who everybody calls "Pink," (as in "Pink Floyd). Pink is a social magnet; his company is always an assurance of a good time. "Hey, Pink!" The phone crackled to life.

"Wow, Angie! Long time!" His friendly voice was a warm breeze of familiarity.

"I am a free woman for maybe a couple of weeks!" My words brimmed with the untapped excitement of independence.

"No Mama? She moved?" Pink's surprised response made me chuckle.

"Just for the moment! She's on a vacation. Any parties or music jams happening?" I queried. Pink's expertise in the local social scene was legendary.

"Actually, Gainesville's own Tom Miller is having an art opening on Friday, and my new band is performing!"

Tom Miller, who was running for mayor of Gainesville, is a local comedian and musician who also hosts open mics around town. Tom Miller was the first person to host an Angelina, the Polka Queen nightclub show.

"Tom Miller is signing and selling butt prints of himself to fund his political campaign!" Pink chuckled. The absurdity of the idea was so typically Tom Miller. "You know he's running for Mayor of Gainesville?"

"Sounds like Tom Miller," I laughed. "What a character," we both simultaneously replied.

"Yep! And we have a new guy in the band I've been wanting you to meet!" Pink added. "His name is David Newman, and, you know what, come to think of it, I think you two might be the perfect match! He is a bad ass harmonica player!"

The prospect of meeting this mysterious newcomer, coupled with the chance to let my hair down, made the upcoming art opening even more enticing.

Soon, it was a rainy, cold October night when I dressed in my highest high heels, curled my hair, and headed out to see Pink, his band, and the butt prints.

****

And there, up on the stage, center right, was a harp player wailing out the blues, down on one knee, clad in a dark medieval costume which contrasted perfectly with his neatly trimmed gray beard and mustache.

He wasn't the lead singer, but his charismatic style certainly dominated the stage. His piercing blue eyes sparkled under the stage lights.

When I waved at Pink, David flashed me a long, seductive wink in between two melancholic tones. I instantly felt feelings that I thought had evaporated from my body forever. Indeed, David immediately captured me.

At the end of the first set, Pink introduced me to the members of his band. One hand reached out with an excited powerful grin.

"I'm honored to be meeting at last face-to-face World Famous Angelina, the Polka Queen!" David announced. We both erupted in laughter.

"I've heard so much about you! And, actually, I've seen a couple of your shows," David added. His words were like notes strummed on the strings of my heart.

Soon, the band members and me were all chatting about Pink's upcoming birthday party.

"You know, I could host Pink's annual birthday bash at the Castle this year," I suggested. I knew this would be a good excuse to get David over to my house to help with the party set-up.

A few days later, David arrived in his gray pick up truck, and we began moving heavy speakers from the back bedroom and up onto the stage. Soon, my Ketron keyboard was set up, and David wanted to know what the Ketron sounded like.

"I use it for my background music."

I quickly put on a polka and started to play along on my accordion. "Do you know any polkas?" I asked David.

"Not really," he replied. But soon, David was whipping a few harps out of his black case, and our impromptu music jam began. Just the two of us. David wiggled his knees from side to side as he blew into the harps and shook his head. It was too good to be true. The past two years of bleakness seemed to be erased from my mind, as I dashed into the garage and took one of Jud's former costumes off of a hanger.

"Here! Try this on!" I said, handing the lederhosen costume to David.

It was a perfect fit. David is almost exactly the same size and height as Jud.

Standing there, up on my castle stage, wailing into the harps, dressed in green lederhosen, I knew that David had captured my heart.

***

Being with David was easy. He enjoyed life and I was enjoying an easy moment with him.

A very short moment. Just three months into our relationship, I got the call from my mother in Ohio, her voice trembling.

"You gotta come to Youngstown and rescue me!" my mother sobbed into the receiver. Her voice trembled over the line, a harbinger of the challenges to come.

Rather than putting my mother in a room in their home, as they had promised her, the Mascarellas had tricked my mother into signing dreadful documents at the nursing home. The documents, unknown to my mother, were allowing the Mascarellas to control every aspect of my mother's life.

"It's just temporary," Shirley Mascarella had falsely assured my mother. "We're decorating a room for you in our home, and then you can come live with us. It will be just a few short weeks."

"We can't wait! We love you sooo much!" John Mascarella had craftily added.

But a week had turned into a month. And a month had turned into three months. I did not realize how dire and desperate my mother's situation had become. Here was my mother, The Master Manipulator, being manipulated by The Mascarellas.

"Please come get me!" my mother begged.

I was, of course, inclined to go rescue my mother, as usual. It had been my lifetime duty. But now there was another reason. Based on all the fun time we had had in Albuquerque, I was convinced that my mother had changed. I felt the Youngstown experience would make her grateful.

A judge had once asked me, "How would you describe your mother?"

I replied, "She is every adjective in the dictionary."

There was tender Louise. There was supportive Louise. There was altruistic Louise, in addition to all of the other not-so-nice Louises. I assumed that the fateful trip to Youngstown had erased all of the gnarly and nasty Louises forever.

Now, here was my mother, begging me to rescue her from Youngstown, Ohio.

The nursing home had intentionally summoned her into a large conference room, surrounded by staff members, an attorney, and the Mascarellas.

"How do you want to leave your money, Louise?" they inquired.

They had put an ankle bracelet on my mother that beeped if she tried to leave the facility. There was no escape.

"I changed the will, Ang. They were putting so much pressure on me. I changed the will to get them off my backs. Now, come get me, Ang, and then we'll go to the banks and put everything back the way it always has been. I don't want them to have my money!"

But rescuing my mother from Ohio was not going to be an easy task, I soon discovered.

Soon, I was on a plane to Youngstown.

****

Ascension of Ambivalence

My thoughts were like flickering slides, switching back and forth between the fresh joy that was David and the impending dread of confronting Shirley's treachery. Each heartbeat seemed to resonate with the rhythm of their names, creating a symphony of conflicting emotions.

David, my newfound solace, was more than just a lover; he was a partner, a friend. The novelty of our romance was still fresh, the intoxicating rush of shared smiles, whispered sweet-nothings, and stolen kisses were my new normal. The joy of doing mundane tasks together, of shaping our daily routines around each other was strangely comforting. It was the promise of a future, of shared dreams and aspirations. We had even indulged in a whimsical trip to Disney, immersing ourselves in the magic of love while envisioning a happily ever after.

But in stark contrast to the bright bubble of happiness that David represented, there was a darker, more foreboding shadow that loomed large. Shirley. Her name alone evoked a wave of anxiety and fear, a dark specter haunting the periphery of my joy. Her calculated maneuvers and devious intentions were a grim reminder of the lengths she could go to.

Even though miles separated me from my mother, I could feel her frailty and distress as if it were my own. The imagined image of her wasted form, the result of Shirley's cruelty, sent a sharp pang of grief through me. This wasn't just about the inheritance; this was about the woman who birthed me, nurtured me, whose life was now being methodically snuffed out.

The plane began its descent, and with it, my heart plummeted. A knot tightened in my stomach, my palms felt clammy. My mind was stuck in a tumultuous limbo between the euphoria of a budding romance and the dread of a looming family crisis.

Every passing minute took me closer to Youngstown, closer to the reality of my mother's plight, pulling me away from the blissful bubble of love that David and I were building. The dichotomy was as clear as the changing landscapes below, and the more I dwelled on it, the more it felt like I was being torn in two. The flight was not just a journey in physical space; it was an emotional journey as well, a test of my resilience, my love, and my duty.

As the plane touched down, the stark reality of my situation bore down upon me. I had arrived, but the journey was far from over. My heart clung to the memory of David's smile as I steeled myself to face the truth of my mother's predicament. I knew I was in for an arduous battle, one that threatened to overshadow the light of my newfound love, and the thought made the descent all the more chilling.

I was now up in Youngstown, Ohio with my lifetime friend, Richard Filisky, who had picked me up from the Akron Airport.

As we drove down the interstate, Richard described how frail my mother had become.

It was no exaggeration. At Meridian Arms nursing home, we found my mother in a small bed, curled up on her side, fast asleep. She looked like a living skeleton from Auschwitz.

I had always known my mother to be a resilient woman, brimming with life and vitality. So, the sight that met me when I reached the nursing home was nothing short of heartbreaking. She was a shadow of her former self, a frail figure lost within the stark white sheets of the hospital bed. The hollow cheeks, the dull eyes, and the grey pallor of her skin bore testimony to the gross neglect and mistreatment she had endured.

Upon investigating, I uncovered a horrifying truth - Shirley and the nursing home had been working in cahoots, exploiting my mother's health for their sinister intentions. Louise was diabetic, and they had deliberately mismanaged her condition, plunging her into a diabetic coma as soon as she had signed a will favoring Shirley.

The medical negligence didn't stop there. Due to poor hygiene and lack of proper care, she had contracted C. Diff, an infection that further deteriorated her health and left her so utterly thin.

I touched her shoulder to gently awaken her. My mother looked up in shock.

"Oh, Ang! You're here!" she said, with relief dripping from her every word. "I'm so happy to see you! You've got to get me out of here! I want to go home!!!" But before I could reply . . . .

Soon, there was a man standing in the doorway of my mother's nursing home room wearing a navy peacoat. He sported a thick mustache, his gray hair slicked back with a lot of hair spray holding it in place, a gold Italian horn on a chain around his neck, his shirt unbuttoned, showing off the massive curly gray hair on his chest. The short man stood there with his hands in his peacoat, his feet spread apart.

"Yeah, I know all about you, Angie," he stated, looking at me with disgust.

"Who are you?" I inquired.

"I'm John Mascarella," the man stated in sarcastic tones. "Shirley's husband. I know all about how you were mistreating your mother in Florida. So, believe me, you ain't taking your mother nowhere! She's gonna stay here and get good care!"

I looked down at my mother who was now seated in a wheelchair.

"Mom, did you hear what he said to me?"

"No. What did he say?"

"He said I used to abuse you in Florida."

"That's not true!" my mother stated to him.

A nurse walked by and took notice of the tension in the room.

"One of you is going to have to leave," she stated.

"Well, it's not going to be me!" I replied.

"I'll be back, Aunt Lou," the short man stated. "Shirley and I love you."

The man flashed me a dagger, and then departed.

Down at the nurse's station, I explained to the staff that my mother wished to go home.

A supervisor was called from the intercom.

Now standing in front of me was Kathy Fine, the social worker/administrator.

"If you try to take your mother out of here, we're going to charge you with kidnapping. I know all about you," Fine stated.

****

Back in my mother's room, she opened the phone book to the Yellow Pages.

"Find me an attorney, Ang! You've got to get me out of here!"

She already appeared more alive than when I had first arrived just an hour prior.

For the next several hours, I phoned all of the attorneys in Youngstown that specialize in elder law. No one had immediate availability. They were all booked up for weeks on end.

I phoned all of the A's. All of the B's. All of the C's. All of the D's. All of the E's. No one had availability. Finally, I reached the F's.

"Mom, I really don't think it's going to be possible to find you a lawyer on the spur of the moment,' I told her.

"Well, keep trying," she said.

F – Fleming.

We were in luck. An attorney in downtown Youngstown, Alfred Fleming, was willing to speak with my mother and me the very next day.

On the morning of January 25, 2008, Richard Filisky and I arrived at Meridian Arms to chauffeur my mother and me to the law office of attorney Al Fleming in downtown Youngstown, Ohio. My mother was quite excited to see Richard. (Richard had been my high school teacher at Cardinal Mooney Catholic high school. He had been a priest during the Sixties when he was my religion teacher, but he had left the priesthood in 1968, married, and now has three lovely grown daughters.)

Trying to get my mother out of the nursing home that fateful morning had been quite a challenge. Kathy Fines, the nursing home social worker/administrator, had told me the previous day that I was forbidden to take my mother anywhere. (I had believed her, although I later found out this was illegal.) However, a nurse who had overheard the heated conversations from the previous day at Meridian Arms had whispered to me, "Just go to the front desk tomorrow and sign out your mother—she can't stop you." The compassionate nurse was aware of how badly my mother wanted to go back to Florida.

I rolled my mother up to the front desk, as Richard looked on.

"We're going out for the day," I said to the nurses on staff.

"Where is the sign out sheet?" I bravely asked, assuming there was going to be resistance. But one of the nurses simply handed me the clipboard.

I signed out my mother, my heart racing, and the three of us headed out of the building, and got inside Richard's car. It felt like an escape from Alcatraz, and the three of us were brushing away sweat beads and laughing nervously as Richard pulled out from the parking lot.

Soon, we arrived in downtown Youngstown. We rolled my mother into the elevator and pushed the "up" button. My mother was softly praying to the Virgin Mary, her hands clasped together, as the elevator whisked us up to the tenth floor.

We stepped out of the elevator, and there was an old frosted door on the right which read in bold black letters "Law Office of Alfred J. Fleming, Attorney at Law." Richard opened the heavy old door widely, as I pushed my mother inside. The secretary greeted us with a polite grin, in between her keystrokes, and told us to have a seat in the waiting room.

"May I get you some water or coffee?" she politely asked us.

Mom nodded, "Coffee, please, just black."

Richard asked for a cup of tea, and I grabbed a small orange juice. We sat there nervously, sipping on our beverages. My mother looked quite pleased, as though she had, indeed, escaped Alcatraz.

"I'm so happy to be out of that terrible, terrible place, Ang. There was nobody for me to talk to. Most of the old people there can't hear or have lost their minds," she said.

I listened and nodded, but I also wondered, however, what would transpire next. Being threatened with an arrest for taking my mother to see an attorney did not settle well with me. I also knew that the Mascarellas were only a phone call away.

"What exactly do you expect this attorney to do for you, Mom?" I asked her, as we were waiting.

"I want him to give me a piece of paper!" she replied, as though the answer was quite obvious.

"What kind of piece of paper do you expect him to give you exactly?" I inquired, a bit baffled.

"A piece of paper that allows me to go home!" she replied, sounding a bit agitated.

We continued sipping our beverages in silence, taking notice of the picturesque scenes on the walls of the waiting room. It was a nervous silence.

My visit to Al Fleming's office was an experience both unsettling and surreal. His office, a study in understated elegance, was situated in the heart of downtown Youngstown. I peered out the window. And there, dominating the view from his large, grand office window, stood a stoic sentinel of history – the imposing, ten-story building where my mother, Louise, and her sister had a dramatic falling-out five decades prior.

In that very structure, my mother had threatened to throw her sister out of the window amidst a fiery disagreement over their father's will. The building's austere brick exterior and towering silhouette were silent testaments to the fierce conflict that had played out between the sisters years ago.

Gazing at the edifice, I could almost feel the past echoing around me. The heated argument, the tense atmosphere, and the threat looming in the air were almost palpable, casting an uncanny shadow over the present. It was an unsettling thought - the same fiery blood that had boiled in the veins of my mother and aunt also flowed within me.

And then, a chilling realization struck me - the betrayal I was dealing with now could have been simmering on a slow burner for years, possibly even decades. Could it be that Shirley, my cousin, had been harboring a grudge, fueled by her mother's stories of that day, right from her early adulthood?

Was it possible that she had been nursing this resentment, waiting for the perfect moment to claim what she thought was her due? The plot of revenge, jealousy, and entitlement - was it passed down from mother to daughter, ingrained in Shirley from the moment her mother stopped speaking to mine?

Looking across the street at that historic building, a sense of dread washed over me. It felt as though history was repeating itself, the roles had shifted, and the stakes were alarmingly high. But now it was not just about inheritance, it was about my mother's life, her dignity, and I was resolved to fight for it.

And what about John Mascarella? Could he be the puppeteer, pulling the strings, stoking the fires of Shirley's latent animosity towards my mother, Louise? Was this his idea of revenge or greed? As I pondered these thoughts, the challenges ahead became clear, and the fight I had in my hands felt all the more vital.

It felt like a daunting challenge. As the excitement of my newfound relationship with David became a distant echo, the urgency of my mother's plight took center stage. I was now in the eye of the storm, my happiness marred by the grim reality of my mother's condition, the budding romance now eclipsed by a deep-set fear for my mother's life. After about an hour's wait, a secretary came over to us and led us to join her inside Al Fleming's conference room, which she unlocked for us.

The three of us entered the stately old room and were seated at this long, dark conference table, in leather lined chairs, legal books surrounding us upon the three walls.

After anxiously waiting ten minutes, Attorney Al Fleming entered the conference room, a tall older gentleman with thinning gray hair and glasses. My mother sighed softly.

Attorney Fleming seated himself at the head of the long, conference table.

"And how may I help you?" he inquired, scanning the three of us with a slight, official smile.

My mother looked at me and nodded.

"Well, I really don't know what this means," I told him, "but my mother wants you to give her a 'piece of paper' that will allow her to return to her home in Gainesville, Florida. She was placed against her will in a nursing home up here in Youngstown by an estranged cousin of mine. She thought she was going to their house for a visit, but they made her sign some paperwork, and now the nursing home says she's not allowed to leave."

My mother smiled widely and winked in agreement.

"Well, let's talk about this," Fleming responded, and he picked up a pen and opened his yellow legal notepad.

"Mrs. Falvo, how did you end up in Youngstown?" Fleming inquired. "I find it very odd that a woman who lived in Florida for more than 40 years is suddenly back up here in Youngstown, Ohio. Do you enjoy the cold weather up here, Mrs. Falvo?"

"No. Not particularly," my mother replied.

"The Mascarellas then took my mother to see an attorney named Charlene Burke in Canfield, Ohio" I explained.

Fleming then wanted to know what happened when my mother was taken to Burke's law office.

"What papers did you sign, Mrs. Falvo, in Charlene Burke's office?"

"I really don't know," my mother replied.

"Did you give Shirley Mascarella any type of power of attorney?" Fleming inquired.

"I really don't remember," my mother confessed. "I just know it was a lot of papers," my mother stated.

"And do you have copies of any of those papers?" Fleming asked her. "No."

"Would you like copies of those papers?"

"Yes, I would," my mother responded.

Questions turned into hours, and hours turned into the entire morning. There were times when Attorney Fleming appeared baffled by the entire situation. He got up from his chair at the head of the long conference table, and paced the length of the entire room, then stared out the window.

"I'm going to have to think about this," Fleming stated. He then added, "Let's break for lunch and then meet back here in my conference room at 1 p.m."

••●●●●••

Richard, my mother, and I then went down the elevator and inside a little pub/restaurant on the ground level, and ordered some hot sandwiches for lunch.

"Well, what do you think, Mom?"

"I like him!" my mother said. "I think he will get me that paper!"

I still had no idea what kind of paper my mother was expecting, but she seemed determined, nonetheless.

Businessmen and construction workers entered the busy, dimly lit pub. We watched the flickering TV as the weatherman reported more rain, mixed with snow, was about to come.

A few minutes before 1 p.m., we went back up the old elevator to Fleming's office.

When we returned, Fleming's secretary stated that only my mother should re-enter the conference room. Richard and I were instructed to wait outside in Attorney Fleming's waiting room again. We had no idea what this meant. Richard and I looked at each other, and shrugged. We picked up magazines and thumbed through them while passing the time.

Attorney Fleming then entered his conference room with my mother, who was wheeled in by one of his secretaries. Then two additional assistants also entered the conference room and quietly closed the door.

While we waited, Richard, who had been one of my high school teachers, informed me why he had insisted I come to Youngstown to rescue my mother.

"I think they're trying to kill her at that nursing home," Richard stated. "Your mother looks so gaunt. I can't believe how much her health has deteriorated."

"Yes," I agreed. "Just three months ago she was robust and raking leaves in my yard every day."

Several hours passed. It was now past closing time at Al Flemings law office. Richard and I stared at the closed conference door, looked up at the big, round clock on the wall, then looked at each other with disquiet resignation. Another half an hour passed.

Then suddenly, the closed conference door sprang open and there stood Fleming, with his three assistants, and my mother in a wheel chair. They all appeared quite pleased. There was a large stack of papers in one of the secretary's hands, and she approached me, smiling, and handed the stack to me.

The papers, all legal documents, had all been signed by my mother and notarized by one of the secretaries. The papers included several powers of attorney, a general power of attorney, a durable power of attorney, and limited powers of attorney over all bank accounts at both Bank of America and Wachovia.

"Can we leave right now for Florida?" my mother eagerly inquired.

"Actually, I would prefer you not do that just yet, Mrs. Falvo," Fleming replied. "If it is at all possible, I would like you to stay until

Friday. At that time, I would like you to come back to my office so we can videotape your wishes and memorialize them. Would that be all right, Mrs. Falvo?"

"I think it's a great idea!" I said. But my mother did not look too pleased.

Fleming then faxed the powers of attorney documents to Banks of America and Wachovia.

On the ride back to Meridian Arms, my mother inquired. "So, when are we leaving for Florida?"

"On Friday, after the videotaping," I assured her. But my mother looked extremely displeased. She was not too excited about being videotaped. "And who will see this videotape?" my mother inquired.

"Anybody who wants to see it shall see it, Mom." I told her.

My mother scowled.

After a beat of silence, she asked, "Even Shirley will be able to see it?"

"Yes, even Shirley will be able to see it,"

My mother had wanted to tell the Mascarella's that it was "Angie's idea" that she go back to Florida so that they would not be "angry" at her.

"Oh, no, Mom. If you blame it on me, I guarantee you that I **shall not** be taking you back to Florida. And that's a fact. You're going to have to come clean and tell them it is YOUR idea." My mother shifted uncomfortably.

When the three of us arrived back at my mother's room, it was about 7 p.m. and the Mascarellas were waiting for her, sitting on her bed. They appeared very agitated.

I wheeled my mother into the room, then left the room, closing the door behind me. I stood outside the door of my mother's room for a few minutes and eavesdropped. I overheard my mother saying, sheepishly "Well, the weather is much nicer in Florida." I felt pleased to know my mother was telling them the truth.

Richard and I walked down the urine-smelling hallways to exit the building.

On the way out of the building, I bumped into an old high school classmate of mine who was working as the assistant activity director at Meridian Arms. I was so surprised to see her.

"Mary Ann! Is that you?"

"Angie Falvo?" she replied.

We nodded and hugged each other.

Suddenly, I had a much-needed ally.

"Can you do me a favor, Mary Ann?" I asked her. "There is a manipulative niece, and her creepy husband, inside my mother's room. Can you phone me and let me know when they have left?"

"I will most certainly do that for you, Angie," she replied with a smile.

I scribbled my cell phone number on a Post- It note, and then Richard and I quickly departed.

Back at Richard's condo, four tense hours passed. Still no word from Mary Ann. Finally, I phoned the nurse's station and asked them to page her.

"Have the Mascarellas left?" I asked Mary Ann.

"Let me check," she replied. A minute later, "Nope. They're still inside the room with her!" It was well past 11 p.m.

On Friday, February 1, 2008, Richard and I returned to my mother's room and drove her to Fleming's office for the video deposition. Richard and I once again waited in Fleming's waiting room during the lengthy video deposition. Somewhere around noon, when the deposition was finally over, Richard and I were in the process of taking my mother down the elevator when my mother asked "Where is the paperwork that authorizes me to go back to Florida?"

Richard and I gave each other a disquieted look. We then pushed the "up" button and went back upstairs to Fleming's office. Fleming was about to step out for lunch. "My mother still wants that paper that authorizes her to go to Florida." But Fleming simply motioned with both of his hands, like a "shooing away" motion. I really didn't realize how powerful a "power of attorney" document could be. Neither did Richard.

Back at Meridian Arms, I showed Kathy Fine the powers of attorney my mother had executed at Fleming's office. Fine quickly glanced at the documents and dismissed them.

"Powers of attorney or not, I will be calling the police and having you charged with 'kidnapping' if you attempt to take your mother out of Meridian Arms." Not truly understanding the authority that had been bestowed upon me via powers of attorney, I went back to my mother's room and explained the situation to her. "I cannot take you back home with me, Mom," I sadly explained.

My mother was terribly disappointed and somewhat disbelieving.

"You just don't want me to be with you," my mother cried.

"That's absolutely not true!" I replied. "But with Shirley and John making 12 calls to Elder Abuse over the last year, and now Kathy Fines threatening to call the cops if I take you out of here, what am I supposed to do, Mom?"

She looked up at me with sad eyes.

"Promise me you will find a way to take me home."

"I promise you, Mom. I will."

•••●••

On February 14, 2008, Shirley and John Mascarella took my mother back to see Attorney Charlene Burke, falsely telling her that "all" of her money had been closed out by me and that there was "nothing" left and that the "only way" to get back at least part of her money was to make yet another Will with Charlene Burke.

Prior to driving my mother to Burke's office, there was a forced meeting held at Meridian Arms on or about February 8, 2008 in which my mother was hounded by an entire group of people which included staff members of Meridian Arms, the Mascarellas, an ombudsman named Kathy Janecko, and Charlene Burke – all hounding my mother, putting her on the spot, and asking her how she wanted to leave her money. Imagine what is what like to be my mother during this meeting and have this many people all at once hounding you. My mother already knew and had stated many times that she wanted to go home to Florida. With this much pressure, however, my mother felt that if she told them the truth any further that they would further prevent her from returning home and she most certainly did not wish to be placed under a guardianship. To foil their attempts, my mother agreed to go back to Burke's office and execute yet another Will favoring Shirley Mascarella. But my mother was a clever woman. My mother already knew that all of her assets were already safely ITF and POD at banks of America and Wachovia to her daughter, Woodhull, so it mattered little what a Will might state. The banks trump any will.

Burke also explained to Falvo that what my mother had done at the banks would defeat any Will that Burke was creating. My mother replied, "I know."

I drove to Orlando from Gainesville, Florida and checked into the Knight's Inn on International Drive. Then, I went through the Yellow Pages calling multiple attorneys, describing the precarious situation up in Ohio, and explaining that my mother wanted to come back home. But no attorney wanted to help. All of them told me that Gainesville was too far away, and that I need either a Gainesville or an Ohio attorney to assist with the sticky situation. Somewhere toward the end of a full day of phone calls, some attorney suggested that I phone an attorney in Oviedo, Florida by the name of Attorney Evelyn W. Cloninger. I had never before heard of Oviedo, Florida.

Exhausted from a day's worth of futile phone calls to Orlando attorneys, I reluctantly decided to phone this one last attorney. I had literally phoned at least 50 attorneys prior to reaching Evelyn Cloninger.

And now, here she was – an attorney live on the phone, late in the day, who was claiming she could help.

Cloninger had such an odd plan. It made me sit up straight in the hotel bed and listen carefully.

"Now, here's what I want you to do!" she stated. "First of all, I want you to go back up to Ohio and tell the staff at Meridian Arms that you are simply taking your mother out to lunch. And since no attorney in Gainesville is willing to help you, just come back here to my county [Seminole County], rent a hotel room for you and your mother for about one week, and we'll put your mother under a guardianship so that cousin Shirley can never bother your mother ever again."

I remained silent. There were a few long beats of silence.

"I hear you hesitating," Cloninger stated. "Why are you hesitating? That is your **_mother_**, for gawd's sake! You are her **_only child_**! If that was my mother, I'd be in my car right now on my way to Ohio! In fact, if I didn't have such a heavy case load, I'd be in my car right now on my way to Ohio to retrieve your mother."

"***Really***?" I asked.

Cloninger stated that she had a reputation for rescuing elderly people from nursing homes and from hospitals and that she (Cloninger) used to have cottages on her property in Seminole County where she would house rescued senior citizens and put them under guardianship with herself as the appointed guardian.

At this point, I didn't even really realize what a guardianship is, or what it actually entails. I thought it was like getting a driver's license, or a power of attorney.

I knew guardianship had something to do with mental competence, so I assured Cloninger, "My mother will not qualify for guardianship. She is manipulative, but she is not mentally incompetent."

"Well, ***we'll see***," Cloninger chirped, her voice rising with confidence and delight. "You'll be here on **my** turf with **my** judges."

"I don't know," I replied. "I'll have to think about this," I said.

Cloninger then provided me with her private, personal cell phone number. Quite an unusual thing for an attorney to do.

"Call any time of the day or night, if you do decide to go get your mother," she said.

****

THE QUARIES

Three weeks passed, and then I had finally made up my mind. I had been somewhat reluctant to go rescue my mother with all of the past drama memories. But additionally, I was in a brand new relationship with David A. Newman. It was my first intimate relationship in more than four years since my divorce from Jud, and I just didn't want to risk losing my new beau because of mother drama, police calls, false reports, and Elder Abuse visits. I had had to think long and hard about Cloninger's odd rescue mission suggestions.

I knew it was time to have a serious talk with my new love and tell him about the sticky, precarious situation my mother was in up in Ohio. It was only the third month of my and David's fledgling relationship. I knew this might be the end of our relationship. Afterall, David was a party boy and loved playing harmonicas. I just didn't see him wanting to be involved in endless Mother Drama.

For this difficult conversation, I selected a very secluded spot, late at night, under the moonlight. It was a very romantic setting. There, under the stars, David and I surreptitiously walked down the long wooden staircase that led to the quarries, a sinkhole in an upscale neighborhood. The sign we passed before we descended the long staircase read, "No trespassing after sundown."

David put his arms around me as we gazed into the sparkling lake, the stars above us reflecting light into the calm waters. A few long kisses later, David asked me, "So, what is it that you want to tell me?"

Immediately, tears fell upon my cheeks.

"Ah, come on. It can't be THAT bad!" David said, grabbing my hands.

"I'm afraid I'm going to lose you," I sobbed.

"I'm not going anywhere," David replied with a big smile.

I looked at David slowly, not wanting to ruin this sweet moment, and told him I had some things to figure out and I wasn't sure what that meant for us. I told him of my estranged cousin Shirley and her crooked husband, John, and how my mother was left in a nursing home, and conned into rewriting her will. He hung onto every word and gave me the ear I needed. When I finished with all the little details I told him my mother's health had rapidly deteriorated in the last three months and she would need a lot of care from now on. I think David could sense the hesitation in my voice. He stopped me without a thought, grabbed my hands tightly, and said "Let's go get your mother."

"You would be willing to help me take care of her?" I asked him, astonished.

David did not hesitate to respond. He had previously been married for ten years to a woman in a wheelchair whom he had cared for. He had also worked for more than 10 years in a hospital as a surgery equipment set up specialist. In other words, David A. Newman was a natural caregiver.

I suddenly realized he was much more than just a long haired guy playing the harmonica. Alas, I was in love . . . and I could take care of my mother with his help and his kindness.

CHAPTER TWELVE:

THE RESCUE MISSION -- OFF TO

YOUNGSTOWN, OHIO

On March 2, 2008, I rented a large RV and hired five people to accompany me for the journey up to Ohio to rescue Mom. The rescue team consisted of Andre Wickes (also a natural caregiver who works with mentally handicapped people (and a professional drummer)), Olivia Hill (a longtime girlfriend and musician who raised six children, also a natural caregiver), Steve, who was attending Santa Fe Community College at the time to become a nurse (Steve brought along some medical equipment and was supposed to be the one to change diapers, etc.), Christopher Wolfe, a native of Youngstown who had moved to Gainesville after having been involved in my production of "**Remember Idora**!" Wolf was 21 years old at the time and he said, "I'll be the one to drive in the middle of the night when all of you old people are sleeping."

And then there was David and me.

And Nini, the cat. Nini was an all-white kitty with bright blue eyes and a little pink nose I had adopted when I was staging **Remember Idora**! I have never known such an easy-going cat. Nini loves everybody. And Nini loves music. She curled up on one of the pillows on the bed in the back of the RV and went to sleep.

And so, on a rainy Florida evening, the six of us commenced our journey to Youngstown, Ohio to rescue Mom!

"My mother will be so proud of me!" I thought!

Andre was super excited. A native of Florida, he said he had never seen snow before. He brought along his camera so he could snap photos of the white wonderland when we reached our destination.

Meanwhile, someone must have been eavesdropping on my mother's telephone conversations in her room at Meridian Arms. My mother had now been moved back to the assistant living side of Meridian Arms, but when lifetime friend Richard Filisky went one evening to take Mom out to supper, he was surprised to find out that she was "not allowed" out of the building. Meridian Arms (or the Mascarellas) (or both) had put another ankle bracelet upon my mother so that she would "beep" if she attempted to leave the building. (This was actually highly illegal.) Frustrated with the situation, my mother finally told the nursing home staff that if they didn't take off the beeping ankle bracelet, she was going to call the police. They took it off.

I had first met Andre Wickes when I was staging a children's musical show called "The Learning Castle." Andre had been my drummer. Andre and I had also been in the Thai Elvis band; Thai Elvis is a man from Thailand who is an Elvis impersonator. Andre entered the RV with a set of drumsticks in his back pack. "Mama, we're coming to get you! Hell ya!!" he said, flashing a peace sign, as he climbed aboard.

David then backed out the big motorhome, and we headed over to the southside of town where Christopher Wolfe was living. With the engine still running, I dialed Christopher on my cell phone. "We're here! Are you ready?"

And soon, there was Christopher exiting his apartment with a backpack and carrying a cooler.

He climbed aboard and announced, "I got enough snacks here to feed an entire army! Who wants some cheesy popcorn?"

Andre, seated in a padded chair next to the sink said, "Sure, man!" They clasped hands, and smiled. "Rescue mission. Here we come!" Christopher bellowed. "Oh, hell ya!" Andre replied. "***Mama, here we come!***"

"Woo! Hoo!" I cheered.

Next, it was time to make a round on the North side of Gainesville, where we would be picking up Olivia Hill, my dear friend of many years. Olivia is an expert guitar player and the mother of six. Although born in England, she lived many decades in Ireland, and she knows all of the favorite Irish tunes. She sings well. She is jovial and polite. Olivia was already waiting outside of her front door when we pulled up in the motorhome.

"Olivia!!!!!!!!!!!!!!!!!" I yelled, with glee. Olivia stepped into the RV with her luggage and a guitar.

Everyone cheered.

Last but not least, we picked up Andre's friend, Steve, the Santa Fe college nursing student. Olivia was already strumming a folk tune on her guitar, seated on the foot of the bed at the back of the RV.

"Hey, everybody, this is Steve!"

"Hey, man, good to see you," Andre said, standing up to greet Steve.

And now, the rescue mission was about to begin.

With a Scrabble board, snacks, a litter box, plenty of soda, a box of maracas, and a stack of diapers, we embarked around 7 p.m. on the evening of March 2, 2008 for Youngstown, Ohio.

I removed my accordion from its case, and said, "Come on, everybody, sing along!"

In Heaven, there is no beer!

NO BEER! (everyone shouted)

That's why we drink it here!

DRINK IT HERE! (everyone shouted)

And when we're gone from here!

GONE FROM HERE! (everyone shouted)

Our friends will be drinking all the beer!

ALL THE BEER! (everyone shouted)

[IT'S SING-ALONG TIME! IN HEAVEN THERE IS NO BEER!

Olivia strummed along on the guitar, and David wailed out some bluesy notes on his harmonica.

Andre played "drums" on the table top, and Steve shook maracas!

La, la, la, la, la, la, la, la, la, la, la, la!

Suddenly, my cell phone was ringing. It was mom.

"Ang, where are you? Are you really coming?"

"Yep, we sure are, Mom!"

"Everybody, say, 'hi' to Mom!!"

"**Hello, Mama!**" everyone bellowed.

"**Mama! We're coming to get you!**" Andre yelled.

"Did you hear that, Mom?!"

"There's six people here, Mom! **Six people!** And we're all coming to get you!"

Everyone cheered!

Soon, it was pitch black outside, and soon, it was about two a.m. We had stopped for supper. We had stopped for gas many times. And now, everyone was asleep, except for Christopher, who was driving, and David, who was seated shot gun.

Steve had claimed the bed overhead up front, while Olivia and I curled up on the double bed in the back of the RV with a purring Nini Cat snuggled between us.

Throughout the long night, the motorhome continued to chug along. Periodically, my friends woke up to use the bathroom, then went back to their sleeping positions.

Long-legged Andre was asleep on a long bench in the dining room area.

"Are you comfortable like that?" I asked him in the middle of the night. Groggily, Andre replied, "It's all good, and re-closed his eyes and fell back asleep."

Soon, the sun was up, and David was at the wheel. Christopher was now riding shotgun, his mouth agape, head back, slightly snoring.

By 7 a.m., we had now reached Kentucky.

Everyone seemed to wake up at about the same time. Everyone appeared tired, but happy and excited.

"About eight more hours, everyone, and then we will be in Youngstown, Ohio!"

The group cheered and clapped.

I removed my accordion from its case. It was time for a good morning song!

"Look ahead everyone!" David suddenly announced. David pointed at a large green sign on the side of the highway, which announced . . .

WELCOME TO OHIO!

In unison, everyone bellowed "**Welcome to Ohio! Woo! Hoo!**" "***Mama! We're comin' to get you!***" Andre yelled. "***Woo! Hoo!***" Within about four more hours, we would be reaching our destination of Youngstown, Ohio.

****

When the Rescue Team arrived, we first found a cheap, funky hotel in the outskirts of Youngstown where we could all stay. I rented three rooms for the six of us. We then phoned Mom to let her know that we had arrived. But, instead, John Mascarella was staked out in my mother's room and picked up the phone.

"Hello?"

"Hello, is this John?"

"Yep, it sure is. (sarcastically) So, this must be . . . (**sounding disgusted**) . . . Angie."

"Yes, it's Angie. Please put my mother on the phone."

There was a long, hostile pause.

[The following conversation is an actual transcript of the actual conversation that has been filed into the Alachua County Probate Court records.]

"Nope. I ain't puttin' your mother on the phone."

"Why is that?"

"Because she said she don't want to talk to you."

"I don't believe, that, John. Now, where is my mother?"

"She's sitting right here."

"And can she hear what you are saying?"

"She sure can. She can hear every word. And she wants you to know that we have put secret cameras in her room, so you better not trying any stuff, Angie."

"Try anything? Like what?"

"Well, you know, like tryin' to take her outta here, Angie. She's quite content here. And she don't want to go back to Florida."

"How do you know that, John?"

"Because we was down there. And we took her to the banks. Believe me, I go into the banks and, believe me, I was surprised to no end when I found out her money had $320,000 in one account in Bank of America. And then we went over to Wachovia and they had

$379,000.00 I was flabbergasted!!! I couldn't believe it!!! In fact, when we went over to Regions Bank, I expected another $300,000, but it was only $39,000.00."

"Really? So what has happened to the rest of it, John?"

"Okay, so I don't know what has happened to the rest of it. But that's all that there was there. And I told Shirley, 'You know, we got big, big problems.'"

"Yeah? What's your problem, John?"

"I said, 'Shirley, there's no way Angie's gonna allow us to leave Florida with her mom with all that money.' So, while you were up in Tallahassee making that movie, we barricaded the door every night. I even moved out and went to a hotel and left Shirl alone with your mom. I said, 'You know, some goon with a gun is gonna show up any minute and wipe everybody out.'"

"Really? That's what you thought? A goon with a gun was going to wipe you out?"

By now, David had taken out our video camera and was taping the conversation.

"Yep. So you'd better not come up here and try some hanky panky, Angie. You don't know what might happen next."

And he hung up.

Several days passed. There was a big snow storm outside in Youngstown, nearly reminiscent of that fateful snow when I was first born. We waited inside our hotel rooms, and ordered pizzas every day. On the third day, Andre and Steve said they couldn't stay any longer. "We've got to go back to Florida. We didn't know it was going to take this long." I provided them with money for bus tickets, and they took a taxi to the Greyhound bus station from the motel.

When the Mascarellas were not staked out in my mother's room, my mother would surreptitiously call me on her room phone and whisper into the receiver.

On day four, I received a phone call from my mother at about 10 a.m. By now, the Mascarellas were convinced that I really wasn't coming to Youngstown. There was too much snow, and too many days had passed.

My mother whispered into the receiver, "Come tonight, Ang, and get me." "John and Shirley will not be here tonight because it is Brian's (Shirley's grown son) birthday, and they are taking Brian out to dinner. They invited me to come along, but I told them I was too tired. So, please come get me tonight."

In preparation for the rescue, David and I rented a car. We figured it would be a lot easier to put my mother in a rental car than pull up with a huge motor home. Olivia stayed back in the hotel room, watching TV. Christopher decided to take a taxi over to the west side of Youngstown and stay with his parents.

Around 6 p.m., David and I entered the side door of Meridian Arms and began searching for my mother's room. We didn't know where it was. We walked briskly down the first hallway, peering into each room to see if a small gray haired Italian lady was sitting in her bed, anticipating our arrival. The last time I had seen Shirley Mascarella was at her mother's funeral, more than 15 years prior.

But I recognized her immediately. As we walked briskly down the hallway, I peered into the laundry room on the right. And there was Shirley Mascarella perched up on top of a washing machine with a video camera in her hands and a walkie talkie by her side.

"Keep walking," I whispered to David. And then we rounded the bend and with my arm locked on his arm, I directed him back outside the building and out into our rental car.

"What's going on?" David inquired.

"Did you see that woman sitting on top of the washing machine?"

"Yes, a little."

"That's Shirley!"

"So, she's not at her son's birthday party after all?"

"Nope!"

Right then, we saw John Mascarella round the bend in the parking lot, talking on his walkie talkie.

It was another foiled attempt. We were unable to rescue mom. David and I drove back in through the snow-covered streets and re-entered our motel room, where Olivia was lying on the bed watching TV.

"What happened?" Olivia inquired.

"It's a no go. Shirley was staked out on top of a washing machine with a video camera."

"Did she see you?"

"I think so. Our eyes locked for a second, but I don't think she recognized me. I look much different these days."

David and I munched on some stale, left-over pizza, and Olivia texted her grown children on her cell phone.

Suddenly, I felt very discouraged and tired. It had been a long, bleak four days in Youngstown. For the past three months, I had been enjoying my life with my new beau. Now, a plethora of horrible memories was flooding my mind. Between John and Shirley Mascarella, cameras in my mother's room, "goons with guns," 12 calls to Elder Abuse, police calls, Fire and Rescue calls, I had had enough.

I curled up in the bed that David and I were sharing and began to softly cry. Olivia and David did not notice my tears. They were laughing and watching an old re-run of Seinfeld on the motel's TV.

Suddenly, my sniffles caught their attention. Olivia snapped off the TV.

"What's wrong, Angie?"

"I can't take it anymore. I just want to go back to Florida," I told them.

David and Olivia looked at me in shocked silence.

"We came all this way," David stated.

There were a few more beats of silence.

Olivia came over and rubbed my back empathetically.

"You know, Ang, if that's how you feel, I respect that."

My soft tears turned into sobs.

"Okay, good!" I said. "Can we just go tomorrow and say good-bye to my mother after a good night's sleep?"

"If that's what you want to do, then that's what we shall do," David said.

Olivia nodded in agreement.

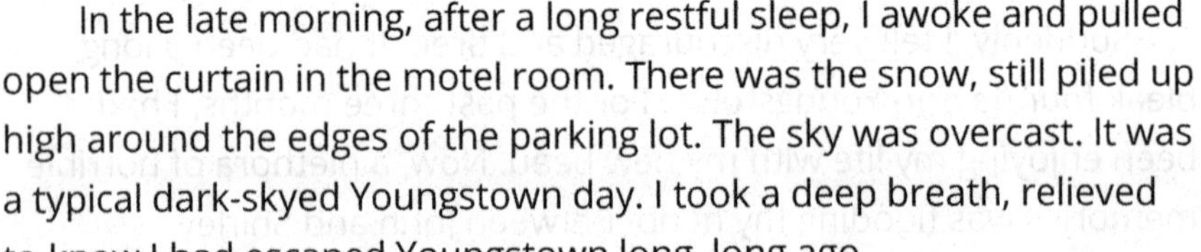

In the late morning, after a long restful sleep, I awoke and pulled open the curtain in the motel room. There was the snow, still piled up high around the edges of the parking lot. The sky was overcast. It was a typical dark-skyed Youngstown day. I took a deep breath, relieved to know I had escaped Youngstown long, long ago.

Soon, David and Olivia started to stir. Nini Cat was curled up on the bed, asleep.

"Shall we go out for breakfast? My treat!" I announced.

"Sure, what's open on a Sunday morning in Youngstown?" David inquired.

"I'm sure we'll find something."

Not far from our motel on south Market Street, we found a breakfast house across from the mall. On the menu, it read, "We serve the famous Idora Park French fries."

"French fries for breakfast?"

"Hell yeah!" I replied enthusiastically.

It was scrambled eggs with a side of Ethyl's famous fries for me.

When our breakfasts arrived, David and Olivia noticed that I was once again brushing away tears.

"What do you want to do, Angie?"

"I don't know. Maybe we should at least go there and say good-bye to my mother."

"I think that's a great idea," Olivia said.

"We can go there and play some songs for her!"

"Yes, how 'bout some Italian songs?" Olivia chimed in.

Soon, we were back at our motel room, gathering up our musical instruments. While David grabbed his case of harmonicas, Olivia placed her guitar back in its case, and David then picked up my accordion case and put it in the back seat of our compact rental car.

Resigned, I stated, "This will probably be the last time I ever see my mom alive."

We were off to Meridian Arms, to bid farewell to Mom.

****

At the Meridian Arms nursing home, it was no secret that we had arrived. When we entered the front door on a Sunday mid-morning, carrying our musical instruments, we saw Kathy Fines (the administrator) inside her office. Although it was a Sunday mid-morning, she was in her office near the front foyer, organizing her files.

"Hi, Kathy. Where is my mother's room?" I inquired.

"It's right there," she replied, pointing to a room adjacent to her office.

There on the door of the room, it read "Louise Falvo."

We tapped gently on the door and then walked in.

There was my mom, seated in a wheel chair and looking quite despondent. "Oh, Ang!" she said, lifting her head up. "I thought you already went back to Florida!"

"We're on our way back this morning, Mom. But we thought we would stop and say good-bye to you first."

"Oh, Ang!" My mother hugged me and burst into deep heart-felt tears.

I brushed away my tears and opened my accordion case. My resolve had already been made, so it was no use spending our short time together crying. This would be our last happy memory together.

"Mom, this is my friend, Olivia. Do you remember Olivia? You met her at my house in the past. She has six kids."

"Hello, Louise," Olivia smiled, then hugged my mom.

Olivia opened up her guitar case and began tuning the strings.

And there was David, meeting my mother for the first time. I was so happy that he would have been able to meet my mother at least once.

"Mom, this is my new boyfriend, David. I love him so much! He is so wonderful!"

David stood up and greeted my mother with a tight squeeze. "Hello, Louise! I'm so happy to meet you!"

"Hello, Honey!" My mother embraced David.

"Mom, we're going to play you some of your favorite, old Italian songs before we go, okay?"

And then the orchestra began!

C'è 'na luna mezz'u mare
Mamma mia m'a maritare
It's the butcher girl! She's got a bundle in her hands!
Hey, Mama! Go get that girl for me!
Hey, Mama! The butcher girl for me!!

While we sang, Mama clapped her hands and giggled.

Kathy Fines peeked into the open-door room, and then carefully closed the door shut.

Now it was time for the Tarantella.

Olivia knew all of the famous, old songs.

David, who plays by ear, was able to pick up the tunes quite easily.

Soon, my mother was laughing out loud. She brushed away happy tears and clapped her hands.

A few songs later, she opened her little white pocketbook, and took out a little, folded paper to show me.

"Ang, what is this?"

I quickly scanned the paper.

"Mom, this paper says you don't want to keep your homestead in Florida any more."

My mother looked shocked.

"Why would they send me that paper?"

"I don't know," I replied. "I guess Shirley and John did that."

"Well, what can we write back to them, Ang?"

"I guess tell them you want to keep your homestead, Ma. Don't check that box."

"And will you give it to them when you're back in Florida?"

"Sure, Mom. I'll give it to them."

My mother then carefully across the bottom of the paper wrote, "I wish to keep my homestead in Florida. Louise Falvo." And she handed me the paper.

•••●•••

When I took the paper from her, she suddenly grabbed it back.

"What now, Mom? What is it?" I asked her.

With tears filling her eyes, she said, "I don't want you to give them this paper."

"You don't?" I felt confused.

Then my mother added, looking up at me, with tears in her eyes. " I want to hand them this paper myself. I want to fo home."

And she burst into loud tears, loud enough for Kathy Fines to hear her.

I turned and looked at Olivia and David. They, in turn, looking at my mother, brushed away their own tears.

"Ang, please," my mother stated in a low voice. "Take me back home."

I sat back down and sighed heavily.

The balance of joy and despair I felt was unsettling, to say the least. I knew I would have to tread carefully, balance my roles, and fight to restore my mother's health and dignity, while simultaneously protecting the precious fledgling connection I had with David.

The room was silent, except for my mother's hopeful sobs.

"We can only take a few things, Mom," I told her.

"I know!" she said, her voice rising with hope.

"Can we take my wedding picture?"

There, up on the wall, hung the black and white photo from Carl and Louise's little wedding day from 1946. My mother was dressed in a little beige satin suit and holding a small bouquet of flowers. Her hair in a neat shoulder length page boy with a pill box on top. My father in a suit sporting a thick tie, smiling broadly.

"Olivia, take that picture down from the wall."

"But that will look kind of obvious, Ang. Don't you think so?"

"Just take the picture down," I told her.

Olivia walked over to the wall and removed the old photo and picture frame from the wall.

David was packing up my accordion and putting away his harmonicas.

The sweet music had stopped but the warm feelings continued in the room.

Yes, I would be my mother's hero.

And then we opened the door to my mother's room, into the open hallway, and there was Kathy Fines with two days of my mother's medications wrapped up in a white bag.

"We're going to lunch with my mother," I told her.

But Kathy Fines obviously realized the plans were much bigger than lunch.

"Well, I think you'd better take this bag with you," she stated, handing to me a bag with two days worth of medicines, while taking notice of Olivia cradling the large framed photo.

Back at the hotel room, we hastily packed up our belongings, loaded Nini cat into the RV, and set off across town to pick up Christopher.

And now it was time for the long journey back to Florida!

My mother lied on the bed petting Nini cat while Olivia entertained us with Irish songs.

I joined in on the accordion, and Christopher sat by, smiling.

"You old people know a lot of silly songs!" he said, laughing.

David, our driver, whistled while listing to tunes on his headphones. He was our head mast. The rescue mission was in full swing, and my mom was happily relaxing while watching the passing scenery. We thought all was well.

Suddenly, my cell phone rang.

It was Richard Filisky.

"Angie! I just got a call from the police. The Mascarellas phoned the police. The Ohio state troopers are looking for your mother."

Right then we were on a part of the highway where we could continue heading south through Ohio or veer off into the state of West Virginia.

We decided to head into the Mountain State, even though the ride would be much longer, and much more dangerous. Soon, the sign ahead welcomed us to West Virginia.

Veering through the mountains in an RV on a cold snowy day with Mama bouncing along on the bed, petting the cat, we sang songs, ate chocolates, and played Uno with Mama.

By evening, we had reached the state of Virginia, and Mom was fast asleep in the back of the RV, Nini cat wrapped in her arms.

The stars twinkled as we trucked along throughout the night.

As we left the frosty confines of Ohio, we embarked on a journey that felt symbolic in more ways than one. Our rented RV carried more than just us and our possessions; it carried hope, uncertainty, and the precious cargo of my mother's fragile health. We navigated the curvaceous routes of West Virginia, the RV jostling us like an old wooden rollercoaster.

The biting cold gradually began to lose its grip, replaced by a more temperate climate as we ventured further south.

We pushed on, leaving behind the gray and snow, our path taking us toward warmer pastures. The road unfurled before us, a ribbon cutting through the picturesque landscape. The barren trees of the north gradually gave way to lush greenery and a riot of colors as wildflowers started dotting our route.

There was a gradual shift in the scenery, in the temperature, in the mood inside the RV. The biting chill gave way to a lukewarm breeze, the heavy winter wear replaced by lighter garments. The journey was grueling, but there was a palpable lift in our spirits. We were not just moving through states; we were moving towards a new beginning, a chance at redemption.

Somewhere, around two a.m., while everyone was asleep except for me and David, I noticed that my mother was sitting up in the bed.

I walked over to the RV bed and put my arms around her. "How are you doing, Ma?"

"I dunno," my mother replied, tears falling on her rugged, wrinkled cheeks. I took a corner of the sheet and wiped away her tears.

"What if they try to come get me?" she asked. "What if they force me to go back to Youngstown?"

"They won't happen, Ma," I assured her. "There is an attorney who has promised to help us. I will be your guardian now. I will make sure nothing bad happens to you."

My mother slumped into my arms and I cradled her until she fell back asleep.

••●●••

And then when the sun came up, there was that sign up ahead "Welcome to Florida."

The first glimpse of Florida was like a watercolor painting come to life. Palm trees swaying in the gentle wind, the sun sparkling off the azure waters, people in their summer best – it was a stark contrast to the gray, wintry desolation of Youngstown.

Florida welcomed us with open arms, the sunshine bright and heartening, promising better days. The freshness of spring was in full bloom, painting the surroundings in various shades of green, pink, and yellow. It felt like crossing an invisible line into a completely different world. One where the air was not filled with the sting of cold but with the scent of blossoming orange groves. The warm wind that now whistled through the RV was not just a meteorological change; it was the wind of change itself.

As we drove into the sunshine state, there was a sense of returning home, but also a trepidation about the challenges that awaited us. Yet, for that moment, we bathed in the golden glow of the Floridian sun, a beacon guiding us towards hope and resilience.

•••• ● ●••

Arriving back in Florida, my mother appeared tired but happy. It had been a long journey for a 92-year-old woman. But she was delighted to be back in the Sunshine State.

"What do we do next, Ang?"

"We have to drive now to Oviedo, Florida now and see that attorney I was telling you about, Mom. She is going to protect us," I assured her.

Arriving at Cloninger's Office in Oviedo, Florida

Somewhere in the midafternoon on March 11, 2008, David, and my mother, and I arrived at the Law Office of Attorney Evelyn W. Cloninger. We parked the RV parallel in Cloninger's parking lot. The sign above the building read "Cloninger and Files." I stepped out of the RV and entered Cloninger's office. And there she was.

Evelyn W. Cloninger, a chunky woman with her hair in a bun, snacks all over the front of her messy desk, looking quite delighted to meet me. She stood up from her desk and greeted me with a strong hand shake.

"Angela?"

"Yes, pleased to me you!" I stated.

"So, where is your mother?" she inquired. "You were able to rescue your mother?"

"Yes, she's here – inside the RV. We're all quite exhausted," I told her.

Cloninger walked from around her office desk and joined me outside in her front parking lot. It was a bright, hot Florida day.

"This is my fiancé, David," I told her, and the two of them shook hands.

"Now, would the two of you mind walking over to the other side of the parking lot?" Cloninger asked. "I'd first like to talk with your mother alone."

As David and I moved to the front side of the RV, we could hear Cloninger introducing herself to my mother, in a loud voice.

"Hello, Mrs. Falvo. I'm pleased to meet you!"

"Pleased to meet you, too" my mother replied.

"I'm Evelyn Cloninger, and your daughter has hired me to represent her."

"Yes, I know," my mother stated.

"How are you feeling, Mrs. Falvo."

"I'm feeling fine," my mother replied. "Happy to be back in Florida."

"Yes, I bet you are. Did you enjoy the snow up in Ohio?"

"No, not at all," my mother stated.

"Now, I have a few questions for you, Mrs. Falvo. Is that all right?"

"Sure, that is fine."

First of all, how old are you?

"I'm 92 years old," my mother replied.

"Wow! Such a ripe old age!"

My mother laughed.

"And what is your address of your Florida home?"

"My address is 1920 S.W. 72nd Street in Gainesville, Florida."

"Okay. And let me ask you. If you counted backwards from 99, what would be the next five numbers?"

"From 99?"

"Yes."

"Counting backwards?"

"Yes."

"Well, this is a bit silly question isn't it?" my mother replied.

"Mm. Perhaps. What are those numbers, Mrs. Falvo?"

"99, 98, 97, 96, 95, 94, 93, 92, 91, 90, 89 . . ."

"Okay, Mrs. Falvo. That's enough."

"And who is the president of the United States right now?"

"Well, it's George W. Bush, Jr.," my mother confidently replied. "But in the future, I hope it will be Hillary. I really love her."

"Okay. And one last question. And what did you eat for breakfast this morning?"

"I had some oatmeal with half a banana and some milk, and a cup of black coffee. But yesterday, I had two scrambled eggs and some wheat toast," my mother explained.

"Okay, Mrs. Falvo. Nice meeting you."

Cloninger then exited the RV and came back around to the front of the vehicle where David and I were standing. She ushered me into her office.

"Well, your mother really is quite astute," Cloninger declared. "She's as sharp as a pin."

"Yes, I know. I told you so," I told her.

Cloninger had already prepared some papers to commence a guardianship upon my mother, and she wanted me to sign them.

"I'll probably need to make a few changes first," she confessed, so don't sign these papers yet. "First, I'd like to take you and your mother across the street over to my doctor friend's office," she explained. "Your mother should probably be examined after such a long ride."

Soon, the four of us were over at Dr. Guillermo Marrero's office. Even without an appointment, Evelyn Cloninger was able to get us in almost immediately to see her favorite doctor.

Evelyn got up from her seat in the doctor's waiting room, and grabbed a clip board and some blank medical forms. Cloninger was busy completing all of the forms, asking me about my mother's past health record, current medications, etc.

Then she moved close to me and whispered,

"Now, when you go in to see the doctor with your mother, tell him that your mother has **dementia**."

I stared at her for just a second, then shifted uncomfortably in my seat.

Why would I want to lie to a doctor and tell him my mother has dementia when she doesn't? I thought to myself.

Soon, the door opened and the nurse yelled,

"Mrs. Falvo?" I walked with my mother to the back patient side of Dr. Marrero's office where patients wait in little individual rooms to be seen. Cloninger stayed out in the waiting room. We entered one of the little rooms and noticed that the paperwork Cloninger had created was clipped onto the front door of the exam room.

Soon, Dr. Marrero entered, and I explained to him that my mother had just returned from a journey from Ohio and needed to be examined. The exam showed that my mother was in good health, and Dr. Marrero ordered that some lab tests be done.

Following the doctor's examination, we then went out to a restaurant with Cloninger and my mother and I became further acquainted with Cloninger. She certainly seemed to be spending a lot of time with us. I had never seen an attorney be this involved with a client before.

While driving in the RV in search of Cloninger's office, I had taken notice of a condominium that was for sale and asked David to pull into the condo complex. I peeked into the window and saw that the condo was fully furnished. I asked David if I could use his cell phone. I then called the phone number on the for-sale sign and got in touch with the real estate agent whose name was Dianne Blue. I asked her if she would be interested in renting to us for just one month.

Dianne said she would check with her aunt and uncle who owned the unit at 25 Sandalwood Court, Oviedo, Florida, and see what they had to say; the place had been sitting vacant for a long time, she said.

Dianne called us back shortly and said that a month-to-month rental was fine—even if it were just one month—as long as we provided her with a 10-day notice. I felt so proud to be my mother's hero and make all of these arrangements on her behalf. This would be much better than the three of us staying at a hotel for one month. The price was $850.00 a month plus an $850.00 security deposit that would be returned to us as long as we left the place in the same condition we found it, and provided her with that 10-day notice.

Back at Cloninger's office, Cloninger had already uncannily pre-written all of the legal documents necessary to commence a guardianship. All I had to do was sign all the paperwork and provide Cloninger with a $2,500.00 deposit! I found this to be very odd and unsettling.

"This first document is called an ETG – emergency temporary guardianship," Cloninger explained, handing me a pen. I signed, and handed it back to her.

She then handed me a second document.

"Now, this document is called "Petition to Determine Incapacity," she stated. "It establishes why your mother needs a guardian." I signed it, and handed it back to her.

She then handed me a third document.

"Now, this document is called "Petition for Appointment as Guardian," she stated, "and it tells the court why you are qualified to be your mother's guardian. I signed it, and handed it back to her.

"And how long should this take?" I inquired.

"It shouldn't take too long," she said. "But then we need to go to all of your mother's banks and remove all of the money as quickly as possible," she suddenly stated, leaning forward and looking at me with a wry smile.

"And why do we need to do that?" I inquired. "Everything right now is "Payable on Death" to me.

"Well, you won't need that anymore," Cloninger stated. "You will be your mother's guardian."

Somehow, it just wasn't making sense to me. I was starting to feel a bit reluctant. (Little did I know it at that time, but Cloninger had previously been in a little trouble with the Florida Bar and had had to take an ethics class. Her law license previously had been suspended for a month. She had also been sued by another attorney for forgery.)

Cloninger then smiled widely and handed me yet another legal document. "This is called 'Application for Appointment as Guardian. You'll need to fill it all out – where you work, where you have worked in the past, all of your past addresses, whether or not you have any criminal record, whether or not you have ever been treated for any mental health issues . . . ."

"Can I just take it with me and fill it out at home?" I asked her.

"Sure," she replied, and she shifted uncomfortably and gave me a stiff smile.

"But let me get some information from you before you go," she added.

After providing me with a blank copy of the guardianship application, form, she then jotted down some detailed information about me on her yellow, legal notepad, and stated, "Now make sure you return this application to me *as soon as possible*," she stated adamantly. "We cannot commence the guardianship upon your mother until I have this document. *We have to hurry*."

I wondered what the rush was all about.

The Surprise Visit

The very next day, as we were getting situated into the condo I had temporarily rented for the three of us, Cloninger showed up at the front door of the condominium with a court paper in her hand. It seemed so odd to see an attorney suddenly visiting a "client" at their home, with no scheduled appointment, unannounced.

In her hand, she held a strange already signed order from a judge at the Seminole County courthouse **approving me as the**

emergency temporary guardian of my mother! I was a little taken back by this, since I had never filled out the guardianship application form that Cloninger said was so necessary and mandatory to commence a guardianship. "And good thing I did this so quickly," Cloninger stated.

"Why is that?" I inquired.

"Because Shirley Mascarella has called Elder Abuse on you, and there is a good chance that you are going to be charged with kidnapping . . . ."

"Kidnapping?" I stammered.

"But as long as you remain your mother's guardian, things should be fine," Cloninger added.

"But I never filled out the form!" I stated. "How did this happen?" I inquired.

Instead of answering my question, Cloninger simply smirked at me and replied, "You might be having to hire a criminal defense attorney."

I looked at her, horrified.

She added, "So, good thing I went to see my favorite judge without you."

At that moment, I was so shocked, confused, and horrified, I didn't know if I should hug Cloninger . . . . or if the three of us (my mother, David, and me) should immediately flee Oviedo and go back home.

Not knowing anything about guardianship laws at that time, I didn't realize it was completely illegal for an attorney to file paperwork in the court without my mother or I even being served that paperwork, or being present -- or a court-appointed attorney being assigned (violations of due process).

As soon as Cloninger left, I checked with an Orlando attorney, Luis Gonzalez, who asked me, "Why did you allow this guardianship to commence in the first place? Guardianships get very expensive and your mother doesn't even need one. They cannot hold you hostage in Seminole County. Just go home."

A Knock on The Door

But a few hours later, before I could even process his advice, there was a knock on the front door of the Oviedo condo. David answered the door, while I was cleaning the kitchen, after having prepared lunch for my mother.

And there entered a tall, extremely good-looking Black man clad in a dark gray business suit, light blue dress shirt, and tie, carrying a small leather briefcase, his long dreads neatly pulled back into a thick pony tail. He spoke to me with a thick, Jamaican accent.

Handing me his business card, he announced, "Good morning, Miss Woodhull. My name is David McKenzie, and I am a case worker from the Orlando Department of Children and Families Services office. It has been reported to our office that you have been abusing your mother."

My mother was in the living room watching TV, eating her lunch.

It seemed odd that a DCF worker from Orlando was here in Oviedo, Florida (Seminole County) with an "abuse" allegation report on mother.

During the ride back to Florida, my mother began stating that she wished to see an attorney as soon as we arrived back to Florida, so that she could undo that February 14, 2008 will that favored Shirley. I spoke with Cloninger about this and told her my mother's wishes. She said, "Your mom can't make out a new will once she is under a guardianship. Cloninger added, "Don't worry about it. You will have already moved all of the money out of the banks. So, there will be nothing left for Shirley."

"Why would I want to move all of my mother's money out of the banks, without her permission, when everything is already 'Payable on Death' to me?" I asked Cloninger. "Additionally, my mother would be furious if I moved all of her money out," I added. But Cloninger had remained silent and swiftly departed.

McKenzie moved into the living room and pulled up a chair next to my mother.

"Are you happy here?" he inquired.

From the kitchen, I could hear my mother's reply, "Yes, I'm very happy to be back with my daughter and her fiancé."

"Do you want to go back to the nursing home in Ohio?"

"Oh, no. Never," my mother replied.

The Next 18 Days in Oviedo

The next 18 days in Oviedo proved to be quite queer. My mother kept needling me about taking her to see an attorney to change her will back the way it was. But I felt it was best to obey Cloninger, feeling that I was now in a very precarious situation.

An Orlando DCF Worker Started Coming Around Repeatedly

Meanwhile, this Rasta-looking Man with long dreads, kept appearing every few days. The first time McKenzie came over, I was very happy to see him so that he could document that my mother was safe and sound, but as he continued to come around, I really questioned who he was actually working for and what was going on.

The False Accusations Begin

The first time McKenzie came out to the condo, he accused me of not taking my mother's medications from Meridian Arms. "That is elder abuse," he stated.

I assured him that we had a two-day's supply with us from Kathy Fines, and that Dr. Guillermo Marrero had written out all new prescriptions as soon as we got back.

McKenzie walked over to the tray next to my mother and wrote down all of the prescriptions.

The second time McKenzie came out, he stated that "someone" had reported that I had left Meridian Arms without paying an outstanding bill of several thousands of dollars. "And that is Elder Abuse," he added.

This time, I was a little defensive with him. I stated to him that I did not even know that such a bill existed, that we were just getting settled in and that so much was happening all at once.

McKenzie always exited with a smile and a warning, "You know, you could be removed as your mother's guardian any day now."

The following day, and the third time McKenzie came around, he stated that it had been reported that my mother had been seen "dirty and dehydrated" in public.

"In public? Where?"

I glanced at the anonymous report, which specifically stated that Louise Falvo had appeared "dirty and dehydrated" in **Gainesville, Florida**.

"Gainesville?" I replied. "We haven't even been to Gainesville!"

McKenzie arose from his chair and headed to the front door. "You know, you could be removed as the guardian."

Fraudulent Guardianships and the Tricks of the Trade

When we had first seen Dr. Guillermo Marrero, Cloninger had whispered to me that I should ask Dr. Marrero to put my mother on some type of sedative for her "anxiety" and Clonigner then stated that doctors would be testing my mother for competency and that I should make sure she had a double dose of the sedative when the doctors would be testing my mother.

Cloninger also stated that I should try to find some reason to have my mother admitted to the hospital and then she would qualify for 20 or 30 days or 60 days for free in a nice nursing home of my choice.

David McKenzie then came out a fourth time and accused me of having a bad credit history (which was not true) and that I could be removed as the guardian for having a bad credit history.

By this time, I thought it was **so odd** what he was doing and the frequency of him coming out that I started to type up on the computer every word he was saying.

McKenzie was laughing openly and nervously, as he watched me type, and stated that he wanted a copy of what I was typing up. I then told him I wouldn't save it, and I closed the file without hitting "save" hoping that I would be able to retrieve it, but it truly was gone, unfortunately.

The next time McKenzie came out (fifth time), he accused me of not complying with a doctor's order. But my mother had been taken off of a medication that had been prescribed to her in Ohio, so, once again, there was no truth to the false allegation.

Finally, an attorney in Gainesville, Florida, Scott Toney, advised me to "Go home." "Just go home," he said. "Since your mother has not been examined for mental capacity, and it has been over 18 days, the Temporary Guardianship has now expired. They didn't follow the laws. Just go home."

The clock had ticked past the 15-day mark and on the 18th day, the emergency hearing commenced - an egregious bending of the rules that hung over the proceedings like a shadow of deceit. The temporary guardianship order, initiated by forgery, should have lost its validity.

Instead, it was as though the deadline had been invisibly stretched, the date on the calendar altered with the same audacious impunity as the signature on the guardianship application.

••●●••

Back in Gainesville, Florida, Pink stayed overnight at my home, with my mother, while David and I drove back to Oviedo to gather up all of our belongings. Exhausted, we spent the night in Oviedo at the condo.

In the morning, there was a knock on the door. It was David McKenzie again. But by now, I had researched David McKenzie (the evening before) and made a startling discovery. "David, come here and look at this!" I announced with utter excitement to my fiancé.

I had discovered a resume of David McKenzie's online, with his photo attached, so I knew it was really him (the right "David McKenzie"). The online resume announced that David McKenzie was actually a professional semi-truck driver seeking long-distance driving gigs. It even provided his license number, which I verified.

With this knowledge in mind, I decided to play a practical joke on David McKenzie.

"Grandmother, What Big Eyes You Have!"

I quickly slipped into one of my mother's nightgowns, and pulled the covers up over my head.

Meanwhile, David Newman opened the front door and David McKenzie entered, asking, once again, to see my mother.

"Come this way," David Newman announced. "She's in her bed, taking a nap."

David McKenzie entered the bedroom and appeared startled to see the sheets covering "Mrs. Falvo's" head, as though she had already been pronounced dead.

"Mrs. Falvo," he called. "Are you all right?" He tip-toed closer to the edge of the bed.

David Newman simply stood at the entrance of the bedroom and watched the scene, grinning widely.

Slowly, reluctantly, as he slithered forward, McKenzie reached over and pulled the sheets down from over my head.

Covered in my mother's bedwear, I popped open my eyes, and while feigning my best old lady quivering voice, I replied, "Oh, David! David McKenzie! Please drive me in your semi truck back up to Youngstown, Ohio! I want to go live with Shirley Mascarella!"

David Newman began chuckling loudly, as David McKenzie did an about face and headed to the front door.

"You've been punked, asshole!" David Newman announced, slamming the front door shut, as David McKenzie sped away.

****

We then spent the entire day mopping, cleaning, and packing everything into the back of David's covered pickup truck and the back of my SUV. It was quite late when we set back out onto the highway to return to Gainesville.

What happens next is so odd that, to this day, David and I still wonder why we are still alive.

THE NINJAS

(***David and I still occasionally talk about this incident, and we are still very surprised, to this day, that we lived to tell this story. It was an unexpected rendezvous with danger, an encounter that we still find hard to believe***.)

We were returning back home to Gainesville, Florida from Orlando (Oviedo) where we had been living for a few weeks. We were driving in separate cars. It was about two o'clock in the morning. David was in his pickup truck in front of me. I noticed he kept weaving on the highway, so I called his cell phone and said, "Look. It's too dangerous for you to be driving while you're that sleepy. Let's get off at the next exit. We'll park your truck somewhere for the evening and then drive back for it tomorrow afternoon after you've had a chance to get some proper sleep."

David agreed. The next exit was a lonely two-lane road in the middle of nowhere on the way to Leesburg, Florida. We drove and drove, looking for a place to park his pickup truck, but there were only trees and shrubs on either side of the completely unlit lonely, eerie county road.

Suddenly, we saw a closed convenience store. It was now about three a.m., and we were both quite exhausted.

Although completely closed, the convenience store was brightly lit, including the outside area where the closed gas pumps were located. There were no other businesses around in that area. There were no cars in the parking lot of the closed convenience store. This was a convenience store located in the middle of nowhere on this lonely, spooky two-lane county road. The alarm had been set off. Lights flashed and loud bells were ringing. We thought nothing about it. We assumed it was a false alarm, caused by the wind. David backed in his truck in a parking spot in front of the convenience store and then hopped into my SUV. I had parked directly across from the front entrance door of the convenience store while I was waiting for him to get a few belongings out of his truck and then join me.

David was now safely inside my truck and we were just about ready to back out of the parking space when suddenly –our drowsy stupor was shattered by an unexpected and surreal spectacle. Six men, dressed head-to-toe in black, akin to movie-style ninjas, burst out of the convenience store, uzis upright in their hands. Their faces, under the shadow of their hoods, registered surprise at our unexpected presence. We were sitting ducks, a mere few feet away from these armed robbers, a stark tableau of crime unfolding before us. Why they didn't fire at us, remains a baffling mystery to this day.

The band of ninjas sprinted to their waiting getaway car, an old maroon beast that roared to life, and tore down the intersecting road, disappearing from our sight. The abrupt adrenaline rush left us both frozen in our seats, our hearts pounding against our ribs. It was a close encounter of the dangerous kind, one that took us a few moments to even comprehend.

"Holy shit," was about all David could to manage to say, while I sat beside him in stunned silence.

Managing to regain our senses, we drove onward to Leesburg where we dialed the local police from an open convenience store, relaying the strange episode. We were asked to return to the crime scene, where we were met by a formidable array of six police vehicles. However, their choice to stay put rather than pursuing the ninjas struck us as odd. We furnished all the information we could, hoping our encounter could aid in capturing the criminals.

In the ensuing days, we didn't hear from the Leesburg police. The chilling eye contact with the robbers, their unmasked faces, their potential decision to let us live, still sends shivers down our spine. Every time we recall the incident, we marvel at the thin line that separates the ordinary from the extraordinary, and the fine thread of luck that helped us escape unscathed.

Cloninger was pissed.

The illusion of peace was soon shattered.

In our innocence, we had believed the worst was behind us. We had braved the storm, faced down the vultures, and emerged on the other side. My mother was safe, nestled in our care, and we thought we had seen the last of probate court, the last of Evelyn Cloninger, the last of the Mascarellas.

My mother wore victory like a warm cloak, contented in the knowledge that David and I were now with her in the Castle, just as she had wanted.

But the vultures had not retreated, merely bided their time. A knock on the door and a delivery from an Alachua County deputy process server snapped us back into reality.

Cloninger had appealed to her ally at the court, Judge Nancy Alley, for an "emergency" hearing. **Emergency**. According to her tall tale that she placed in the court records, Angela Woodhull was about to vanish into the winds, my mother's wealth in tow. She urged the court to replace me with a professional guardian, Rebecca Fierle. As further ammunition, she claimed I had never signed a mandatory bond, a fallacy she wielded to call for my removal as my mother's guardian.

An Odd Scene in Cloninger's Officer -- Even James Bond Would Be Shocked

Prior to our escape from Oviedo, Cloninger had called me into her office, and the scene was terribly odd. A bond had arrived for me to sign, which is why Cloninger had demanded I come to her office. But when Cloninger opened the manilla envelope with the express mail bond inside, lo and behold – to her surprise and horror, the bond had been accidentally written out for another "ward," -- "Edith Taylor."

Certainly, my mother was not named "Edith Taylor."

Cloninger suddenly threw a conniption fit right then and there, on the spot, in her office. I had never witnessed such unbecoming, unprofessional, and undignified behavior by an attorney. It was reminiscent of the time when Nikita Khrushchev historically wacked his shoe upon the podium. Cloninger rose up, slammed down the palm of her hand on the table, and then shouted for her secretary, who immediately rushed into the conference room.

With extreme panic in her voice, she yelled at her receptionist, "Go get Alex Hanley from Jurisco on the phone *immediately! Immediately!* And tell him that he needs to reissue this bond immediately! Immediately!! Have him reissue it right now! *Right now!* Have him hire a driver to drive it from Tallahassee to my office *immediately!*

The sheer panic and rush of it all certainly caught my attention.

Cloninger reseated herself and began fanning her flushed face.

"Wow. Courier express from Tallahassee to *here*? That sounds very expensive," I commented.

Without missing a beat, Cloninger said, "Now, where are you going to be tomorrow, Saturday?" Cloninger wanted to know, panic rising in her voice. "I will come to your condo tomorrow. *We need to get this bond signed first thing in the morning and then on Monday, we need to go to all the banks and remove all of the money into a guardianship account!"*

Instead of replying with my availability, I inquired, "When do my mother and I get to go back home to Gainesville? You said it would be about one month."

Cloninger shifted uncomfortably, then looked me straight in the eyes and replied, "I never said you get to go back home."

I looked at her in utter disbelief. There was an uncomfortable silence in the air, and so Cloninger continued.

"You're not allowed to go back home until your mother passes."

I raised my eyebrows and stared at Cloninger, as she reached for her high blood pressure medication and dowsed down a pill.

"And given her health, I don't think that's going to be too much longer."

The plot to terminate my mother's life and hijack a million dollars was already in motion. And once in motion, it does not stop.

------------ ··•●●●•·· ------------

The Emergency Hearing

The fraudulent guardianship commencement that you're about to read is so shocking and so unbelievable that your mind is going to struggle to accept that things like this exist. But they do. And they are happening right now all over the United States. In small towns, as well as in big cities, elders are being confiscated, their properties stolen, their natural heirs hijacked, as their lives strangely end while their assets are being depleted.

My mother's own story begins with Evelyn Cloninger, a well-connected small-town attorney who fraudulently induced me to commence a guardianship upon my mother to "protect" her from the Mascarellas.

Dirty attorneys don't work in isolation. In order to rob the elderly, they need a comrade, a judge who will protect them and assist them. In Evelyn Cloninger's case, her buddy was Judge Nancy Alley. Both women had previously been disciplined by the Florida Bar for serious ethics violations. (see appendix)

On the outside, the guardianship players try to appear as pillars of their communities. For example, when initially advising me to go get my mother and bring her back to Oviedo, Florida, Cloninger boasted to me that she plays organ at her nearby Presbyterian church and that she also heads the local branch of the Republican party in Seminole county.

On the inside, guardianship players are truly evil human beings.

I appeared telephonically for the "emergency" hearing. I had already been warned by Dr. Robert Sarhan and Bonnie Reiter (guardianship victims) that "emergency" is all part of the predictable plot. I began to suspect that the hearing would be rigged, but I didn't yet know the depth of the sinister plan.

Using the courts, the plot was to remove me as my mother's guardian. That is always the first step. This plot is usually accomplished in one of two ways – by either demonizing the family member and asking the court for their removal, or stating the family member was unable to obtain a hefty, unobtainable bond.

The Bond.

Judge Nancy Alley, after verifying that it was, indeed, me, Angela Woodhull on the phone, said, "I understand that you were supposed to obtain a bond but you failed to do that."

No natural heir, no daughter or son, can trump that well-planned accusation.

"The bond was obtained but it arrived in the wrong name," I replied.

"Well, when are you going to sign that correct bond, ma'am?" Judge Nancy Alley then inquired.

Cloninger suddenly chimed in. "Your Honor, I have already returned the bond to the company, Jurisco. It is no longer available."

Judge Nancy Alley then removed me as my mother's guardian.

With the click of the phone, I was unable to tell the judge that this "emergency hearing" should never have even taken place because the temporary guardianship had already expired. Therefore, the hearing was illegal – and a violation of the Florida statutes -- to begin with.

But additionally, I was not able to tell the judge something even more shocking. "Your Honor!" I was prepared to say. "Evelyn Cloninger committed a felony!"

"And what felony is that?" I expected the judge to reply.

Having driven back to Seminole County in preparation for the upcoming "emergency" hearing, I had asked the Seminole probate clerk to please print out any documents that had been filed by Ms. Cloninger into the court records.

The unsuspecting clerk dutifully began churning out photocopies and handed them to me in one large stack.

Sitting down at a long legal table inside the probate clerk's office, I began reviewing all that Cloninger had filed.

There was that Emergency Petition for a Guardianship. Yes. I remember. I had signed that document in Evelyn Cloninger's office.

There was that Petition to Determine Capacity of Louise A. Falvo. Yes, I had signed that, too.

But then there was a curious paper amidst the stack in the probate guardianship court records. **The Guardianship Application**. The form I had never completed. The form that is mandatory by law to commence a guardianship upon another. No, I had never filled it out or turned it back in to Cloninger.

And there, staring back at me, as I looked at the legal document in horror, at the guardianship application – all filled out – **and** signed! With **my** signature!

Only it **wasn't** my signature. I stared at the signature – a jig-jagged attempt to duplicate my sloppy handwriting. Except the author of "my" signature had taken my whimsical scribbles and turned them into jig-jagged peaks.

I arose from the table and went back over to the clerk.

"Who filed this paper into the court record?" I inquired, pointing at the forgery.

The clerk glanced over the document, adjusting her glasses, then replied, "Your attorney. She filed in all of these papers at the same time."

I looked at the clerk in shock, speechless, but she did not understand my speechlessness and the apparent look of horror registered on my face.

Following this forged document, next in the court record, had been a court order approving me as my mother's guardian.

And then following this approval of me as my mother's guardian, a guardianship I had never fully requested, was now Judge Alley's ominous "Order Removing Guardian."

With the stroke of a pen, Judge Nancy Alley removed me as my mother's guardian and **Rebecca Fierle** replaced me.

The well-calculated plot had been breezily executed.

And there it was. The commencement of a guardianship. Within 24 hours, my mother was whisked away to Palm Gardens Assisted Living via a deputy sheriff and one of Rebecca Fierle's assistants. My mother would never set foot inside the Castle House ever again.

Long *Before . . . .*

Long before Rebecca Fierle was arrested for placing a "Do Not Resuscitate" ("DNR") on one of her "wards," Rebecca Fierle was routinely placing DNRs on all of her "wards," including my mother. After all, when the money is all spent, the "ward" becomes just a "waste of space." She understood a disturbing calculus: once the wards' money was exhausted, they were rendered worthless in her eyes.

Before Fierle's office was raided by the Florida Department of Law Enforcement, she maintained a grim collection in her workspace. Among her routine business documents were the cremains of nine humans and a dog, a chilling testament to the value she placed on the lives entrusted to her.

And long before she found herself in handcuffs, Fierle was part of an extensive network of professionals across multiple sectors. Attorneys, judges, social workers, hospital and nursing home administrators, police, bankers, brokers, and DCF caseworkers all existed within her sphere, complacently ignoring or actively participating in her actions.

So, how does that enormous level of power commence in the first place?

The following tragic story of my mother, Louise, is simply a generic story that anyone familiar with guardianship fraud could tell you. Just switch out the names; the story will be the same.

Having already been snatched from her home by Rebecca Fierle and the deputy sheriffs, my mother, now confined to Palm Garden assisted living and nursing home, called me on the phone a few days later.

"Ang, there were just three doctors here in my room at the nursing home! It was the strangest thing!"

"What did they want, Mom?"

"I dunno," my mother replied. "They asked me the dumbest questions."

"Like what?" I inquired.

"Like what is the address of our home."

"And what did you tell them?" I asked her.

"Well, of course, I told them it is 1920 S.W. 72nd Street, Gainesville, Florida. I even told them the zip code —32607."

Neither my mother nor I knew the significance of this intentionally contrived inquisition.

"Well, that's good!" I told her.

"They also asked me how much money I have in the banks!" my mother continued.

"And what did you say?"

"Well, of course, I lied to them. There's no way I'm going to tell a bunch of strangers I have a million dollars in the bank!"

"So, what did you tell them?" I asked her.

"I said, 'Well, I don't know. Maybe ten thousand?"

My mother and I chucked.

Little did we both know that this joke answer would soon strip my mother of all of her civil rights – and that she would soon have less rights than a prisoner on death row. (While Death Row inmates can hire their own counsel, a person under guardianship cannot. The Court appoints one, and in this case, it was one of Rebecca Fierle's own attorneys and a friend. While Death Row inmates are entitled to read their own mail, a "ward's" mail is directed to and read by the corporate guardian. While death row inmates can have visitors, "wards" are so isolated that their only contact may be the nursing staff, doctors, and other care givers at the nursing home.) "Isolate, Medicate, Take the Estate," has become the slogan used by Guardianship Reform Advocates.

"Louise Falvo does not realize the extent of her bounty" they wrote in their three twisted, fake reports.

So, here was my mother, already confined against her will to a marginal nursing home, telling me about this curious conversation that, unbeknownst to me and my mom, was just simply routine. This curious conversation commenced the beginning of a living death sentence for my mother.

Soon, There was A Court Hearing Based on That Curious Conversation, and I was Served Court Papers to Attend

Anyone who has ever been served court papers announcing that a **total stranger** is about to become your mother's guardian is going to have the same, identical, easy solution -- **Hire a lawyer! Presto!**

Yes! Just **hire a lawyer** and the whole thing will end, right? After all, your mother made out legal documents favoring you, her daughter. Right?

Our stories are all the same.

"Oh, they're just getting started," stated Bonnie Reiter, a woman from South Florida I found on the internet when I Googled "guardianship fraud" after David McKenzie started snooping around frequently.

"After they take away all of your mother's civil rights, then they will spend her million dollars as quickly as possible, and then, suddenly, **bam!** your mother will be dead. They will kill her."

Of course, my immediate impression of Reiter was that she was some kind of nutcase. After all, this is America, and all judges are noble, and all attorneys help their clients, right?

Isn't that what my parents had taught me?

The pivot point of our lives stood before us, looming like an ominous leviathan: the probate courtroom. As I entered, I felt like I was stepping into quicksand, the world shifting under my feet as I descended into the surreal chaos of legal jargon and skewed justice.

A blatant act of forgery had lit the fuse on this disaster, and the explosion of events that followed was consuming everything in its path.

It was akin to a wildfire, ferociously devouring everything in its path, ignited by a single spark. Once lit, it is nearly impossible to extinguish a terrifying, unstoppable force.

The events unfolding within those cold court walls felt similarly unstoppable. This was a decisive moment, a turning point that would set the stage for the disturbing events to follow. The machinery of the guardianship process had been set in motion, its gears grinding relentlessly forward, its progress unimpeded by truth or justice.

As we entered the probate courtroom, there was Attorney Ann Marie Giordano Gilden seated to my left, her face a blank canvas of professional decorum. She had been appointed by Judge Nancy Alley to represent my mother's "best" interests.

Behind Gilden walked in Rebecca Fierle, the puppeteer of this macabre performance, armed with her little attorney, a short guy who somewhat resembles Dustin Hoffman, clad in glasses, his gray hair slicked back, carrying his briefcase. He appeared to be in a jovial mood. I was soon to find out that Attorney Anthony M. Nardella, Jr., also doubles as a fundamentalist preacher in Clearmont, Florida. Yes, the Reverend Nardella was there with the sacred task of delivering the three fabricated doctor's reports to the judge, at God's request.

There was an undercurrent of the sinister in the room, like being slowly buried alive, each scoop of dirt a fraudulent document, each thump on the coffin lid a deceitful accusation. I wanted to scream out, to protest the injustice unfolding before me. The feeling was eerily reminiscent of Bonnie Reiter's forewarning – her words no longer felt like an alarmist's cry but a chilling premonition.

And then they walked in, Shirley and John Mascarella, who would swear to the judge that my mother was fully mentally capacitated just a few weeks before when she wrote out that February 14, 2008 will leaving all of her worldly belongings to the Mascarellas. But Shirley and John were now prepared to prove that, as of March 8, 2008 (the day Cloninger had forged my signature on the guardianship application), Louise A. Falvo needed a guardian because she was suddenly a total looney tune – just three weeks later!

In walked the "Honorable" Judge Nancy Alley.

All rise! The Bailiff announced.

"You may be seated," Alley stated.

I had never before seen a judge with such messy hair. Her hair appeared as though she had not taken a comb to it since the turning of the new millennium. Her disheveled appearance mirrored the chaotic proceedings about to unfold, her gaze scanning the room like a hawk circling its prey.

Attorney Reverend Nardella handed the three ominous reports to the bailiff who, in turn, handed them to the judge.

"So, what do we have here?" Alley stated, shuffling through the papers. Her brows furrowed as she sifted through them, each sheet a potential verdict on my mother's looming horrific fate.

"Your Honor," I said, standing up, interrupting, approaching the Bailiff.

"I have video footage here proving my mother's mental competency."

I handed three CDs to the bailiff, who gave them to the judge. The ripple of surprise in the courtroom was almost palpable, as if a stone had been tossed into a still pond.

"Objection, Your Honor!" Reverend Nardella stated. "My client, Ms. Fierle, and I do not have copies of those videotapes!"

"It doesn't matter," Alley stated. "We'll just play them here in the courtroom for everyone to see, and then you can object at that time."

"Where is Mrs. Falvo?" Alley added, looking through the sparsely occupied courtroom.

Attorney Ann Marie Giordano Gilden, seated in front of Nardella and Fierle stood up and replied.

"Your Honor, I interviewed Mrs. Falvo at the nursing home, and based on my findings, I determined that it was best that Mrs. Falvo not attend today's hearing because she would not have comprehended. Her dementia is too severe." She handed her report to the judge.

"Your Honor! That's a lie!" I stood up and stated in a heated voice.

Judge Alley looked at me sternly over her bifocals, as she whisked back her tangled hair from her left eye.

"Miss Woodhull!" she stammered. "I won't have you interrupting this Court!"

"I'm sorry, Your Honor! But the videos will prove it's a lie!"

The Court Reporter tapped on her keys furiously, trying to keep up with all of the commotion.

Alley turned to the Bailiff. "Do you know how to plug this thing in and turn it on?" She handed him the three CDs I had given her.

The Bailiff reached down and plugged in two extension cords, then inserted the CD into the side of a computer at the far end of the courtroom where a screen loomed overhead.

And there was Louise, talking from her bed at Palm Gardens.

"Mom, what day of the week is it?" I asked her.

"Why, it's Friday, of course! What a silly question to ask me!" she added. "Why wouldn't I know what day of the week it is?"

"And what DATE is it, Mom? Do you know the actual month and date?"

"Why, of course," she said. "I always know the month and date! Today is April 11, 2008." My mother smirked and shook her head from side to side.

"And who is the President of the United States?" I asked my mother.

With that question, my mother rolled her eyes to the ceiling, feigning exasperation, as David Newman continued to videotape her.

My mother tsked and replied, "It's Nini, your cat!"

Everyone in the courtroom suddenly chuckled, (even the judge) as it became quite obvious that this was a woman who had no dementia, but instead had quite a keen, sarcastic sense of humor.

Bonnie Reiter had encouraged me to videotape my mother upon my phoning her again. I had come to realize, though our multiple phone conversations, that Reiter was not crazy after all.

"This is what they do," she said, in accurate prediction. "Your only hope is that the judge is somehow honest and will watch those videotapes."

I looked intensely at Judge Alley after the laughter subsided, as if to say, "See? I told you so!" But I had been silenced.

Soon, it was Reverend Nardella's turn to speak.

"Your Honor, all those tapes prove is that Ms. Woodhull is wielding **undue influence** over her mother. Ms. Woodhull most certainly prepared her mother for all of those answers.

"Your Honor!" I stood up.

But before I could speak a word more, Judge Nancy Alley said, "Ms. Woodhull, one more word out of you, and the Bailiff will remove you from the courtroom!"

I sat down and brushed away angry tears of frustration.

Bound by judicial decree, I was powerless to interrupt this farcical act. I couldn't rectify the address discrepancy or challenge the unjust diagnosis of dementia. It was as if I was gagged, my protests swallowed in the cavernous silence of the court. It's an oppressive sensation, to witness an untruth about to take flight and yet be restrained from clipping its wings.

"In fact, your Honor, Mrs. Falvo did not even know her own address!" Nardella added.

(Note: Silenced, I was unable to tell the judge that Attorney Ann Marie Giordano Gilden had told the three medical professionals that Mrs. Falvo resides at 25 Sandalwood Court, Oviedo, Florida.)

"She couldn't even draw the hands on a clock!" Nardella scoffed, pointing at the amateur inaccurate, drawing.

Ang, they wouldn't let me have my glasses, and asked me to draw the hands of a clock!

This rigged system has predictable outcomes.

It's like reading a movie script, and you already know the plot, and the ending.

At one point, Judge Nancy Alley was shuffling though the papers, while blowing her hair out of the front of her face, when Reverend Nardella asked her, "Your Honor, did I hear you say that you find Mrs. Falvo to be mentally incapacitated?"

Alley looked up from the papers and said, "***No. I almost said the opposite.***"

There was hope for a moment, and I squeezed David's hands.

But soon, there was that fateful pronouncement that Louise A. Falvo had only limited capacity, and as such, she needed Rebecca Fierle to become her full-time Plenary Guardian.*

Ann Marie Giordano Gilden turned around and looked at Nardella and Fierle. They actually squealed in delighted, and cheered while they gave each other a high five.

"And this court is now adjourned." Alley stood up and started walking away.

"But Your Honor!" I cried out.

But she had already disappeared behind the black curtain.

As we all shuffled out of the courtroom, I passed Reverend Nardella, who was now standing next to the metal detector in the front of the courthouse, waiting for Fierle who had slipped into the restroom.

"You're disgusting!" I shouted.

Nardella chucked and replied, ***"We're not finished with you yet*!"**

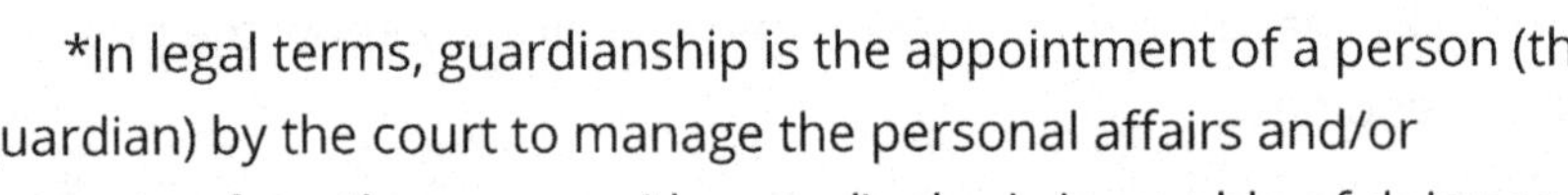

*In legal terms, guardianship is the appointment of a person (the guardian) by the court to manage the personal affairs and/or property of another person (the ward) who is incapable of doing so themselves due to certain circumstances such as minor age, incapacity, or disability.

1. **Plenary Guardianship:** In a plenary guardianship, the guardian is given complete authority to make decisions on behalf of the ward. This involves all aspects of the ward's life, including healthcare decisions, financial matters, and living arrangements. This form of guardianship is generally reserved for situations where the ward is considered to be fully incapacitated and unable to make any informed decisions for themselves.
2. **Limited Guardianship:** Conversely, a limited guardianship only gives the guardian authority to make

decisions in specific areas where the ward is deemed
incapable. The ward retains their rights and the ability to
make decisions in all other aspects of their life not
covered by the guardianship. Limited guardianship
respects the autonomy of the ward, upholds their dignity,
and encourages the development and utilization of their
remaining capabilities.

CHAPTER THIRTEEN:
"I'll Soon Be Dead"

After Rebecca Fierle took over as my mother's Plenary Guardian, we continued to legally fight. David continued to videotape my mother, and on April 21, 2008, my mother stated, on tape, "***Ang, you've got to get me out of here, or I will be dead soon***."

My mother was right. She was very right. Three months to the date, (on July 21, 2008) she died in another nursing home where Rebecca Fierle had confined her, of a morphine sulphate overdose. All alone and so frightened, my mother was not even allowed to have any visitors in her final days.

Here's what happened next after the May 8th, 2008 court hearing with Judge Nancy Alley.

"Isolate, Medicate, Take the Estate"

The more David showed up at the nursing home and videotaped, the more Rebecca Fierle and Reverend Nardella felt threatened.

And so, Rebecca Fierle reported to Attorney Reverend Nardella that David Newman had been seen **having sex with my mother's roommate at Palm Gardens**!

Yep, right there, in the room, a 52-year-old man, with nurses running in and out of the room, allegedly raped a 94-year-old woman.

Never mind that there were no police reports written about this. Never mind that DCF was never called. And never mind that this allegation never even showed up in the Palm Gardens medical notes.

No. It was simply a statement for which Reverend Nardella decided to bill, bill, and bill.

"Investigating allegation of Angela Woodhull's boyfriend sleeping with Mrs. Falvo's roommate." $1600

"Continuing investigations of boyfriend David Newman sleeping with Louise Falvo's roommate." $2300

"No further information available regarding David Newman sleeping with Louise Falvo's roommate." $1200

In other words, my mother was billed nearly six thousand dollars based on a false and libelous allegation. Cleverly, the allegation was nowhere else to be found, except in the court records.

It had a dual effect. While Nardella used it to bill, bill, and bill, Fierle used her made-up tale to have us banned from the nursing home. Nancy Alley granted Fierle a court order based on a request from Nardella. According to this new court order, David and I were never allowed to see my mother unless the guardian, Rebecca Fierle (or one of her employees), was paid $120 an hour, out of my mother's bank accounts, to have us watched. And videotaping was forbidden.

Indeed, Reverend Nardella was not finished with us.

••●●●••

On June 7, 2008, Reverend Nardella marched into court with Rebecca Fierle and held an unusual (and illegal) hearing in front of Judge Nancy Alley.

"Your Honor," Nardella began, his voice carrying a mock earnest tone, "we find ourselves uncertain of Mrs. Falvo's true intentions regarding her wealth distribution. We suspect that Ms. Woodhull may have exerted undue influence on her mother, persuading her to alter her will and disinherit her cherished niece, Shirley Mascarella. Consequently, we propose that the Court nullify any 'Payable on Death' and 'In Trust For' bank account designations favoring Ms. Woodhull."

Of course, Judge Nancy Alley granted this illegal order, a decision that sent a shockwave through my body. A county judge has no authority to destroy federal bank account designations. "Payable on Death" or "In Trust For" accounts typically avoid probate as they directly pass to the beneficiary upon death. On the federal level, the "Payable on Death" accounts, also known as Totten Trusts, have been recognized as a means to avoid probate. These funds are beyond the reach of probate courts.

Soon, all the money that was in Wachovia Bank, Payable on Death to me, had been transferred to an account under Rebecca Fierle's name at Bank of America. All of my mother's money that was In Trust for me at Bank of America also was placed into this same Fierle guardianship account.

•••●••

Feasting on the Spoils: A Raging Tempest

Nardella and Fierle went into overdrive. Day by day, the ravenous duo orchestrated a ballet of transactions that siphoned funds from my mother's assets with alarming haste. Every detailed invoice was immediately approved by Fierle, dispatched to Judge Nancy Alley, and ratified with equal urgency. It was a voracious cycle, a feast of self-enrichment under the guise of guardianship.

Expenses were drawn for protracted phone conversations with Shirley Mascarella, for Fierle's purported visits to my mother, which, to my knowledge, were nothing more than fabrications. They even carved out substantial payments from my mother's wealth for a heated dispute with Wachovia Bank officials, who initially resisted the transferring of the funds to Bank of America. But Reverend Nardella, brandishing threats of litigation like a sword, succeeded in breaking their resistance, and the bank capitulated. He conveniently billed for that, too. The million-dollar treasure was rapidly depleting, drifting away in the relentless current of their greed.

Meanwhile, I was chained to my workstation, my days consumed in a ceaseless battle against the storm. The whirring of my computer became a familiar symphony, accompanying the drafting of court papers, poring over case law, reaching out to law enforcement, and penning pleas to congressmen, senators, and even the president of the United States. My resolve ignited a beacon of resistance, striving to expose the sordid saga unfolding before me.

In addition to these efforts, I lodged a formal complaint with the Judicial Qualifications Commission (JQC) against Judge Nancy Alley for endorsing an order that, by my understanding, infringed upon federal banking laws. While it seemed the JQC barely stirred in response, a startling event unfolded: Judge Nancy Alley, amidst the maelstrom, abruptly and mysteriously announced her retirement.

But . . . **A New Dirty Judge Appears**

The Shadows Deepen: Enter, the Second Judge

A new puppeteer, Judge John Galluzzo, entered the theatrical production, orchestrating the same tune as his predecessor. He became the new benefactor approving the substantial legal fees Nardella and Fierle claimed, penning his approval to monthly invoices that often reached an astonishing sixty to one hundred thousand dollars with a seemingly careless flourish of his round "O" signature.

A term used in the legal world, *'in camera'*, became a crucial point of conversation between Nardella and Judge Galluzzo. In Latin, 'in camera' means 'in private', and in a legal context, it refers to a hearing or inspection of documents that takes place in private, often in the judge's chambers. Nardella requested Judge Galluzzo to permit him to bill 'in camera', which essentially meant he could bill another $50,000 without publicly detailing his services that merited such a sum. The judge assented without hesitation, thus plunging the transparency of the entire operation into murky waters. The invoices, hidden from public scrutiny, were allegedly reviewed by Judge Galluzzo before he rubber-stamped the legal fees.

Undeterred by this impenetrable fortress of injustice, I relentlessly appealed each order approving the attorneys' fees. However, the Court of Appeal seemed to be caught in a state of inertia, delaying any rulings on my appeals. My grievances were left hanging in an abyss of indecision, silenced by the cogs of bureaucracy.

Only once did my efforts yield fruit. I implored the Court of Appeal, arguing that it was inappropriate and potentially unlawful to keep the invoices hidden from me, permitting Nardella to bill 'in camera'. As the rightful heir to my mother's bank accounts, I maintained that I deserved transparency regarding Nardella's billing.

In a surprising turn, the Court of Appeal found merit in my argument and accorded their agreement, casting a tiny beam of light into the sprawling shadowy saga.

A Tale of Empty Pages and Empty Promises

Then came the moment of revelation that rendered me both speechless and incensed.

And there in the file . . . .

Attached to each request for another $50,000.00, $60,000.00, $100,000.00 were the invoices. I blinked hard as I looked at each and every invoice that Judge Galluzzo was allegedly reading prior to approving the hefty fees.

And there in the file . . . .

Blank pages. Yep. Blank pages. Pure, unadulterated blankness.

I blinked hard as I paged through hundreds upon hundreds of blank pages. These were the very invoices that Judge Galluzzo was allegedly meticulously studying before approving the exorbitant fees.

I could hardly believe my eyes, blinking hard as I rifled through an unfathomable pile of nothingness - hundreds upon hundreds of vacant pages. This supposed evidence, which should have been overflowing with justification for such massive payouts, held nothing but silence.

Nardella had not filed **anything** for Judge Galluzzo to even read. But Galluzzo was approving the hefty fees anyway.

Nardella hadn't bothered to put pen to paper; he hadn't bothered to submit anything for Judge Galluzzo to scrutinize. Yet, in an act of unmitigated audacity, Galluzzo was validating these enormous fees without a shred of substantiation.

This revelation brought home the stark reality of how low they were willing to stoop, the true depth of their underhanded tactics. I had ventured so close to unveiling this scandalous affair to the highest court of our land, falling short by just one vote from the six judges in Atlanta.

While the slim hope of justice through the Supreme Court eluded me, I remained resolute, driven by the raw emotion that arose from the blatant robbery being perpetrated by these so-called pillars of justice.

•••••••

A Dark Day in the Courtroom

At long last, on July 21, 2009, after over a year and a half of Nardella's rampant billing, I summoned a special hearing before the judge. I went all out, inviting ABC Action News from Orlando and securing expert witnesses – a skilled attorney, a professional guardian, a highly-regarded psychiatrist – each prepared to provide undeniable evidence that Louise A. Falvo's guardianship was a sham from the very beginning. The experts had cost me $20,000.00

Notably, I had also tipped off the Florida Bar about Judge Galluzzo's potential misconduct. They took the allegations seriously (or so I assumed, in my naivete) and sent two young representatives to bear witness to the court proceedings.

However, to my profound disappointment, the hearing became a farce. Barely five minutes had elapsed when Judge Galluzzo abruptly terminated the proceedings. My expert witnesses, for whom I had paid $5,000 each, were left sitting on their hands - not given a moment's chance to testify, their voices silenced in the courtroom.

At one point, Galluzzo threatened to put me under a guardianship, claiming that I had filed a "frivolous pleading" that had wasted his time, Nardella's time, and Fierle's time, and that I was obviously "mentally unstable" and perhaps needed a guardianship myself.

The reporter from Orlando ABC Action News walked out of the courtroom in disgust. "Thanks for wasting my time!" he yelled.

For filing the "frivolous motion," I was fined $25,000.00 by Judge Galluzzo. I was ordered to pay $25,000.00 to Reverend Nardella. Stealing my inheritance wasn't good enough. Now, he wanted another twenty-five thousand. Of course, I had no intention of paying that bill, and Reverend Nardella knew it.

The hearing ended on an even more disheartening note. Judge Galluzzo, with laughter in his voice, invited the representatives from the Florida Bar and Nardella behind the austere black curtain that stood at the front of the courtroom, hinting at some form of celebration or party. The corruption I had been fighting against appeared to run deeper than I could have ever imagined.

A Hasty Pledge and a Perilous Game

Two blocks away from my Castle House is my townhouse that I had purchased at auction for a mere $25,000.00. It was here that David Newman had taken up residence.

Reverend Nardella, keenly aware of my transfer of the property's title to David's name, protested before Judge Galluzzo that such a transaction was illicit. He argued that he had the right to claim the property as compensation for the $25,000.00 that I now owed him. (How 'bout that – the **same price** as the recently purchased townhouse!) Galluzzo, predictably, sided with Nardella and green-lit him to sue David Newman for the title to my townhouse.

We Became Escape Artists

Legally, a lawsuit cannot commence until the defendant is served with the initial complaint.

Before long, the Alachua County deputies were banging on David's front door. They would bang with ultra force, and simultaneously ring his cell phone demanding that he open the front door. Terrified, we would tip toe into the bathroom and not come out until we were certain they were gone. This terror went on for weeks, and then suddenly, the deputy sheriffs stopped coming around.

The Little Blue Sentinel

And that's when we noticed a little blue car parked outside in the driveway at the townhouse. Through the narrow lens of our front door's peephole, we kept an apprehensive watch. A license check of the tag revealed that, indeed, the car was registered to a private process server. Nardella had shifted tactics, now billing my mother's assets for this new adversary who sat waiting, ready to strike at $75 an hour. Sometimes he lay in wait at the Castle, sometimes he lurked across the street from David's townhouse.

The Secret Exit

There were times when we had to get out of David's townhouse, so we devised an ingenious plan for avoiding the process server.

In David's backyard is a fence that totally encloses the backyard area.

Using an electric saw at night, after the process server in the little blue car had left for the day, David took the saw and cut the fence vertically in two places. We then put hardware on the fence, enabling that piece of the fence to operate as a door without looking like a door. Latches were put on the inside only.

On one particular day, we had some emergency errands to run. As the process server was hammered on David's front door, we snuck out through the back fence. David had parked his Mazda truck a few doors down from the Castle House. We ran through the streets, holding hands, until we reached the Castle and his Mazda, and then sped away.

In this way, we evaded service, and my townhouse remained out of Reverend Nardella's covetous grasp.

Her Blank Eyes

She stared at me blankly as I stood at her bedside in the emergency room of a large, private hospital.

"Mom! What happened? Why can't you speak!?"

My mother looked at me with sad, soft eyes and shrugged her shoulders.

I gave her a piece of paper. She wrote, "I LOVE YOU" in all capital letters—each word written on top of the other.

"What has happened to her?" I inquired of an emergency room nurse.

"Well, we're not sure yet. We do know for sure that your mother did not suffer a stroke. However, she does have a slight urinary tract infection and that can make a person stop speaking," the nurse replied.

"Stop speaking? From a slight urinary tract infection?" I thought.

I scratched my head in disbelief as the nurse briskly walked away.

The nurse turned around as she continued walking. "The good news is her speech will probably return as the infection decreases."

It was not making sense. A bladder infection -- affecting my mother's vocal cords?

From my work as a private investigator, it sounded like a drug overdose to me.

Soon, Cousin Shirley was on the phone. "How is your mom?"

"She's not doing well, Shirley. She can't even speak."

"Well, I spoke with the guardian. They think she had a slight stroke."

I already knew this was not true but I said nothing. My mother had been overmedicated so they could whisk her back to Seminole County—an attempt to legitimize an illegitimate guardianship.

The "guardian." The word made me bristle.

I stroked my mother's forehead while she continued to stare at me with intense fear in her eyes. She would somewhat recover from this one particular drug overdose, but she would never really recover. The guardian had her marked for destruction. Within six weeks, she would be dead from a morphine sulphate overdose.

My mother always, always stated she would live to see 100. She didn't believe in death. Death was for other people, not her, and by her feistiness and strong-willed nature, I had to agree with her. I just couldn't imagine that day ever coming.

She had been a hearty 91-year-old who cooked her own meals, paid her own bills, and bagged tons of yard leaves every day—though she feigned disdain.

"These damn leaves! Every day I rake them, and by tomorrow, there's trillions more all over the yard!" As Shakespeare stated, "Me thinks the lady doth protest too much."

She loved to rake the leaves, while feeling the outdoor Florida breeze on her wrinkled, chiseled face. Some called her "cute." She was less than five feet tall and wore her chin length hair combed to the side with a bobby pin to hold it back from her face.

She was a simple woman who loved every minute of living.

Fiercely independent and always outspoken, she enjoyed, cooking, cleaning, gossiping, and planning her daughter's daily activities.

"First we'll go to Family Dollar and pick up Honey Buns. I'm almost out of Honey Buns and I don't give a damn that I'm diabetic and the doctor and Shirley say I shouldn't eat them. I'm 91 years old, so I get to eat whatever I want!" Then we'll go to Publix and get some orange juice, spaghetti, and frozen dinners. I love those turkey breast dinners. Then we'll go shopping at Wal*Mart. They always have good things on sale. I love their electronic shopping carts. Then it will be time for lunch. I'll treat you to lunch and after that, my prescriptions should be ready at Walgreens. We'll pick them up and then maybe we'll go to that thrift store and if you like and I'll buy you a $1 skirt that we saw yesterday."

•••••

"David, My Hero" "The Unlikely Clergyman"

He walked the hallways of the nursing home in an ingenious disguise. Toting a Bible in his left hand and wearing little round spectacles, his salt and pepper hair was slicked back into a neat, little ponytail. His high rise baggy trousers and plaid shirt let you know that he was truly a man of the Lord.

The nursing home staff came to know him as "Reverend Newman," a benign figure who roamed the facility in apparent devotion.

After briefly praying with several of the residents, he always made his way into Louise A. Falvo's (my mother's) room.

The kind-hearted "Reverend" Newman was none other than David, my fiancé, in a calculated guise. We'd outfitted him with baggy trousers, white socks, a skinny black tie, and those convincing spectacles, purchased for a pittance at Goodwill. Alongside a Bible, these humble props transformed David into Reverend Newman, our only means to evade the restrictions and visit my mother, whom we were now forbidden to see.

When Rebecca Fierle, the guardian, and Reverend Anthony M. Nardella, Jr. secured a court order barring us from visiting my mother without Fierle's surveillance, we understood the grave peril she was in. When Rebecca Fierle, the guardian, and Reverend Anthony M. Nardella, Jr. had obtained a court order from Judge John D. Galluzzo stating that we were not permitted to visit with my mother unless the guardian, Rebecca Fierle, was watching us, we knew that my mother's life was gravely in danger.

While posing as a minister, David was able to secretly videotape the wretched conditions in my mother's urine-smelling Welfare nursing home room where Rebecca Fierle and Reverend Nardella had confined her against her will. She had been hooked up to a feeding tube and there was an IV drip by her bed that had been cruelly disconnected.

Her body had been ravaged by neglect and cruelty. Her skin was thin and fragile, stretched taut over the bones that protrude from her emaciated frame. Her eyes were sunken and dark, conveying a sense of resignation and despair. Her mouth was agape, dry and parched, as if begging for even a single drop of water to soothe the pain. Her breathing was shallow and irregular, as her body struggles to maintain the will to live. Her veins were visible through her papery skin. She is a shell of the vibrant person she once was just a few months before, now trapped in a world of suffering and neglect that no human being should ever have to endure. Yet she hung on, waiting for me to rescue her.

"Don't worry," David whispered. "Angie is at home writing court papers as quickly as possible. She's trying to get you out of here."

My mother stared at him with frightened eyes and whispered softly, "Good. I want to go home."

On July 21, 2008, my mother had eaten her breakfast by mouth, despite this unwarranted and unnecessary feeding tube. Within twenty minutes after she had consumed her breakfast and was previously reported as "awake and attentive" by the nursing staff (in nursing medical notes), my mother was suddenly found dead. The shock was brutal.

It was very strange and heart-wrenching how I found out about my mother's sudden death.

My mother and I had a pact from long ago. I had once told my mother, "Mom, I don't really totally believe in the afterlife."

My mother had replied, "It is real, and I will come to you in a dream upon my death to show you it is real."

On the morning of July 21, 2008, while still asleep, I had a very strange dream that suddenly woke me up. I dreamed that David and I were driving my car, when suddenly, I looked in the rearview mirror, and there was my mother in the back seat, smiling! There was just a big smile on her face.

I turned around and looked at her in amazement (in the dream). She was glowing. "Mom! They tried to kill you, you know! How did you escape the nursing home?"

But she just continued to beam and stare at me. She did not reply.

Startled, I woke up.

Blinking into the harsh light of my computer screen, an email from Reverend Attorney Nardella caught my eye. Its terse message read, "I think you had better go to the nursing home immediately."

****

When I arrived at the nursing home . . . .

I cradled my dead mother in my arms and sang songs to her.

Sing for me! Dance for me, Ang!

We then smuggled the urine-filled bag out of her room and had it tested in a lab. The lab confirmed that my mother had been over-medicated. She had died from a morphine sulfate overdose.

⸺ ••●●•• ⸺

At her funeral, I hired three flute players to come and play lovely songs.

I invited Shirley and John Mascarella to the funeral, but they didn't even bother to show up.

I laid a bouquet of yellow flowers in my mother's arms prior to the mortician closing the casket. Yellow had always been her favorite color.

A flood of memories accompanied my tears.

There were those truly hilarious moments I had shared with my mother during the last three years -- like the day I gave her a tour of Gainesville when she had first come to live with me.

"Mom!" I said, pointing at the campus buildings. "Over there on the right is the University of Florida."

"It's pretty big," my mother said, as she looked on.

"Yes!"

"Ang, what are those really tall buildings over there?" she inquired.

"Those are the dorms, Mom!" I replied.

"The **what**?"

"Those are the **dorms**, Mom!" I replied, again, slightly shouting. My mother refused to wear hearing aids, so there was always this fine balance between getting her to hear you and not ruffling her and then being accused of shouting at her.

"What are dorms?" she inquired.

"Dorms are where the students live," I responded.

My mother keenly looked on and then suddenly stated, "***Oh! There must be a lot of marijuana in there!!***"

I suddenly gave my mother a surprised and dashing look.

"Mom. How do you know about marijuana? Have you ever smoked marijuana?"

"Nope," she replied. "Of course not!"

Then, with a wry smile, she turned to me and added, "But I know what college students do in those dorms!"

And then there was that time when she had been overmedicated in Palm Gardens and ended up in the emergency room of North Florida Regional Hospital.

My mother, somewhat delirious, stared at the wall, as I held her hand. Then she whispered in a low voice, "I don't think I'm going to Heaven."

I squeezed her hand, although I don't think she was truly aware of my presence. I think this was the closest my mother ever came to apologizing to me.

And now, I tucked a big beautiful bouquet of yellow flowers under her rigor mortis arms with her in her coffin.

And I kissed her good-bye, and the mortician lowered the lid.

****

There came a time when I put down my accordion and tucked it away, into its old musty, leather case. I didn't realize I would not squeeze the bellows or tickle the keys again for more than a decade.

I'm normally a comedy musician. I play sing-along music on my accordion at nursing homes, restaurants, and kids' birthday parties.

Weeee-oooo! It's polka time! Roll out the barrel! We'll have a barrel of fun!!!!

The polka beat commences, and I make my grand entrance clad in my eighties prom dress and donning a tiara with pink lace gloves. All bow before me -- ***The Queen***! -- with bubbles blasting in the background and everybody shaking maracas. And the show begins!

But now the stage was barren. There was only the sound of a gavel in my daily life.

My mother, a millionaire, had been killed (intentionally over-medicated) in a run-down nursing home for Welfare recipients. Medicaid fraud at its best.

I had subsequently been robbed of approximately one million dollars through "legal" court maneuvers.

My inheritance money -- one million dollars – had been stolen from me.

It was time to put down my accordion and pick up my magnifying glass. You see, I'm not just Angelina, the Polka Queen.

I'm also a licensed private investigator.

<hr>

CHAPTER FOURTEEN:
MY UNDERCOVER INVESTIGATIONS

Going Undercover: Visiting Isolated Guardianship Victims and Their Family Members

Warning: Some readers may find the contents of this chapter to be very disturbing, so caution is advised. The following are true life stories regarding a few of my undercover investigations detailing nursing home neglect, financial exploitation of the elderly, and documented elder abuse.

Once the guardianship of my mother took off like wildfire, I hired myself as my own licensed private investigator. After nearly six years of investigations, I submitted a 300+ page report to the FBI, the FDLE, the Florida attorney general, and other agencies, which I thought could have had Fierle arrested 300 times over for Medicaid fraud, financial exploitation, and elder abuse. In this chapter, you will read a sampling of my undercover investigations.

We walked together in the hallways of nursing homes searching for Rebecca Fierle victims. Each case was different, yet they were also all the same. We witnessed dozens of elderly persons, dehydrated, neglected, robbed.

Here are some of the hair-raising events we witnessed.

We Will Not Forget What We Witnessed (Veda Jones)
Veda Jones

Our journey led us to the tragic story of Veda Jones, a mere 60 years old and diagnosed with dementia. Statistically, the average age of onset for dementia in the United States is 83.7 years old (Plassman et al., Aug 3, 2017). As we delved into her history, we wondered how this relatively young woman, who had previously been a nurse at a residential treatment center, had ended up incapacitated, her assets in the hands of a guardian.

From the court records, it appeared that Veda Jones had no relatives. She had been working as a nurse in a private residential treatment center when she suddenly was placed into a Fierle guardianship. She had owned a condominium in the Orlando area that, during the real estate boom, had been worth about $250,000.00. Veda also owned a bank account, furniture, a car, and other assets. So, how had she ended up in a nursing home at such a young age?

The answer is better understood after watching the Netflix movie, "I Care A Lot."

The Netflix hit, I Care A Lot, was released on February 19, 2021. The film's protagonist, "Marla Grayson," is portrayed as a seemingly saintly court-appointed guardian who targets elderly folks who possess substantial assets.

Grayson systematically defrauds her clients, conspiring alongside doctors and nursing home administrators to identify susceptible targets. With the assistance of her attorney, she then seizes legal control of their lives, then takes possession of all of their assets.

Prior to watching "I Care A Lot," I couldn't understand how a guardian would allow her "ward" to go unattended, without food, without water. We were now watching, in real life, a slow death in progress when we met Veda Jones, but we didn't realize it. And we didn't know what to do.

Veda Jones was the first court file I decided to investigate thoroughly.

We went to Life Care of Altamonte Springs and located Veda Jones, who was strapped in a wheelchair and sat in front of a TV in the community room. Just six months prior, she had been working as a nurse.

We attempted to talk to her.

"Veda? How are you?" Veda stared up at the ceiling, her eyes rolling around from side to side as though she was attempting to find our voices.

"Veda? What happened to you? How did you end up here? You used to be a nurse?" Veda attempted to speak with us but the words came out jumbled and garbled. There was drool running out of the corners of her agape mouth.

"She's overmedicated," David whispered to me. David had previously worked in hospitals and nursing homes. He knew the signs.

A staff member walked by the TV room, curious to notice that Veda Jones actually had two visitors.

"Can I help you?", she asked tersely.

"Oh, no. We're fine. We're just here to visit Veda."

"How do you know Veda?" she inquired, suspiciously, approaching us.

I had to think quickly.

"Oh, we lived in the same condominium complex off of Pine Hills Road. She was our neighbor."

The nurse eased up her stiff pose, assured that we knew personal information about Veda that only authentic neighbors would know.

"We just learned that she's here. What happened? How did she end up here?" I inquired.

"That's confidential information," the nurse snapped, appearing defensive again. "I am not permitted to discuss her medical diagnosis."

The nurse made a quick about face, but then she went to a nurse's station and picked up the phone, as she continuously eyeballed us.

So, we stayed only a bit longer. She probably was phoning Rebecca Fierle, so we wanted to get out of there before we got caught.

Besides, it was difficult to carry on a conversation with someone who is tongue-tied and unable to respond.

Her hands were warm. I squeezed her hands. I held her hands. I attempted to make eye contact with her. I stroked her hair. I sensed that there was more to this story than what we had just witnessed. So, after our brief visit, it was time to go back to the Seminole County Courthouse and review her court file in more depth.

••●●••

Back at the Seminole County Courthouse, I gave Veda Jones's file a more careful look.

Ann Marie Giordano-Gilden, the same attorney who had been appointed to my mother, had also been appointed to the Veda Jones case. Gilden was frequently listed as the "court-appointed attorney" on Rebecca Fierle cases during that time period.

Most of the time, the reports filed in by the court-appointed attorneys have been redacted. But we found that Seminole County Courthouse is disorganized and many of the "Reports to the Court" that were not supposed to be uploaded for public view were scanned in anyway. I sometimes brought along my lap top and typed up entire reports, verbatim, that I was not supposed to see.

A careful read of Attorney Ann Marie Giordano-Gilden's secret "Report to Court" revealed that Veda Jones had been diagnosed with Parkinson's disease.

Parkinson's disease?!

I did a double take. I was certain that I had previously read that Rebecca Fierle had filed a petition for guardianship stating that Veda Jones had dementia.

I flipped back to the first entry in the court records. Indeed, it stated that Rebecca Fierle was claiming that Veda Jones had **dementia**.

Treatment for Parkinson's disease would not leave one speechless and somewhat of a living vegetable. David was right.

It appeared that Veda Jones was simply being given a cocktail of psychotropic drugs on a daily basis that left her speechless. With treatments for Parkinson's disease, Veda Jones could most likely have remained an active member of her community, just like Muhammad Ali or Michael J. Fox.

Minus the drugs, I wondered what Veda Jones would look like and act like.

It was time to go pay another visit to Veda Jones.

The next time we checked in on Veda Jones, she had been left alone in her bed. A tray of lunch food had been delivered to her room, which was now cold to the touch, and remained untouched on a portable table adjacent and parallel to her bed. We wondered how she was supposed to eat this food, since it was out of her reach.

We concluded that she wasn't. Soon, a nursing home worker came and removed the untouched tray. Veda stared out into space, unaware that lunch had been delivered, and then the untouched meal had been removed.

••●●●••

There was nothing in the Seminole County court record to indicate what happened to the $250,000.00 from the sale of her condominium, plus the money from the sale of her car, or the sale of Veda's personal belongings.

Within less than a year, Rebecca Fierle then petitioned the court to not have to file any further annual financial reports because all the money was gone, according to Fierle and her attorney. (A guardian can ask the court to not file any more annual financial reports once the money is all gone.)

Shortly after Judge Alley gave Fierle permission to not have to file any more financial accountings, a death certificate for Veda Jones, age 62, was filed into the court record.

••●●●••

We Will Not Forget: What We Witnessed (Debra C. Duffield)

It was a lovely spring day when Debra Duffield finished teaching her morning class at the University of Central Florida. As she briskly walked back to her black BMW, a text message suddenly appeared on her phone. "Margaret is interested in you!" Debra clicked on the link and saw a photo of a smiling young woman with long, curly dark hair and green eyes.

Debra opened her driver's door, tossed in her briefcase, and began reading.

"Your profile really caught my eye! I have been wanting to visit America for a long time. I live here in Chester, England. It is a very historic city, once owned by the Romans. Perhaps you can come visit sometime. I see that you live in Florida! I have always wanted to visit Disney World!" Margaret messaged.

Soon, the two women were chatting in real time. The flirtations quickly turned into cyber- sexting, and within a few weeks, Debra had purchased a plane ticket for Margaret.

At the Orlando International Airport, Debra eagerly awaited with a large bouquet of pink roses, lilies, tulips, and daisies cradled in her arms.

"Are you Debra?" a woman approached and asked her. Soon, they were hugging, as Debra handed the large, lavish floral arrangement to her new lover.

Debra and Margaret quickly became inseparable, visiting Suzanne McCord's custom jewelry shop together in downtown Winter Park, Florida. Suzanne and Debra had become close friends a few years before, ever since Debra inherited more than $3 million, a fully paid-off house, precious antiques, and a valuable coin collection from her adoptive, now deceased, parents.

The two women entered Suzanne's jewelry boutique, laughing and holding hands.

"Suzanne! This is Margaret, my fiancé! We're getting married in three weeks. Isn't she so beautiful? Can you make us matching custom wedding bands in time for the wedding?"

Suzanne was a little taken aback. "Wow. Congratulations! When did this happen? You never told me!"

"Oh, yeah. Margaret and I just met two weeks ago, but I know she's the one!"

As the two women began looking at photos of Suzanne's unique designs, Suzanne pulled Debra aside into her back room. "I have to show you the custom bracelet I've been working on for you! Let's go have a look."

Once safely in Suzanne's back room, Suzanne asked Debra, "Are you sure you are doing the right thing? If you marry her, she will be entitled to half your estate."

"Yeah, I know," Debra replied, with a smile. "She's really a good person and would never take advantage of me."

But just two days after Debra made Margaret a joint account holder on her bank account, Margaret disappeared on a plane back to England with $60,000 in cash, leaving Debra devastated.

Debra never heard from Margaret ever again.

Debra grew despondent and depressed. She stopped eating. Soon, she was frail and anorexic. She walked into Suzanne's jewelry store appearing haggard and distraught. That's when Suzanne offered her help.

"You look so gaunt," Suzanne stated.

"Yeah, I know," Debra replied. "I just can't believe she did that to me. I have felt suicidal," she confessed.

"I think maybe you should move in with me and get some therapy," Suzanne suggested. "I have that spare bedroom on the back side of my home. There is a private bathroom. Why don't you stay there for a while?"

Soon, Debra moved in. She enjoyed the homecooked meals Suzanne was providing for her and the warm companionship.

"Truthfully," she told Suzanne, "I don't ever want to go back to my house. It is too big and too lonely now that my parents are gone."

Shortly thereafter, Debra granted Suzanne a power of attorney to sell her home. The proceeds would be used to pay rent to Suzanne and update the dilapidated back bathroom.

Debra was starting to eat a little and gain a little weight. But one day, a few weeks after moving into Suzanne's house, Debra slipped on the wet kitchen floor and ended up breaking her right hip. Suzanne called for an ambulance.

Debra was rushed to the hospital, where a social worker discovered that Suzanne held power of attorney over her.

That's when an ominous phone call was made.

"Hello, Rebecca?" the social worker stated. "I think you need to come down here to room 225. There is a 56-year-old woman who is bipolar and anorexic. She gave her friend a power of attorney, and she's worth millions."

Within 24 hours, an emergency petition had been drawn about by Rebecca's lawyer, the most holy Attorney Reverend Anthony M. Nardella, Jr.

Following hip replacement surgery, Debra was transferred to a nursing home. She would never see her home, her possessions, or Suzanne McCord ever again.

As we searched the Seminole County court records looking for additional cases where Rebecca Fierle had been appointed as the plenary guardian (which, in legalese, means that she was in charge of everything – the person and the person's property), it was difficult to know where to begin. There were so many, many cases that came up on the docket under Rebecca Fierle's name. So, we decided to search for cases where the victim seemed too young.

Soon, we found a case in the records that had all the elements of suspicion. The victim, Debra C. Duffield, was being confined to a nursing home where the average age of the residents was about 76. Duffield was only 56.

She had been diagnosed, according to Rebecca Fierle, with manic depression and anorexia nervosa.

Manic depression and anorexia nervosa?!

I had to do another double take again. "They're putting people into guardianships for manic depression and anorexia nervosa?" I asked David.

"What the fuck?" he replied, as he looked over my shoulder and read the bizarre Petition for Guardianship paper that Fierle's attorney had filed into the court record, to commence a guardianship on Debra. "All I can think is 'She must be loaded,'" he added. David was right.

I nodded in agreement. As an artist and musician, I certainly know a lot of artistic-type people who could qualify for guardianship if manic depression and anorexia nervosa were the sole criteria. But most artists are broke and penniless. They are safe from the predatory guardians of the world.

Prior to being institutionalized, Duffield had been living with a good friend at her friend's home, Suzanne McCord, in Altamonte Springs in a lovely lake-surrounded neighborhood.

We set off to interview Suzanne McCord.

We arrived at her lovely house and knocked on the door.

"Suzanne McCord?"

"Yes."

"My name is Angela Woodhull. I am a licensed private investigator." I flashed my badge. "And this is my fiancé, David Newman. We are investigating Rebecca Fierle for financial fraud. May we come in and speak with you?"

Suzanne was delighted to see us and opened the door widely. She had also been conducting her own background research on Rebecca Fierle.

Suzanne, in her early sixties, appeared attractive, thin, clad in elegant attire with nicely styled hair and wearing lots of interesting silver jewelry. She lived in a uniquely furnished small home that is very artistically decorated, with unique paintings and gorgeous rugs.

Suzanne owned and operated her own custom jewelry store where she crafted and sold her own unique creations. Debra had been a frequent customer. And that's how Debra Duffield and Suzanne McCord had first met and struck up a friendship.

"So, what is the back story on Debra Duffield?" I inquired.

Orphaned at birth, Debra Duffield had been adopted by a wealthy childless older couple, now deceased, who had left her a significant fortune. Debra owned a lovely, fully paid-off $300,000.00 home, several expensive antique furnishings, and a trust estimated, by McCord, to be worth about $3 million. She had been working part-time as an adjunct college professor at the University of Central Florida, just for fun.

"So, what's the full story?" we asked Suzanne. "How did Debra go from wealthy, independent woman to living in a dumpy nursing home?"

Suzanne was eager to tell all.

According to Suzanne, a few years back, Debra had fallen in love with a woman who had emigrated to the United States from England that she had met online. Soon, the lovers, within weeks of meeting each other, were living together. But shortly thereafter, the English woman took advantage of her, robbed her, broke her heart, and then swiftly returned to England with about $60,000.00 in cash that she had stolen from Debra. Debra subsequently went into a deep depression and stopped eating. That's when Suzanne McCord offered her help.

According to Suzanne, Debra simply could not cope with the loss and betrayal of her lover and, as a result, was feeling quite lonely and suicidal. Debra did not wish to live alone and so that's when she offered Suzanne a power of attorney to sell her home. Suzanne did her best to find a seller for Duffield's house and then moved Debra into a wing of her home, using the proceeds of the sale to pay for Debra's ongoing living expenses. The wing had been used for storage for many years, so Suzanne used part of the proceeds from the sale of Debra's home to furnish the wing. Suzanne also refurbished a private bathroom for Debra --$18,000.00 – using Debra's money, all with Debra's alleged permission.

"She was happy not to be alone," Suzanne explained.

Truthfully, the price seemed a little high -- $18,000 just to update a bathroom? But Suzanne seemed nice enough. She was a grandmother of two and had a daughter with whom she was very close. She did not appear to be the kind of person who would take advantage of another. Her cell phone rang frequently from her daughter and other friends as we sat and sipped on herbal tea and ate cookies while visiting with her. She was also on good terms with her ex-husband who just happened to be a licensed private investigator. It was through Suzanne that we obtained an extensive dossier on Rebecca Fierle that had been compiled by McCord's ex-husband, the private investigator.

Rebecca Fierle's dossier provided us with many more interesting pieces of information that we had not previously known. We discovered that "Fierle" is not even her real last name. Her full real name is Rebecca Fierle-Santoian or Rebecca Santoian, depending upon which legal document she was signing. Fierle is married to her second husband, an older man about 20 years older than her who is a cardiologist based out of Ocala, Florida. Fierle's first husband, Jeff

Fierle, filed for bankruptcy in 1997 with her. The two of them also went through a home foreclosure. So, from 1997 to 2007 --just ten short years-- Rebecca Fierle went from totally bankrupt and homeless to a multi-millionaire. Most people working ordinary jobs cannot make such a claim. The guardianship business is certainly lucrative, we concluded.

We also learned from reading the dossier that Fierle owned a fleet of Mercedes, carries a concealed weapon, and owns several million-dollar properties in Windsor, Florida.

So, how had Debra Duffield ended up in a Fierle guardianship?

According to Suzanne McCord, Debra had slipped and broken a hip on the slippery tile floor in Suzanne's kitchen while Suzanne was at her jewelry store. Because she was so thin from not eating, she broke a hip. Suzanne then called an ambulance and Debra was taken to the emergency room for hip surgery. It was while she was in the hospital that a social worker discovered that Debra was living with her friend, Suzanne, who held a power of attorney. Professional guardians, social workers, and law enforcers generally tend to view mostly anyone who holds a power of attorney as a suspicious person. And, hence, a social worker at the hospital alerted Rebecca Fierle regarding this power of attorney, and the subsequent sale of Duffield's house by Suzanne.

Fierle then immediately placed Debra under an emergency temporary guardianship using the "Reverend" Attorney Anthony M. Nardella, Jr. as her counsel. Ann Marie Giordano-Gilden, my mother's court-appointed attorney, became the court-appointed attorney in the Duffield case.

We learned of another player who was frequently on the scene when it came to Rebecca Fierle guardianship cases: a DCF (Department of Children and Families) worker by the name of David McKenzie. (You'll recall reading about David McKenzie in my mother's fraudulent guardianship case, as well.) It seems that whenever Fierle was about to become the guardian or had already been appointed as guardian, there was this David McKenzie to step in and do the shakedown. McKenzie arrived at Suzanne McCord's house on several occasions threatening her with criminal prosecution. "All you have to do is give back all of the money you took," McKenzie told Suzanne, "and we won't prosecute you."

McCord, frightened, had money in a bank account for Duffield which she hurriedly provided to Fierle in a brown paper bag. Fierle had requested all the money be given to her in cash.

Before we left, Suzanne showed us photos of Debra at the family dining room table, seated among McCord's family members and grandchildren, enjoying a Christmas dinner.

"As you can see from these photographs, Debra was doing quite fine while she was here with me. She was capable of carrying on a bright and intelligent conversation."

The photos depicted a vibrant woman seated at the dining room table among Suzanne's relatives. The photos were taken only six months prior.

It was time to go see Debra Duffield. We invited Suzanne to come along, but Fierle had obtained a court order stating that McCord was not permitted to see Debra Duffield.

Isolate. Medicate. Take the estate. That is the three-part slogan that guardianship fraud victims use to succinctly describe what transpires in a fraudulent guardianship.

At the nursing home, we quickly learned that it was best not to ask the location of an "inmate". It raised too much suspicion, especially if it was someone without friends or relatives. Such a person is not expected to have visitors.

David and I learned to simply walk briskly down the hallways with him checking on the left and me checking on the right for the victim's name to appear on one of the doors. Alas, we came upon a room labeled "Debra Duffield."

The young woman was lying in bed in the middle of the afternoon watching television. She didn't make a lot of sense at first but snapped back into reality once we started speaking with her at length. She appeared lethargic and resigned to the fact that she had been placed against her will in a nursing home. She strongly smelled of fecal matter and she frequently adjusted her body from side to side to attempt to avoid the uncomfortable waste in her disposable diaper. The sound of the crinkly diaper was ever present as she kept adjusting herself from side to side. Debra Duffield had nothing negative to say about Suzanne McCord. In fact, she asked how she was doing and asked to give her regards.

"Would you like her to come and visit you?" I asked.

"She's too busy," Debra stated. "She has a jewelry store to run."

We asked Debra if she knew who Rebecca Fierle was. She said that she did not know Rebecca Fierle; that she had never met her. There were several beats of silence. Debra sometimes nervously switched the channels on TV and then commented on what she saw. It seems she was highly embarrassed and really didn't want to talk with us.

My body tightened. This frail woman was once an adjunct college professor, just like me. She was a peer. No wonder she felt embarrassed by her current situation.

I walked out to the nurses' station where they congregated and were talking and laughing with each other, sharing jokes as they sat in front of computer screens or stood about.

"Is there anyone who can help my friend?" I asked, pointing to Debra's room.

A nurse responded. "Ma'am, which room?"

"Room 325," I replied. "Her diaper needs to be changed."

But no one came during the next two hours to change her diaper.

I was standing there witnessing this thin, gaunt woman with scrambled hair lying on a cot, smelling of fecal matter, with a 90 year-old roommate who moaned and made babbling noises the entire time we were attempting to talk with Debra. At one point, I left the room, nauseated not only from the smell of defecation and urine that this woman my age was forced to sit in for more than an hour, but just to imagine that here was a woman, one year younger than me, in this horrible situation. It was upon meeting Duffield that I realized, "This could happen to me! Rebecca Fierle could place me—or anyone else—in one of these places." All it takes is an allegation, a dirty lawyer, and a corrupt judge.

When I returned to the room, I whispered to David, "Let's go. I can't take this anymore." We bid farewell to Debra C. Duffield. It felt like I was abandoning someone on the side of the road, leaving them to die.

****

Back at the Seminole County courthouse, we read Debra Duffield's file a little more carefully. We discovered that Rebecca Fierle had listed some of Duffield's antiques on an inventory list. The listed prices for the antiques seemed awfully low. We then returned to Suzanne McCord's home and showed her a copy of the list filed into the court records.

"Does this seem right?" I asked her, pointing to one of the items.

Suzanne assured us that these valuables were greatly undervalued in the court records; for example, an antique table allegedly was sold by Fierle for a mere $30. "This can't possibly be true," McCord stated. "I remember that table. That table is worth at least $3,000.00."

McCord then named at least a dozen antique items that had belonged to Duffield that didn't even appear on the inventory list. Fierle had confiscated a key from McCord where all of Duffield's antiques had been held in storage.

In addition to taking a bag of cash from Suzanne, worth more than $120,000.00, Fierle had also obtained a judgment against McCord for an additional $120,000.00.

"How am I supposed to pay back $120,000.00?" Suzanne asked, "when I've already given back more than $120,000.00 in cash?"

That was the last time we saw Suzanne McCord. The next time we went to visit her, there was a For Sale sign on her home. Neighbors stated that she had already moved.

Checking the court records periodically, we learned that nothing—absolutely nothing—was being done to benefit Debra C. Duffield. "Reverend" Attorney M. Anthony Nardella, Jr. was simply putting in regular billing statements for doing such things as trying to find and track down Suzanne McCord, read and review the court file, and run periodic property checks on Suzanne.

At this writing, Duffield's money has all been converted to attorneys' fees to benefit Reverend Attorney Anthony M. Nardella, Jr. There is no one disputing this guardianship.

And now the taxpayers of the state of Florida are paying for a relatively young woman to rot away in a nursing home while Rebecca Fierle was seen on Facebook smiling, showing off her new pool.

We also learned later from taking the guardianship certification course with professional master guardian, Irene Rausch, that antiques are supposed to be appraised.

"A guardian can't just list antiques for the price they were sold. By law, you have to have them appraised," Rausch informed us.

Fierle had not bothered to do this court-required mandate. And no judge had punished her.

I also later learned from one of Debra Duffield's cousins that she had actually inherited approximately $5 million from her deceased parents. The vast majority of the $5 million was never reported to the Court.

—••●••—

FAYE ELIZABETH ARNOLD AND HER SON, WILLIAM HAROLD ARNOLD

Early on a Sunday morning, Tina Holland was driving her Mustang north on John Young Parkway, heading toward Silver Star Road. As she approached the red light at the intersection, she gunned her accelerator pedal, as she simultaneously looked down on the floor board, passenger side, at her bag of fresh doughnuts.

(After all, viewing a bag of doughnuts is certainly what a driver would be doing when driving full charge through an intersection where the light has just turned red. Right?)

Turning right from the perpendicular corner was William Harold Arnold, age 53, on his motorcycle, on his way to his church where he plays the piano. Tina struck him broadside, and the motorcycle skidded to the side of the highway. Arnold lay unconscious on the side of the road.

Soon, an Orlando police officer arrived and questioned Holland.

"What happened?" the officer inquired.

"Oh, I'm sorry!" Tina replied. "I got distracted. I was eating a doughnut!"

****

Four hours later, the accident investigation was closed out and completed. The officer snapped a few photos of the bag of doughnuts, and the smashed motorcycle.

He charged Tina with running a red light and issued her a simple citation. Tina drove off in her dented car, and waved at the officer.

****

A tow truck removed the demolished motorcycle from the intersection.

****

An ambulance arrived and took the severely injured and unconscious William Harold Arnold to a . . . ***nursing home***. (Not to a hospital. Not to an emergency room.)

****

At the same time that Tina was charging through the intersection, an ambulance arrived and broke into the home at 907 Silver Drive. Eighty-year-old Faye Elizabeth Arnold was then removed from her home on a stretcher.

"Why am I being taken to the hospital?" Faye protested. "I did not call for an ambulance." "Why did you break into my house? I'm quite capable of answering the front door!"

The EMT workers did not respond.

****

Faye was then transported to the same nursing home facility where her son, William Harold Arnold, (unknown to her) was being held, unconscious, in an adjacent room.

****

While all of the above activities were simultaneously occurring, a grinning Rebecca Fierle was at the probate division of the Orange

County Courthouse filing in a death certificate **for the alive** (though unconscious) William Harold Arnold. *Why the rush, Rebecca?* Her attorney was simultaneously petitioning the court for Fierle to be appointed the curator of the "deceased" Arnold's estate (even though he was not deceased).

****

Faye phoned one of her neighbors from inside her tiny nursing home room where she was now being held hostage.

"Sophia, I haven't seen my son, William, and he's not answering the phone! Can you check my house?"

Sophia peered out of her kitchen window.

"Oh! There's movers at your house right now, Faye," Sophia replied.

"Movers?"

"Yes," Sophia stated. "And there's a FOR SALE sign out in the yard. I didn't know you were selling your house."

Stunned, Faye replied, "I didn't know either! Where is William?"

****

Faye grew a bit hysterical. "Nurse! Nurse! Help me! Help me! Get me out of here! I need to go back to my home and find out where my son is!"

The nurse approached with a syringe.

Faye slumped over in her wheelchair and all was quiet.

****

The Story Starts Taking a Weird Twist.

A careful look at additional police reports and court records revealed some peculiar information. The story was now taking a very weird twist.

William Harold Arnold, a 53-year-old bachelor, had lived his entire life with his mother, Faye Elizabeth. Arnold was the neighborhood pariah. And his mother, Faye Elizabeth Arnold, had been placed in and out of guardianship on several previous occasions.

LETS GO BACK IN TIME THREE YEARS PRIOR TO THE MOTORCYCLE ACCIDENT

Here's how Fierle would periodically confiscate Faye Elizabeth Arnold for three years before the motorcycle accident.

Faye Elizabeth would periodically check herself into an Orlando hospital for ultra swollen legs.

While Faye was at the hospital, Rebecca Fierle would apply for a temporary guardianship (the first step prior to permanent guardianship). Faye's son, however, would then throw a conniption fit at the nursing home, disturbing and harassing the nursing staff to such a point that they would refuse to keep Faye. Faye Arnold would then happily return to her home, and the temporary guardianship would expire. No more guardianship.

The yard at the Arnold's home was very unkempt. The exterior of the house appeared very dilapidated. The unsightliness irritated the neighbors who felt that their surrounding properties were being devalued because of the Arnolds.

There were frequent disputes with the neighbors, according to various Orlando police reports.

The neighbors called the police several times on gnarly Arnold. One report stated that Arnold threatened to shoot some neighborhood children because they had cut across his front lawn.

Another report, initiated by Arnold, stated that the neighbor children were spraying a chemical on his car.

"This is 9-1-1. What is your emergency?"

"There's some kids outside vandalizing my car!" William Arnold told the dispatcher.

A police officer arrived at the tattered home, once again.

The officer interviewed the kids who said they had been spraying only water on Arnold's dirty car.

To better understand what happens next, I must deviate and inform you of a similar situation.

On March 11, 2020, the TV show ***Dirty Money*** aired an episode titled "Guardians, Inc." The episode is about an elderly man who is removed from his home and placed into guardianship because he failed to make repairs to eight homes he owned in his neighborhood, including his own home. The run-down properties were creating a health hazard and were an eye-sore to the neighborhood. Concerned neighbors kept phoning the police and code enforcement. Finally, a professional guardian, and her attorney, took possession of the elderly man and placed him under guardianship. Once the guardianship was in full swing, they demolished all of his tattered houses, built a high rise, and made millions of dollars (none of which was ever given to the elderly man). Instead, John Savanovich was confined to a marginal nursing home and given an allowance of $200 a month, where he has remained ever since.

••●●••

It appeared, from reading police reports and court files about the Arnolds, that the City of Orlando has also adopted a guardianship strategy for ridding neighborhoods of problem folks like the Arnolds.

Soon, another guardianship petition was taken out on Faye Elizabeth. But, once again, Faye's son, who raises holy hell at the nursing homes, successfully used his boisterous, pushy style to get his mother removed from the nursing home.

"I'm taking my mother out of this rat hole right now!" Arnold screamed at the nursing home staff, as he wheeled his mother out.

"You can't do that!" a supervisor stated. "Your mother has a guardian."

"Yeah! And I own a lot of guns!" Arnold replied, as he wheeled past the administrator's front desk.

Arnold somehow was always able to bail Mom out of these emergency temporary guardianships and bring her back home. Then the emergency temporary guardianships would expire.

This back-and-forth scenario continued for about three years, while the weeds grew tall in the yard at the dilapidated house at 907 Silver Drive.

And then, there was that strange motorcycle wreck....

****

It was time to conduct a background check on Tina Holland and learn more.

A background check on Tina Holland revealed that Holland had actually been in jail on several occasions for DUI, possession of crack cocaine, and prostitution. On the morning when she hit William Harold Arnold, however, she was just merely eating a doughnut.

A background on her work history also revealed that she used to own a dumpster rental business with her ex-husband—the type of business that a professional guardian, like Rebecca Fierle, would use when she guts a house.

Over the next two years, following the accident, Tina Holland's court date was pushed forward continuously, with the officer who wrote the four-hours-later report always being the one who requested the date change.

Almost three years had elapsed when the court convened for a hearing. The room echoed with silence, punctuated only by the rustle of paperwork and the officer's steady breathing. Tina Holland was conspicuously absent.

Squinting at the files spread out in front of her, the judge queried, "Where is Mr. Arnold?" Her gaze skimmed over the donut-scattered photographs, pausing momentarily on each one.

"Is he alive?" Her question hung in the air, unanswered for a moment.

The officer casually responded, "Yes, your honor."

Ignoring the confusion, the judge pivoted back to the initial point of interest, "And where is Ms. Holland?" Her gaze swept across the near-empty courtroom, unmet by the defendant.

Upon the silence that followed, the judge issued an order: a fine of $400 on Tina Holland for the red-light infringement and a mandate that she attend traffic school.

The absurdity of the situation crystallized when the judge found a peculiar detail in the file. William Harold Arnold, the man supposedly summoned for this hearing, had been declared deceased two years prior, a fact confirmed by the death certificate filed by Fierle herself.

The legal dance continued as if he were still alive and capable of attending the hearing. A subpoena had been served to the late Mr. Arnold, summoning his ghost to yet another traffic court date. This surreal spectacle of bureaucracy, oblivious to the mortality of its participants, drew to a close with no less confusion than it had begun.

That death certificate was then voided out and a new death certificate was created for another date—approximately one month later—when William Harold Arnold actually died.

Furthermore, the court records also showed that Fierle placed William Harold Arnold on Medicaid, even though she had sold his home for $190,000.00 (which would disqualify him from Medicaid). Fierle then was appointed as personal representative of his estate.

•••●●●•••

We then visited Elizabeth Faye Arnold in person at the nursing home. She appeared alert and astute. Fierle had tucked her away in a marginal nursing home and Faye had been trying to figure out just exactly what happened to her. "They came with an ambulance to my home the day that my son was hit on his motorcycle—even though I had not called for an ambulance." Like David and I, she felt baffled.

Faye removed the blanket that was covering her legs. "Look at my feet," she said. Her feet were so red and so swollen that there were stretch marks on them. "I've never met Rebecca Fierle," she stated, "and she does nothing for me and does not give me any answers. I've looked out the window and I see her nice Mercedes that she drives. Can you get me out of here? Can you find out what has happened to my possessions, my furniture, my photographs? I don't have even one picture of my son."

Suddenly, her hands started to quiver as she wiped tears from her eyes.

Then she looked up at me with woeful eyes. "Would you be my guardian?" she asked me, her voice shaking. "I want you to be my guardian," she whispered to me, squeezing my hands.

****

I found the names and addresses of the only two witnesses who were allegedly at the accident scene on the day when Tina Holland was "eating her doughnut." The one witness just happens to be **an Orlando city council member. And his wife just happens to be the secretary for the state attorney's office in Orlando**. We tracked him down at his office. He appeared to be extremely defensive when I ask him to recall what he witnessed at the accident scene. "Whatever it states on the report. That's all I remember," he stated. "Read the report." And he walked off hurriedly.

The other witness is a **real estate broker**. He, too, appeared to be extremely defensive when I knocked on the door of his home and attempted to interview him. "How did you find me!?" he inquired. "I don't remember what I saw," he stated.

"It was too long ago."

This is a tragic and bizarre story of a woman who was placed into a predatory guardianship and her son was killed. Upon looking into the court file for witnesses, I found it odd that the only two witnesses listed were an Orlando city council member and a real estate broker. It seems highly unlikely that these individuals would be the witnesses at the accident scene, and their behavior when questioned about the incident was suspicious.

Realtors often work with guardians, which could explain the convenience of the real estate broker as a fake witness. It is equally strange that the other witness happened to be an Orlando city council member, and his wife just happened to be the secretary for the state attorney's office in Orlando. This connection raises questions about their credibility as witnesses.

In conclusion, the presence of these witnesses in the court file seems bizarre and unbelievable, and their behavior, when questioned about the incident, further raises suspicions about their credibility.

•••❮❯•••

I then visited Silver Drive and interviewed some of the neighbors. It turns out that the neighbor directly across the street from the Arnold's home is good friends with the mayor of Orlando. "They were real problem people, the Arnolds," he stated. "I'm glad they're gone. The yard and the exterior of the house were always in shambles. Nobody liked them."

•••❮❯•••

I then tracked down one of Tina Holland's former landlords, the manager of a trailer park. I was never able to actually locate Tina Holland herself. The landlord told me that everyone in the trailer park neighborhood was aware of the motorcycle accident. "She killed a man on a motorcycle and got away with murder," he stated. "It was the talk of the neighborhood." "She's a real problem person—a drug addict. Didn't pay her rent."

•••❮❯•••

Elizabeth Faye Arnold's house has been repainted, repaired, and sold. The yard is now pristine.

The neighbors no longer call the cops. Everything is now happy and tidy on Silver Drive in Orlando, Florida.

Faye Elizabeth Arnold is now deceased.

313

We Will Not Forget: What We Witnessed (Lawrence Long)

The next victim that we visited was a man in his early sixties living in an assisted living facility, Lawrence Long. Long was in the process of being sued by professional guardian, Rebecca Fierle.

Long's crime? Rebecca Fierle had lost in her bid to become Long's guardian. She was now **suing Long** for the unwarranted attempt at becoming his guardian—**and charging Long for the cost of her hiring an attorney and pursuing an involuntary guardianship against Long.**

Her attorney, Karen Goldsmith, who had assisted Rebecca Fierle in her quest to become Long's unnecessary and unwanted guardian, had been sending threatening letters to Long. Using their favorite judges in Seminole County (Nancy Alley and John Galluzzo), Rebecca Fierle and Karen Goldsmith had managed to obtain a court order demanding that Long pay thousands of dollars to Goldsmith for their foiled attempt at taking away Long's civil rights. A judgment had already been entered against Long—even though he had never been successfully served or appeared in court.

It was time to meet Long and ask him how he had managed to become victimized by this precarious and frightening situation.

We found Long alive and well and living in an upscale assisted living facility. He had his own efficiency apartment and seemed quite happy and fine in his surroundings. He enjoys playing on the internet, driving his car, and going shopping. It turns out that Long had suffered a mild stroke, which is what had put him on Fierle's "radar" but he had now fully recovered (or appeared as such).

Fierle found her hunting grounds in hospitals, snaring veterans like Long through involuntary guardianships, guaranteed by Florida law to siphon off five percent of their monthly incomes. The sum might seem paltry at first glance, yet multiplying it across 20 victims every month paints a stark picture of manipulation and greed.

"Greed is an uncontrolled longing for increase in the acquisition or use of material gain; or social value, such as status, or power. Greed has been identified as undesirable throughout known human history because it creates behavior-conflict between personal and social goals." ~Wikipedia

Long was aware that Rebecca Fierle had sued him for the money she had spent in her foiled attempt to become his guardian.

Stacks of unopened mail lay ignored in a corner of Long's living room - court notices and threatening letters from Fierle and Goldsmith. Long said he didn't want to open the mail because it was "too stressful" to deal with and he didn't really know what else he could do except ignore the situation. He hoped that the problem would somehow disappear on its own.

How was Long lucky enough to get out the unwarranted guardianship? Luckily for Long, he had been seeing his own personal psychiatrist for most of his adult life, and his personal psychiatrist went to bat for him and wrote a letter to the judge stating that he would not go along with the assessment (by Fierle's medical doctors) that Long needed to be placed into an involuntary guardianship and have all of his civil rights removed.

However, the unpaid bill "owed" to Rebecca Fierle is actually an omen of what is to come. Banking on the "fact" that Long is getting older, it's just a matter of time. Fierle can always re-apply at a later date to become Long's guardian again, having her favorite doctors declare him incompetent at a later date. And then, the unpaid money for the first foiled attempt will be reimbursed to her out Long's lifetime savings, since there is already a recorded judgment against Long.

Our visit with Long was a somber one, spent in the shadow of impending jeopardy. We enjoyed the afternoon visiting with Long, sharing a pizza with him. We opened, with Long, the stack of unopened threatening letters Fierle and Goldsmith had sent to him, which confirmed what I had already read in the court files.

"Let her go f--- herself," Long said, looking over the bills from Fierle and Goldsmith that increased in price every month, due to interest. Fierle's attorney was adding interest for each month that Long had ignored the bills.

Long showed us websites that he likes to visit. Between surfing the web and driving around in his car, he has managed, for the moment, to escape the reality that his freedom will be short lived.

Long seemed to realize that he was a "marked man."

Even though she didn't win the first round, it's just a matter of time before Rebecca Fierle steps back into Long's life to become Long's "guardian."

"I try not to think about it," Long said.

Long had been "marked for destruction."*

At the time of this writing, Long is now deceased. He had been successfully placed in a Fierle guardianship prior to his death – just as I had predicted. And yes, Fierle and her attorney got paid for their foiled attempt.

––––––––––––––––––––––

"Marked for Destruction" is a term coined by John Caravella who became involved with yet another victim of a predatory guardianship. His chilling tale, **Adele's Diary**, can be viewed at www.markedfordestruction.com

We Will Not Forget: What We Witnessed

The Tragic Story of Bobbie Thompson and Her Son, Roy Thompson

How would you like your only son -- and sole heir -- to be forcefully removed from the home he has always shared with you?

You are about to read the sad and tragic story of how Rebecca Fierle took control of a mom, evicted her son, and allowed the home to go into foreclosure -- without Fierle, the legal guardian, having to ever pay even one single dime on the overdue mortgage payments.

It was time to go visit another Fierle victim. According to the court records, Bobbie Thompson had was now in a nursing home, not allowed to return to her home. Her crime? Perhaps it was the tall grass in her front yard. Perhaps it was the tattered exterior of her home. Perhaps it was both.

But the that's not what had been written in the court records. According to Fierle's petition for guardianship, Bobbie Thompson had been found all alone in a hospital, without anyone to help her and assist her in making medical decisions. According to Fierle's petition for guardianship, Bobbie Thompson's only son, Roy Thompson, refused to become his mother's guardian. Do you believe it?

And thus, the only kind soul, willing to help Bobbie Thompson, was this complete stranger to her, Rebecca Fierle. ***Right?***

After skimming the court file, David and I went to the nursing home and found Bobbie Thompson in a room she shared with three other people. She didn't make a lot of sense at first, but the more we attempted to communicate with her, the more her mind snapped back to the reality of her bleak situation – imprisoned in a nursing home against her will, isolated from her beloved son.

"You've got to help my son," she declared, a look of fright in her eyes. "Is he still living in our home? I want my son to have our home," she insisted. "He's been applying for social security disability; he's living at my house all alone. What is going to happen to him?"

She scribbled the correct address for the home on a small piece of paper. It was time to go visit Roy Thompson.

The exterior of the home seemed to be in need of some serious repairs.

The grass also was very tall and needed cutting. In fact, we doubted that anyone lived at the residence. We peeked through the windows and saw that the living room furniture was in disarray with many items, such as a sofa and TV, missing.

We heard the sound of dogs barking when we knocked on the door, so we knew that someone must be residing at the tattered home. Roy Thompson appeared at the door and looked suspicious and concerned.

"Can I help you?"

I asked him if he had heard of a professional guardian by the name of

Rebecca Fierle and I explained that I was the victim of that same guardian and I asked him if he would like to speak with me. Roy's attitude and demeanor immediately improved and he graciously invited us into his home.

We sat down with him at the dining room table and he explained to us how Rebecca Fierle had taken control of his mother when she had gone to the hospital. Roy had lived with his mother for his entire life, and so he assumed that he would become her guardian if one was ever needed. Fierle had written in the court records that Roy did not wish to become his mother's guardian.

Roy had no money for attorneys' fees to fight this inaccurate scenario.

After taking control of Bobbie Thompson through an emergency guardianship, Rebecca Fierle next set off to remove Roy from the home.

Although Roy is handicapped and had been applying for social security disability, Fierle had all utilities turned off at the home, leaving Roy and his dogs to live in the dark without a working refrigerator and no water or air conditioning. Luckily for Roy, he had a girlfriend who paid to have the utilities turned back on. Fierle had been moving furniture and items out of the house but had told Roy that if there was anything he wanted that had belonged to his mother, he could go ahead and keep it, but she had also provided him with an eviction notice. So far, Roy had been ignoring the eviction notices. His girlfriend stated that Roy could move into her condominium with her, but the condo association does not allow for pets and Roy was very concerned about and attached to the dogs that he loves and wanted to keep.

It was obvious that Roy was in a very dangerous situation and I warned him. "You could be next. I envision that if you don't leave this house, Rebecca Fierle is simply going to take an emergency temporary guardianship out on you, too, and then she'll come here with the deputy sheriffs and have you removed to a nursing home, especially since you've been applying for social security disability.

This triggered an alarm in Roy and he said, "Funny you should mention that. A package came in the mail for me just the other day. And when I opened it, it was these purple pills that are for depression. They arrived in my name. **I've never ordered such pills and they are a prescription drug**."

David and I had been suspecting for several weeks that victims are overmedicated, such as my mother and Elizabeth Faye Arnold, and that it might have to do with Rebecca Fierle, who is married to a medical doctor.

"And have you been taking these pills?"

"Yes, I've taken some of these, since I really am depressed," he stated.

"But they make me feel dizzy and disoriented."

David spoke up. "This might be why the mysterious pills showed up in your mail box. If you are removed from this home and tested for mental incapacity during the time you are under an emergency temporary guardianship, these pills would assist in having Rebecca Fierle's doctors assess you and declare you mentally incompetent. I think you should stop taking those pills."

By now, we truly had Roy's attention. "I think we should call my girlfriend on my cell phone. I have very little minutes left this month, but this is worth the call." He dialed Mary Ann's number. "Honey, could you come over here? Well, there's these people here and I want you to meet them." She sounded reluctant to come. "They know Rebecca Fierle."

The girlfriend changed her tune. "I'll be right over."

Mary Ann arrived. "So, what you're telling me is that Roy might be in danger of losing his civil rights if he remains in this house?"

"It sounds like a real possibility," I stated. We told her and Roy of other similar cases, especially the story of the Arnolds.

"Honey, I really think you should move in with me."

"Does Rebecca Fierle know your address?

"No. She doesn't even know that Roy has a girlfriend."

"Good. I think you should keep it that way."

"Most definitely."

"But what about my dogs!?" Roy asked in a distressed tone.

"I think you might have to select between your dogs and your freedom," Mary Ann stated. Roy's eyes became filled with tears.

"But I don't want to lose this house! Once I get onto disability, I will have enough money to make the mortgage payments. And there's not that many payments left! I told this to Rebecca Fierle. But she said she doesn't care and that I have to get out. Maybe I can just wait it out just a little longer 'til I start getting my cheques."

Roy also told us that one of Rebecca Fierle's employees had called him one day and wanted to know when he expected to receive his first disability cheque.

****

Back at the courthouse, we examined Bobbie Thompson's court file a little more carefully. We discovered that rather than making the mortgage payments on Thompson's house, Rebecca Fierle had allowed the house to go into foreclosure. According to the bank, Ms. Fierle could not be found, so they were unable to serve her a lawsuit for the overdue mortgage payments. A guardian would normally be responsible, by law, for all of the overdue payments.

"The process server, on behalf of the bank, could not find the legal guardian?" I asked David, incredulous.

"Yep." David flipped through the court records and found the rhyme to the riddle. "Rebecca Fierle gave the wrong address in the court records."

On her guardianship application for Bobbie Thompson, Rebecca Fierle intentionally had listed an old address – a former residence where she had not resided in more than six years.

Providing a fake address to the court is how she had skirted the process server.

But the clever process server had then found Rebecca Fierle's legitimate address and knocked on the door of her correct address. Fierle's husband, Dr. Santoian, answered the door.

"Never heard of her," Dr. Santoian told the process server.

"Aren't you her husband?" the process server inquired.

"Nope. Never heard of her," Dr. Santoian repeated, and closed the door.

And so the process server left with the unserved papers still in his pocket.

And thus, Thompson's house was able to be foreclosed upon without Rebecca Fierle, as the guardian of Bobbie Thompson, being sued for the balance of the mortgage payments.

We returned to Roy Thompson's residence to let him know what we had discovered in the court records – that the house had already been foreclosed upon. But this time, the house truly was vacant and the cell phone numbers that Roy had given us for himself and his girlfriend were no longer working.

Roy, we concluded, had selected freedom and escape a potential guardianship—at least for the moment, he was "safe."

At the time of this writing, Bobbie Thompson is now deceased.

We Will Not Forget: What We Witnessed

Thomas Chada and his Father, Benjamin Chada Back at the Seminole County probate court records, things were heating up. Rebecca "Fierle's" attorney in my mother's case (Reverend Attorney Anthony M. Nardella, Jr.) actually began billing my mother's estate every time I was observed reading the court files. Imagine that.

"Phone call from probate clerk stating that Woodhull is reading the probate files once again." Charge: $58."

The next file I began assessing was yet another veteran. By now, we clearly understood that Rebecca "Fierle" had quite an appetite for veterans, since she automatically receives five per cent of their monthly income—no matter what she does or doesn't do during the course of a month.

Another veteran, Carlisle Bosworth, we noticed that $250,000.00 of his assets had been spent in a very short period of time.

What about Benjamin Chada, a veteran? First of all, becoming increasingly savvy at ascertaining the court records more quickly, we noticed that "Fierle" had placed Chada in a regular nursing home, rather than a veteran's nursing home. There is a "reason" for this, we discovered. A veteran's nursing home is free. Therefore, there would be nothing to bill for. However, if "Fierle" places a veteran in a non-veteran's nursing home, not only can she bill, bill, and bill, but she can also GENEROUSLY bill. I called the nursing home where Chada was staying and posed as a concerned daughter looking to place my father somewhere in an upscale nursing home. The administrator told me that a top-of-the-line private room, with all the bells and whistles, would cost about $6,000.00 per month at that facility.

And what was "Fierle" claiming to the court? "Fierle" was claiming that she was spending $12,000.00 a month for Chada's care. We wondered:

Where was the other $6,000.00 per month going?

Because of the exorbitant and completely unnecessary spending (to reiterate, Chada is a veteran—between his monthly income and the fact that he could be placed in a veteran's nursing home for free, Chada should have had enough money to sustain himself indefinitely), "Fierle" had initiated a lawsuit against Thomas Chada, Benjamin Chada's son. Thomas Chada was facing being evicted from his homesteaded residence if he could not find the money to purchase his father's half of their trailer home. The real estate title was "joint tenancy with right of survivorship" but that hadn't stopped Rebecca "Fierle" for attempting to make Benjamin Chada's son homeless. It was time to go visit Thomas Chada.

How can I describe Thomas Chada (Benjamin Chada's son)? The words that come to mind are "fun" "vivacious" "opinionated" "strong willed" "straight shooter." Chada likes to drink beer, kick back, tell a few jokes, and use a lot of colorful language, especially when describing his feelings toward Rebecca "Fierle."

After introducing ourselves at his door, one of his first comments was,

"Oh, don't even get me started talking about that c--t." We knew we were in for an interesting evening.

Thomas and his father had lived together quite amiably on several occasions. He described Dad as a "skirt chaser" and had somehow ended up in an expensive retirement center where he could flirt with all the gals. There were some health problems and soon he had been transferred to a nursing home. Thomas had been out of town when he learned, upon his return, that a woman named "Rebecca Fierle" was now his father's guardian.

"What the hell was that shit-- all about!? You tell me. It's gotta be about his money! The bitch just wants his money. Don't even get me started talking on that subject. Then she moves Dad so far away that I can't even get to go see him. I'm on a very limited budget and I suffer from arthritis. How the hell am I supposed to go clear across town to visit my dad? As far as that lawsuit against me, she can go f--k herself! I have an attorney on it and she ain't gonna get a g—d---m dime outta me!"

Thomas told us how his attorney had been very good to him. Thomas had recently been released from a hospital and his attorney had actually been paying for groceries and delivering them to Thomas's door. "What a fantastic guy! I couldn't ask for better."

Truthfully, an attorney going out of his way THAT much for a client just didn't sound right. We wondered what it all meant. We were soon to find out. Thomas was also in the middle of suing someone, a personal injury case.

The "nice" attorney was actually pre-spending the few dollars that Thomas would end up with from the settlement. In the end, there wasn't much left for Thomas out of the settlement money, and at that time, "Fierle" just happened to want to "settle out" with Thomas. She offered to let him stay in his homesteaded home if he would simply turn over $10,000.00 to her—the same, exact amount of money Thomas was about to get in a settlement. (How 'bout that there.)

We asked Thomas, after he cooked us supper and gave us a few beers, if he would like to drive to the neighboring town and see his father. "Would you like to go see your dad this evening?"

"Hell, yeah, I'd love to go see my father! I'm going to get him the hell out of there once I get my settlement money and then I'm going bring him back home. **I'm** going to be his guardian! I mean, what the hell, I am his son! Who ever heard of some f------ c--- stranger being my dad's guardian?! Who ever instituted this crazy f---ed up shit?! I was doing one hell-of-a job taking care of my dad and I know he was happy here. He needs to come home. There's nothing mentally wrong with him. You'll see."

The three of us piled into my van and Thomas directed us to the nursing home. It was late at night and we found his father lying in bed, this tall man who seemed very similar natured to his son. The hugs and tears between these two macho men brought tears to the eyes of both David and me. We were ecstatic to have brought them together. "Honey, let's videotape this because I see no mental incompetence whatsoever," I said to David.

Benjamin Chada seemed a little startled at first that were videotaping him. "Don't worry about it, Dad. These are my new friends. They're here to help you. I wanna get you back home, Dad, and this can help."

Benjamin Chada was then all right with the videotaping. He stated on many occasions that he would like to come home, that he wanted his son to definitely stay in the trailer home and he was definitely upset to learn that Rebecca Fierle was in the process of trying to make his son homeless.

"When you bail me out of here, we're going to sue the hell out of her.

Oh, yeah, just you wait and see," Benjamin declared adamantly.

Staff workers, not used to seeing visitors in Benjamin's half of the room, kept peeking into the room. We would hide the phone camera every time a staff worker appeared.

Soon, it was time to leave. "I don't see any mental incompetence with your dad," David stated. "Neither do I."

"See? I told you so!" Thomas responded. "We got to get him the hell out of there. I've never seen him in such bad physical shape. This place is killing him. I want my dad home."

****

The following day, Rebecca "Fierle" found out that Thomas Chada had managed to go see his father.

Her response? She had Benjamin Chada Baker-acted—put into a straight jacket and medicated on psychotropic drugs. She then contacted her attorney and they wrote a Petition to the court asking the judge to NOT permit Thomas Chada to see his father any more ever again. "Fierle" claimed that it upset the father so much to see his son—and whom he "didn't really want to see" according to "Fierle"— that she had to Baker Act him. Little did "Fierle" know that we have video footage of the father that is so contrary to these claims that are in the public court records that it is rather surrealistic to even fathom that such a statement would be written in the court records.

Lo and behold, at the court hearing, dirty Judge John D. Galluzzo actually decided he would not go along with "Fierle's" petition. He denied the motion and stated that Thomas Chada was free to see his father any time he wanted.

However, Galluzzo's decision did not stop Rebecca "Fierle" from wielding her unlimited authority. Her response? She simply moved Benjamin Chada to yet ANOTHER nursing home **so far away** that Thomas Chada would have to spend the entire day taking a series of busses just to get to the new location.

****

Thomas Chada never saw his father alive ever again.

The next time we saw Thomas Chada, he told us how his attorney was planning on having "Fierle" removed as the guardian—a motion serious enough, that if awarded, "Fierle" could have lost her license as a professional guardian.

"I thought we were moving ahead. Next thing I know, I'm getting a call from one of 'Fierle's' staff members. The b---- didn't even have the nerve to call me herself. Fierle's employee stated to me, 'Where do you want us to drop off your father's ashes?'"

"What!?! My father died?! When did my father die?"

"More than a month ago," the staff member responded in a flat tone.

"You mean to tell me my father has been dead for more than a month and this is the first time you're even telling me about it!?? What the f--- bull---sh-- is this!?"

This big, warm-hearted man, a true man's man, stood there in front of us and wept. He broke down and he literally wept.

"Oh, there's a special place in hell for people like Rebecca 'Fierle,'" Thomas stated. "I didn't even get to say good-bye to my father. My dad had a pre-paid burial plot. He didn't **ever** want to be cremated!

What the f--- kind of sh—is that?!" "Oh, believe you me, there's gonna be a payback time!"

Thomas Chada could not stop weeping.

Shortly thereafter, Thomas became seriously ill – to the point of almost dying. He was hospitalized on several occasions and needed extensive home health care. "I can't focus on any of this Rebecca 'Fierle' bullshit—any further," Thomas told us. "It literally ruined my health. At least that b---- wasn't able to get a f------ dime out of me. At least I have my home."

At the time of this writing, Thomas Chada is now deceased.

"We Will Not Forget Anthony Mieczynski"

Anthony Mieczynski -- Mary Mieczynski (Anthony's mother) is one of the guardianship reform advocates. We have become lifetime friends. Mary feels like kin to me, at this point.

This bizarre guardianship, upon Mary's son (a college student at that time) commenced as a divorce proceeding. Here's how a divorce proceeding turned into a guardianship proceedings which robbed thousands of dollars from Anthony's annuity.

Anthony, age 22, is the son of Mary and Alan Mieczynski. He was not a legal party to a divorce, since he was an adult at the time of his parents commencing a divorce. But he was the recipient of a substantial $3 million annuity.

The divorce attorney for the husband, and the divorce attorney for the wife had both advised their respective clients that Anthony and his annuity needed protection during the divorce proceedings. "Your wife is trying to steal your son's annuity." "Your husband is trying to steal your son's annuity." Both statements were a lie, but when two people are going through a nasty divorce and not communicating with each other, they tend to believe and trust their attorneys. So, both agreed that their son should be place in a temporary guardianship, "to protect Anthony and his assets." "Don't worry; the guardianship will automatically terminate when the divorce is finalized."

But instead of being a "temporary" situation, the divorce proceedings then dragged on for more than four years with no divorce ever granted or in sight. The proceedings seemed to be dragging on and on. Meanwhile, the money from Anthony's annuity was being used to pay both attorneys (which is illegal, of course). Rebecca Fierle had been appointed as the guardian.

When I tracked down Alan Mieczynski, the father, he already knew that something was terribly wrong. He had fired several attorneys, realizing they were all after his son's money, and he even succeeded in getting one of his attorneys disbarred for the fraud. Yet the guardianship was continuing with no divorce in sight. Anthony Mieczynski, who had been attending Seminole Community College when a guardianship was instituted against him using Fierle's doctors, was constantly and extremely stressed out over losing his civil rights. He contacted Rebecca Fierle on several occasions to inquire about his finances and payments to him (which Fierle was supposed to make to him, but never did).

"Rebecca, where is my allowance?" Anthony would inquire.

Exasperated by his numerous phone calls, Fierle replied, "Stop calling me, or I will put you in a crazy house where you belong, and you'll never get out!"

Anthony stopped calling Rebecca Fierle and became deeply stressed.

On the day that I first phoned Alan Mieczynski, he was originally not willing to listen.

"Hello."

"Is this Alan Mieczynski?"

"Speaking. Who is this?"

"My name is Angela Woodhull, and I am a licensed private investigator. I am investigating financial fraud by Rebecca Fierle. My mother and I are also her victims."

Alan was just about ready to hang up the phone on me.

"Fuck off!" he replied. "You're probably some cunt who works for Fierle!"

The phone hung up.

I called him back and got voice mail.

"Alan, pick up the phone," I said. "I'm writing a report for the Attorney General's Office! I swear to God I am for real. Can you just meet with me? I'm trying to help you guys!"

About an hour later, my phone rang. It was Alan Mieczynski.

After all he had been through, after multiple attorneys had ripped him off, he was willing to take a chance on me "They accused me and my wife of stealing from my son. What kind of people make those kinds of fucked up allegations?"

"They do that to everybody," I told him. "They did that to me, too."

"So, what's your plan?" he asked me. Alan is a Vietnam vet and a victim of Agent Orange. As such, his personality fluctuates and he can become intensely angry in a heartbeat. Hence, the reason why his wife of 30 years had filed for divorce in the first place.

"I think you and your wife should call off the divorce."

"Call off the divorce?" he stammered.

"Yeah. At least temporarily. Then they have no excuse for keeping the guardianship. Just tell the court that you and your wife got back together. You don't really have to get back together. Just call off the divorce."

Alan hesitated. Then he said, "Why don't you contact my wife about all of this? Tell her that if she agrees to call off the divorce, I'll go along with it, too. Tell her to call me." Both attorneys had forbade their clients to phone each other. It is a divide and conquer technique that predatory attorneys frequently employ.

I then contacted Mary and Anthony by phone. Mary was not too keen on speaking with me. "I just spoke with your husband," I stated.

"I'm sorry, but I have a new attorney, Grace Glavin, and she's doing a good job," Mary replied, and she hung up the phone.

But luckily for the Mieczynski's, Anthony, the alleged "mentally incapacitated son," had been listening in on another phone line at his mother's house.

"I believe that lady," Anthony told his mother. "I think we should listen to her."

Soon, Mary, Alan, and I were having a three-way phone conversation. "I think you two should reconcile and call off the divorce. I think you should -- at least temporarily. And then I think you should get out of the state of Florida."

The Mieczynskis did call off their divorce and have been caring jointly for their son ever since. They credit me for saving their son's life. Anthony is actually a genius, similar to **Rain Man**, starring Dustin Hoffman. I have no doubt that if Anthony appeared on "Who Wants to Be a Millionaire" or a similar type show, he would make it to the top.

The Mieczynskis had filed in three reports from psychiatrists that state that Anthony is not mentally incompetent. In fact, one psychiatrist actually stated that she thought the idea of Anthony being under a guardianship is "disgusting." However, Dirty Judge John D. Galluzzo said he would not entertain the reports from out of state psychiatrists. (Galluzzo also kicked me out of a public courtroom--a public hearing for the Mieczynskis--when the Mieczynskis two oldest daughters showed up for court and were questioned about Anthony's whereabouts – a hearing that Rebecca Fierle and her attorney initiated.)

"What are you doing here?" Galluzzo inquired of me. "Are you an 'interested person'?

"It's a public hearing," I replied.

"Well, I'm asking you to leave immediately, or I'll have you arrested," Galluzzo replied.

The Mieczynskis temporarily left the state of Florida with their son and fled to North Carolina. We remained in constant contact. Fierle filed a police report with the Lake Mary Police Department stating that when she found Anthony, she planned to place him in an assisted living facility "for his own safety."

"Anthony wrings his hands together and doubles over when he conjures up this statement," Mary told me.

"He tries not to think about it," Mary Mieczynski added.

After meeting me, the Mieczynski's came up with a different plan to try to save their son's annuity from being depleted in a guardianship contest. Instead of hiring an attorney to go up against Rebecca Fierle and her attorney, Ian Gilden, they simply ignored the court case and started filing complaints with every state agency imaginable. They filed complaints with senators, congressmen, police, and the Florida Department of Children and Families (DCF).

Finally, very excited, Mary phoned me one day.

They had returned to Florida and were now residing in a different county.

"Angie! We have found a DCF worker in Vero Beach who is seriously going to investigate Rebecca Fierle!!"

Weeks passed, and then they no longer heard from the DCF worker. Finally, they provided me with his name and cell phone number.

"Hello, I am Dr. Angela Woodhull, the private investigator who has been investigating Rebecca Fierle guardianship cases. Can you tell me where you are at with your investigation of Rebecca Fierle at this point?"

After a long pause, the investigator told me, "Actually, I have quit my job as an investigator for DCF."

In case you're wondering what the investigator's new profession was:

He had decided to become a professional guardian. Fierle had offered him a lucrative job with Geriatric Care Management.

More than a decade passed. The Mieczynski's continued to care for their son and keep their whereabouts hidden. They were now living in St. Augustine, Florida, and Alan was very ill with stage four kidney failure. Alan got up and prayed the rosary every day. He also said, "When I get better, I'm going to have the Mafia from Chicago execute that Cunt." It is no wonder that Fierle carries a concealed weapon. I heard these kinds of statements multiple times from her various victims and their family members.

Alan died, and Fierle was on the verge of being arrested. Fierle then decided to give the guardianship of Anthony to a guardian friend of hers located in Jacksonville name Joy. Joy, in turn, filed paperwork to make Anthony's older sister his legal guardian.

The nightmare is finally over, but never forgotten. Simply by playing a waiting game, and Fierle finally being arrested, the Miezcyskis were able to save Anthony and at least part of his annuity.

"I wish Alan had lived to see this day," I stated.

"I'm sure he's looking down from Heaven, and he's finally at peace," Mary replied.

We Will Not Forget Julia Andon

I was never able to meet Julia Andon face to face, or even talk to her by phone. By now, Rebecca Fierle realized that I was tracking her. She was now placing her "wards" in lock down facilities. She would instruct the staff, "If anyone shows up, call me immediately."

Despite the restrictions to my investigations, I was able to make an all-important discovery in this file. This was an Orange County guardianship case. The Orange County internal auditors were actually reviewing Fierle's guardianship cases and were filing Auditor Reports regarding missing monies. Each time an auditor filed a report, Fierle and Moss, her attorney, would have to go before the judge and give an explanation. In this case, Fierle had been claiming that she was making monthly payments on Julia Andon's lease car, a 1985 Ford Escort. Fierle and Moss showed up for the court hearing and brought along photocopies of all of the payments. The judge adjourned the hearing and all was well.

"It was just a simple mistake," Moss had declared to the judge. "After all, Ms. Fierle has more than 450 guardianship cases. She inadvertently made a mistake."

For several years, I read various auditor's reports, where it appeared that Fierle had been caught red-handed. I would then see proof of payment, or the receipts later filed in, and I would simply turn the page and go to the next document in the file. But on this particular day, I decided to do something different. Using my cell phone, I called the Ford Motor Company and posed as Julia Andon.

When the customer service representative answered, I used my best 85-year-old voice to impersonate Andon.

"Yes, my name is Julia Andon, and I was wondering if you could check on the Ford Escort I have leased. How many more payments do I owe on it?"

"Let me check that for you, Ms. Andon. Would you mind holding for a minute?"

"Oh, no! That's fine!" I stuttered in my best quivering voice.

Soon, the customer service rep was back on the line.

"Ms. Andon, you actually paid off your lease car, in full, three years ago!"

"I did?" I replied.

"Yes." And she provided me with the exact date.

"Thank you so much for that information."

"It was my pleasure."

I then went back and looked at the invoices Fierle had filed in as "proof of ongoing monthly payments."

And that's when I realized what she had done. She had simply photoshopped each invoice with the current year and current date. In that way, she could claim she paid the bill with her own money and then reimburse herself out of Julia Andon's assets.

We Will Not Forget Ulita Edris Lopez

On the morning of March 25, 2008, Ulita Lopez was running across a highway attempting to catch a bus in Gainesville, Florida. She was on her way to work at an assisted living facility where she was employed in housekeeping. She was merely 62 years old.

According to the probate records, Ulita was struck by a car and sustained severe head injuries, resulting in multiple surgeries. According to the probate records filed in by Rebecca Fierle and her attorney, Ulita was now 100% incapacitated and required 24 hour care. She could no longer speak and could only babble. Fierle and her attorney quickly filed an insurance claim against the driver and received a mere $150,000.00 (so they claimed in the court records) for a woman who was now a vegetable, according to Fierle and her attorney.

Having already read hundreds of Fierle files, I was not convinced that Ulita Lopez was a vegetable, and I decided to find her and visit her. I was also certain that Fierle and her attorney had received more than a mere $120,000.00, which was already almost all spent by Fierle and her attorney, according to the court records. The attorney had charged more than $60,000.00 for filing the paperwork on the accident claim. He also had steadily charged Ulita, "the vegetable," for storing her furniture in his law office!

It was time to go visit Ulita Lopez.

Reading through the court records, I discovered that Ulita had resided at Parkland's Nursing Home in Gainesville, Florida (the same nursing home where my mother had mysteriously died). But Fierle had petitioned the court to move Ulita to Orlando.

I went to Parkland's Nursing Home and discovered that Ulita Lopez had actually been working in housekeeping during her stay.

She was not paid. Fierle had told her when she had recovered from the car accident that she would have to work in order to pay for her room and board now that she didn't have an apartment or a job any more.

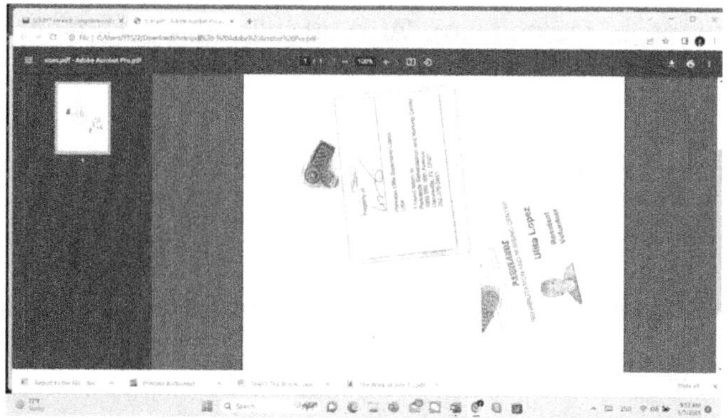

Here is a copy of Ulita Lopez's badge proving that she was working as a slave while housed at Parkland's Nursing Home.

I discovered that Ulita had been transferred to an unmarked home in Orlando (Pine Hills). I had read in the court record that Ulita was from the Philippines and she desperately wanted to go back home and live with her sons. I was on a mission to find Ulita and help her.

The first thing I did when I arrived in Orlando was find a videographer off of Craigslist. His name was Arte Tedesco. Arte and I are about the same age, and we are both full-blooded Italian, and we are both musicians. We hit it off right away on the phone, and I asked him to meet me at the Denny's on the corner of Lee Road and I-4 so I could first discuss with him what I wanted him to do.

"We're going to be undercover, Arte," I told him. "What do you think?"

"Well, it sounds intriguing. But I'd like to hear more before I agree to this," he replied.

Sipping on a hot coffee and scrolling through my phone, I waited inside Denny's – the same Denny's where I had previously spent the day with Dr. Richard Larkin.

Soon, it was half an hour past the time Arte was supposed to meet with me, so I texted him. "Are you still coming? I am here."

There was no reply.

I ordered a taco salad, and soon an entire hour had passed.

I checked my phone. I paged through e-mails.

A waitress approached me. "Is your name Angelina Woodhull?"

"Yes!" I replied.

"Well, there's a man on the other side of the restaurant. He has been waiting for you."

"Oh, my goodness! That must be Arte!" I replied. Arte had assumed I was going to be sitting on the busy side of the restaurant. Instead, I was quietly tucked away on the far side by the counter.

"Arte?" I said, as a man wearing a large black coat approached me. Arte sports a full beard, mustache, and has long salt and pepper hair pulled back in a pony tail.

Arte shook my hand.

"Oh, my gawd! I thought you weren't coming!"

"Yeah, I just checked my text messages. My ringer was accidentally turned off!"

Arte sat in the booth across from me, and there was this instant camaraderie. Arte would be perfect for the job, I thought.

Arte ordered a stack of pancakes, as I continued nibbling on my taco salad.

"So, here's what they do, Arte," I began to explain to him. "They lock a person up, take away all of their civil rights, and spend their money."

Arte ran his fingers through his beard, one eyebrow cocked up.

I leaned forward. "Yeah, I know it sounds like bullshit. And I know you probably think I'm just making this up. But just go there with me, okay?"

Arte leaned back. "What exactly do you want me to do?"

I opened my phone and showed him a photo of the unmarked home we would be visiting in Pine Hills.

"This house here," I said. "We are going to visit this home and pose as a married couple."

Arte gazed at the picture and scratched his head.

"So, you want me to say that I'm your husband?"

"Don't worry about it," I explained. "I will do most of the talking. I've been doing these undercover investigations now for more than four years. I have seen so much crazy shit," I said.

"You'll see," I told him.

We left my car parked in the far corner of the parking lot at the Denny's, and I entered Arte's car.

"Now, remember," I told him, when we pulled up to the residence. "We are looking for a nice place for my mother to reside, okay?"

"Okay," Arte replied.

"We will then walk quickly down the hallway looking for a woman who appears to be Filippino. There is probably only one woman who looks Filippino. Then, when we are talking with her, I want you to secretly videotape."

"Got it," Arte replied. Our hearts were pounding.

We walked up to the front door of the home and rang the doorbell. We waited on the small patio, holding hands, our hands shaking. We knocked and rang a second time after a few minutes.

Finally, the door opened slightly, and we were greeted by a woman with a very thick Jamaican accent.

"Yes, can I help you?" she said.

"Is this Ionie's Assisted Living?" I asked her.

"Yes," she replied, suspiciously.

"We were told there is one room available, and we're here to check it out. We are looking for a place for my mom. My name is Gina, and this is my husband, John."

"How do you know about this place?" the woman replied.

"Rebecca Fierle told us to come here and check it out," I said. My heart skipped a few beats, and I could feel that my face was flushed.

The woman opened the door and let us into the foyer. "Well, maybe I should call Rebecca. She has never sent anyone here before . . ." The woman began dialing a number on her cell phone. We stood in the foyer, holding our breath. Luckily, the call went into voice mail.

"Rebecca, there is a couple here to check out a room for her mother. Is it okay for them to look around?"

The woman then led us into the dining room. I think you should wait in here while we are waiting for Rebecca to return the phone call.

Arte was already secretly videotaping on his phone. We laughed and talked casually with the woman to gain her trust. An hour passed. There was no return call from Fierle.

After an hour of inquiring about the premises, and my showing great concern for the placement of my mother, the woman appeared confident that we were simply checking out the home to see if it was suitable for my fussy mother.

"Who does the cooking?" I inquired. "My mother is pretty fussy about her meals."

"I cook everything," she replied. "The food is fresh. Your mother will be pleased."

Arte glanced at his watch and addressed me. "Hun, it's getting dark out. We have to walk the dogs."

"Oh, that's right," I replied. "Well, it seems pretty nice here," I told the woman. "Would be it all right if we spoke with some of the residents and see if they like it?"

"Yeah, I guess that would be fine," she replied.

Soon, Arte and I were walking down a hallway in the six bedroom home. The doors were marked with the residents' names on them. One door was cracked open. The sign on the door read "Princess."

On the bed was a woman paging through a magazine and sipping on a cup of hot chocolate. She was wearing a jogging suit and a matching head band; she was sitting Indian-style.

We entered the room, and I whispered to her, "Are you Ulita Lopez?"

"Yes!" she replied, astonished.

She seemed to instantly understand that we were undercover and that we were there to help her. I motioned with my index finger to my lips that we should speak in hushed tones.

"How did you end up here?" I asked her.

"One day, Rebecca came to Parklands where I was working. I told her I wanted to go home to the Philippines. She said she was taking me to the airport in Orlando. Then when we reached Orlando, she brought me to this house, here."

"How long have you been here?" I inquired.

"I've been here at least six months now. Can you get me out of here? I want to go home."

"Why did Fierle put you in this house?"

"She said that she was waiting on a letter from President Obama, and that I could not go back to the Philippines under we received a letter from President Obama."

Right then, the worker walked past the room, where we were cozily seated on the bed with Ulita.

"Oh, that's Princess," she said. "We call her Princess. She helps me with the cooking and cleaning."

"Aw, that's great!" I replied.

The woman was looking suspicious again.

"Princess, it's past your bed time," the woman said, sternly.

Ulita was jotting down something on a small piece of paper, which she slipped to me when the woman turned her back. I quickly crumbled the paper and stuck it in my coat pocket.

We walked to the front door, and as we were approaching it, the woman's cell phone rang. It was Rebecca Fierle calling back.

We walked briskly to Arte's car and quickly pulled away, our hearts pounding.

"Oh, my gawd! Oh, my gawd!" Arte said, as he turned the steering wheel and we entered Highway 50.

"Now do you believe me?" I asked him.

Arte was visibly shook up. He waited 'til we were at a red light to speak. "You know, I have to tell you, I really thought you were crazy," he said.

"Yeah, I know," I replied.

When we reached Denny's, we did not go back inside. We sat in Arte's car, and he played the audiotapes for me.

"This is unbelievable," he said. "There's nothing wrong with her. She's as normal as you and me," he added.

"Yep, I told you," I replied.

I opened my purse to pay Arte for his time. We had been together more than six hours.

"Don't worry about it," he said. "I'm just happy I could help."

I took the crumpled paper out of my pocket. Ulita had written the phone number of her son, Joniel Calibo.

Within days, I had received a return phone call from the tearful son from the Phillipines.

At that point, I started contacting congressmen and senators in hopes that they would be able to assist in getting Ulita out of imprisonment and back home to the Philippines. Here's what I wrote:

Ulita Edris Lopez was hit by a car when crossing Sixth Street in Gainesville, Florida, on her way to work at Oak Hammock Assisted Living/Nursing Home. She then underwent head surgery at Shands Hospital where Rebecca Fierle found her and put her under a Fierle guardianship, claiming that Lopez was so seriously injured that she would require 24/7 care for the rest of her life. Fierle and her attorneys then took the $150,000.00 insurance settlement cheque and divvied it out among themselves, leaving only $23,000.00 for Lopez which was then placed in a guardian pooled trust. The court record shows that Lopez asked many times to go back to the Philippines where she has three sons. Her pleas have gone ignored for four years.

I now have an inside "spy," Paula Harriott, whose mother is also at Ionie's Assisted Living Center.

See the attachment. It turns out that before Fierle transferred Lopez to Orlando where she could "take better care of her," she had Lopez working as a volunteer at Parklands Nursing and Rehabilitation Center (where my mother was placed and died of a morphine sulphate overdose). See Lopez's ID, attached, as a pdf. So, while Fierle was claiming that Lopez was a vegetable, Lopez was telling the truth when she stated by phone to me/person who made the phone call for me that she was living at Parklands and working there in exchange for room and board. So, (1) Fierle placed Lopez on Medicaid so that Medicaid was actually paying the bill to Parklands, then (2) stole most of her $150,000.00 (if not all), and (3) had her working every day to "pay for her room and board" while holding her hostage at Parklands and while telling the court that Lopez is a vegetable.

We are now in touch with Lopez's son who is going to the Filippino embassy to apply, once again, for a tourist visa so he can come here and get his mother. We don't know what kind of court battle we will face. We hope you will step in and do something about this situation. Fierle has already paid for a cremation on Lopez and when Fierle pays for a cremation, she uses it, especially when she feels threatened.

Fierle transferred Lopez to Ionie's Assisted Living in Pine Hills, Florida (a sleazy "suburb" of Orlando). Ionie's is an unmarked house in a neighborhood where at least four of the eight residents there are Fierle wards. There are two Jamaican women who run the place and who sleep on the couches on the outside porch. I have now heard twice (from Dr. Larkin and from Paula Harriott) that the women are there against their will and want to go home to Jamaica and are being paid $2 an hour and were told that if they try to run or tell anyone, they will be arrested for being illegal aliens.

Please look into this situation.

Joniel Calibo's cell phone number in the Philippines is 011 63 907 532-7744.

He was told by Fierle that his mother is a vegetable. Now it turns out that not only is Lopez NOT a vegetable but that she was working as a volunteer while placed in an involuntary guardianship against her will. Lopez wants to go home. There were 16 suitcases packed with clothing at the time of her car accident in her apartment and she had already hired an attorney. Sounds like she was planning on going back to the Philippines when this accident occurred. Please help us get Lopez safely home.

When Lopez asked Fierle "when" she might get to go home, Fierle replied that they were "waiting on a letter from President Obama" and that a "letter from President Obama" was necessary before she (Lopez) would be allowed to go home.

Angela Woodhull

(352) 327-2665

I was never successful at getting Ulita back home, and her son, Joniel Calibo, was denied a Visa.

As of May 11, 2023, Ulita Lopez is still under guardianship. She has a different guardian now, since Fierle was removed from all of her guardianship cases. Kelly Pittman has taken over several of Fierle's former cases. The Orange County probate court entry on May 11, 2023 was for none other than . . . a judge's order granting fees to be paid to the guardian -- out of Ulita's money, of course.

At the time of this writing, it has been 15 years since I first met Arte Tedesco.

I am still in touch with Arte, by phone, on occasion.

"I will never forget that day," says Arte.

Ulita remains a permanent prisoner in the United States, estranged from her family in the Philippines, while she is being daily robbed of her own money.

CHAPTER FIFTEEN:

WHITE COLLAR CRIME UNIT – ORANGE COUNTY SHERIFF'S DEPARTMENT, ORLANDO, FLORIDA

In March 2012, I contacted Corporal Gerald Preston, the head of the White Collar Crime Division, and showed him my 300-page investigative report on Rebecca Fierle. The lengthy 300-page report prompted Corporal Preston to say, "Miss Woodhull, if you could **ever** show me just "one" example of EXACT provable theft committed by Rebecca Fierle, I will go arrest her."

Preston had thrown down the gauntlet, and I decided to take up the challenge.

At about this same time, an elderly man, age 72, contacted me by phone. His claims sounded incredulous, preposterous, at first. I really thought he was lying.

"You have to help me!" he stated. "I was kidnapped! I was placed in a white panel windowless van by two men from a convenience store I had just walked to, to purchase some shaving cream, and then I was delivered to the psychiatric ward of a hospital in downtown Orlando. Next thing I knew, my estranged alcoholic sister, who I haven't spoken to in more than twenty years, showed up and was assisting a professional, corporate guardian named Rebecca Fierle. Together, they had me declared mentally incompetent. Then they cleaned out my condo, took all of my belongings, and sold my condo. Now, I'm confined in a house that has been converted into a nursing home close to downtown Orlando that is owned and operated by some people from India. Please help me! There is a computer here, and I read about you on the internet. That's how I found you."

As far-fetched as it sounded, I went ahead and made plans to sneakily pick up Dr. Larkin from around the corner of the nursing home and try to assist him.

Dr. Richard Larkin, Ph.D., was dressed in a plaid sports jacket and wearing sunglasses when I picked him up from a corner in the neighborhood, a few blocks from the home where he was being imprisoned.

Together, we drove to a Denny's Restaurant in Winter Park and were allowed free access to a back banquet room where only the two of us remained for the entire day.

When corporate guardians file paperwork claiming that you are mentally incapacitated, the judge automatically grants these frequently fake and inaccurate petitions. The guardian then has 60 days to prove that you "really" are mentally incapacitated. The way she does this: She hires her regular doctors that she deals with – the same doctors on every guardianship case. These doctors always declare you "mentally incapacitated" whether you are or aren't. As Dr. Larkin explained, "They administered to me a cocktail of drugs that made me feel quite dizzy and drunk. Then three doctors appeared and began questioning me. 'What is your name? Where do you live? Who is the president?'" I already knew from my interviews with several other elderly persons who had also been confined by this same professional corporate guardian that this was her tried and tested ***modus operandi. No one –*** not even you nor I – could pass this mental capacity test while under the influence of these strong psychotropic drugs.

But I had high hopes, in this particular case, that I could help free Dr. Larkin, who spoke to me in clear and coherent tones. He was obviously not mentally incapacitated. In fact, he had just returned from a Navy ship teaching gig, teaching psychology courses to Navy men on the sea.

Together, we entered the Orange County probate courthouse and asked to see the secret records of how the guardian Rebecca Fierle had been spending Dr. Larkin's money. No one is permitted to view these secret records except for the guardian, her attorney, the judge, and the "mentally incapacitated" person – IF he or she can prove identity.

"I need to see proof of identity before I can hand over the file," the probate clerk informed us.

Corporate professional guardians always confiscate your I.D.s when they take over your life. He had no driver's license, no social security card, no credit cards, or any other forms of identity to prove he was actually the real Dr. Richard Larkin.

"Wait a second!" he suddenly declared.

"What about this?"

And then he displayed a "dog tag" that he was wearing around his neck, tucked inside his shirt, that had been issued to him by the U.S. Army decades ago. This silver colored "dog tag" included his name and social security number stamped into it.

My heart was pounding. The clerk adjusted her reading glasses and double checked to make sure that the social security number in her file, and the one on that "dog tag," were identical. Then, she went off and came back with a hard copy of the secret file.

I was so elated that I broke down and cried.

We sat in eager anticipation while she ran off copies at $1 a page of the secret file. The copies came to $10 more than I had on me. We were running out of time. Dr. Larkin had to be back at the nursing home by 6 p.m., in time for supper, or he would be declared a missing person.

I rushed down the hallway of the courthouse and accosted a man. "You wouldn't happen to have a spare ten dollars you could give me? I'm trying to assist an elderly man to get his court papers."

By golly, that man gave me a ten-dollar bill!

I rushed back into the probate office and handed the additional ten dollar bill to the clerk. I was pushing aside additional tears. This was going to be the epitome of my investigations.

Back at Denny's, Dr. Larkin and I combed through the secret files. The Orange County Sheriffs Department, Economic Crimes Unit, Corporal Gerald Preston, had previously told me, "Just find ONE GOOD INCIDENT of absolute theft and we will arrest Rebecca Fierle."

We carefully combed through the records, the billings, the endless billings.

There, on one of the billing statements, was the claim that Rebecca Fierle had paid $500 at **Bobby's Auto Repair** to have Dr. Richard Larkin's 1999 Toyota Corolla painted. It was a somewhat small amount, but it was extremely significant.

"Ah!! *This* one!" Dr. Larkin announced. "This one! She did NOT pay for a paint job on my 1999 Toyota Corolla. I paid for that paint job at **Earl Scheib's** shortly before I was kidnapped from that convenient store." NOT Bobby's Auto Repair. I don't know that guy. Never heard of such a place."

The following day, I went and visited "**Bobby's Auto Repair**" that had been listed in the secret billing file. My goal was to obtain a duplicate receipt, which I knew didn't exist if Larkin was telling the truth. If I could get the owner of "Bobby's Auto Repair" to verify that he had never worked on a 1999 Toyota Corolla in December, and that this was a made up bogus bill, then I could prove that Fierle had pocketed the $500. It was a rather small amount, but it was extremely significant.

So, I went undercover and I posed as an employee of Rebecca Fierle.

When I arrived at Bobby's Auto Repair, the mechanic was backing in a white car. It was about 7 o'clock in the morning. He was a young man covered in tattoos. The tattoos were all over his arms, like sleeves, and all over his neck, and one tattoo ran up onto his cheek. He was tall, and muscular, with piercing blue eyes. Big, black round buttons in his ear lobes.

"Hi!!!!!!!!!" I said, as I stepped out of my van and greeted him in the best ditsy-girl voice I could feign. "My boss sent me here! She lost the receipt for the 1999 Toyota Corolla you repaired in December, and she asked me to stop by and get a duplicate receipt from you."

The tattooed auto mechanic young man appeared quite irritated.

"**WHAT** 1999 Toyota Corolla? I don't remember working on any Toyota Corolla in December. In fact, I normally don't work on foreign cars at all -- ever."

I was on the verge of proving that Rebecca Fierle had totally fabricated a paint job with this unknown auto mechanic.

"Do you paint cars?"

He looked at me like I was insane.

"Does this look like an auto body shop to you?" he curtly replied.

Truthfully, I already knew from the title of his business that this was an auto repair shop, and not a body shop. My heart pounded, as I was about to verify that no such paint job had ever occurred at this random stranger's auto repair shop. This would be the absolute proof that Corporal Gerald Preston was seeking.

I followed the tattooed mechanic into his office where he plopped himself in his chair and opened his computer.

"Now, what's your boss' name?" he asked in haste, still sounding quite irritated. "Let's make this quick. I'm quite busy this morning," the stranger said.

"Rebecca," I replied.

"And what is Rebecca's last name?"

"Fierle," I replied.

The mechanic suddenly looked up at me, inquisitively and blinked hard. The room seemed to freeze as he stared at me, wide-eyed. Then, after what seemed like an eternity, he muttered,

"That's my sister!"

I suddenly felt my face flushing.

The world seemed to spin as my heart pounded in my chest. I was the mechanic was her brother! Panic surged through me, fear threatening to undo me as I envisioned being arrested for impersonating one of Fierle's employees.

"Oh!!!" I quickly added. "I think she sent me to the wrong place! You know, she's so busy . .. . "

He nodded in agreement.

"Is there another auto repair place around the corner on Michigan Avenue?"

"You mean Sloan's?" he replied.

"Yeah! That's it! Sloan's!" I added quickly as I dashed toward his door.

"Now I remember which place she told me!"

And then I hastily exited.

"I'll make sure that I tell your sister that you said 'hello'," and then I hastily rushed into my car, my heart still pounding.

I was driving rather erratically as I quickly backed out of his parking lot.

But now, I had the proof I needed. (Yeah, that's what I thought.)

Unthinkable Turn of Events

I'd finally nailed it. Or so I believed. The proof I'd toiled for was securely in my grasp. I could barely contain my excitement as I headed back to the White Collar Crime division of the Orange County Sheriff's Department, an anticipation fizzing within me like champagne bubbles.

What greeted me there was a bucket of cold water to the face. The truth was almost absurd. "We called the guardian. We provided Rebecca Fierle with a copy of your 300-page investigative report about her," Corporal Preston admitted casually. The sentence hung in the air, an atomic bomb of disbelief.

It was as though a detective, hot on the trail of a serial killer, had decided to send the suspect all the evidence stacked against them. The thought was laughable, as ludicrous as a fox being handed the blueprints to the henhouse. Yet, that was exactly what had transpired. Fierle, the fox in this scenario, was not only privy to the chickens but had been given an intimate insight into their weaknesses.

To add to the incongruity, I learned that Fierle, the very guardian under investigation, was volunteering with the Orange County Sheriff's Department hotline. She was the reassuring voice on the other end when a senior citizen, potentially one of her own victims, called in distress. This was like the wolf volunteering to babysit the lambs.

I stood there, incredulous, as the reality of the situation sank in. The illogicality of it was starkly clear. This was an investigative misstep of massive proportions, a giant leap backwards in our pursuit of justice. If there was any hope of turning the tides, we had to navigate through this paradoxical maze of misplaced trust. And fast.

Dr. Richard Larkin had recently called that hotline and had reported a fire in his condo. Shortly thereafter is when the two men in the white panel windowless truck had kidnapped him. One of the men, he said, was covered in tattoos.

At the time of this writing, Dr. Larkin is now deceased.

The Unseen Weight of Injustice

In the midst of all the chaos that was entangling me at this time, a reminder of the other concurrent battles was like a cruel jolt of electricity. The seemingly omnipresent TOHA was still engaged in its maddeningly relentless quest to wreak havoc, which resulted in more than one sleepless night. The New Mexico lawsuit was still quietly churning in the background like a volcano ready to erupt, its weight bearing down on my shoulders with a relentless pressure. And to add another layer of complexity, Nardella's continuous in-camera billings felt like an unending assault on my resolve.

The severity of these collective strains was invisibly etched into my life, a web of stress spun so tightly that it threatened to suffocate me. I was constantly toggling between various legal documents, attorney meetings, and investigations into the deep-seated corruption. Amid this ceaseless whirl of action, self-care was reduced to a distant memory. I became an emblem of a justice seeker, a warrior battling on multiple fronts, with my health silently teetering on the precipice of collapse.

And then one day, that precipice gave way.

It was a typical winter day in Florida as I walked into the Winter Park Post Office. My arms were laden with court papers, each one a weapon in my relentless fight against injustice. The air conditioning hit me like a cold slap, a stark contrast to the Florida sun outside. The line was long, the weight of the papers in my arms magnifying with each passing second. My head was throbbing, a dull ache that had become my constant companion. My vision started to blur around the edges, the world tilting on its axis.

The last thing I remember was a wave of dizziness washing over me, and then, nothing.

A stranger's quick reflexes saved me from a potentially disastrous fall, a guardian angel amidst the indifferent bustle of the post office. I woke to the concerned faces of bystanders, my body sprawled on the cold tile floor. This was the moment when I truly realized the toll my battles had taken on me, the sheer magnitude of the stress I was under.

And yet, as I sat there, regaining my strength and composure, I was resolute. I picked myself up, dusted off the fears, and resumed the fight, for I was not merely battling for myself, but for the voiceless victims of a system that had lost its way. The weight of my commitment propelled me forward. Through it all, I clung fiercely to one unshakeable belief: the power of truth would eventually unravel the injustices we were fighting against.

LACKADAISICAL STATEWIDE PROSECUTOR

Attorney Nick Cox, Statewide Prosecutor for the State of Florida, stated on March 18, 2020 in a Zoom online meeting with 32 guardianship fraud victims, "A lot of times they [e.g., guardianship victims] are coming across law enforcement who don't really understand the kit and kaboodle of guardianship [fraud]. We need to make sure the government all understands. We need a better understanding -- and resources."

Since uttering this statement in 2020, Cox has done very little to prosecute the plethora of predatory guardians in the state of Florida.

We told Cox that the judges are the real problem.

"Oh, I'm never going to prosecute any judge," Cox assured us.

Since the time of that Zoom meeting, many guardianship victims have phoned Cox's office.

Cox no longer returns victims' phone calls.

CHAPTER SIXTEEN:

Seven Long Years of the Dancing Penis Lawsuit -- The Conclusion

---

THE CONCLUSION OF THE DANCING PENIS LAWSUIT

"Do not dismiss what happened to you or minimize the severity. Be truthful with yourself about the pain you experienced." ~**Sherri Mabry Gordon**, certified life coach, anti-bullying writer and advocate

My beliefs that crime and violation of privacy is wrong come from the <u>Holy Bible</u> *and my relationship with God. Try it -- you'll like it!* ~**Carolyn P. Meinel, happyhacker.org "It Sucks to Be Me"**

Sometimes winning is a sad statement, because, in the end, what did Meinel "win"?

She had spent thousands of dollars hiring two top tier lawyers to prove I stage a lewd and lascivious show. She ended up empty handed. They dumped her.

She also lost at the court of appeals. I went up against her two big, powerful attorneys -- and I had prevailed.

"This is amazing," a New Mexico attorney stated to me. "Even seasoned lawyers rarely win on appeal. This is truly egg on their face at the Rodey law firm."

Additionally, Meinel was stripped of her beloved website, happyhacker.org, where she had previously relished endlessly tormenting innocent people.

Like me, I'm sure her numerous victims felt great relief. Was I their secret hero? I had dared to challenge a dragon. I had stood up to the New Mexican cyberbully and won back my peace of mind.

In my winning appeal, I had stated, in part, " Carolyn Meinel states that her Happy Hacker website is meant to inform and educate the public. However, her website is more about shaming and embarrassing people than informing and educating. To back up this premise, see the selected quotes of Meinel's that appear below.

Meinel is like a sting operation. She announces to the world that she can hack into people's computers. She waits for requests and then, after baiting people, exposes them for their "crimes" on her website. Telling someone, for instance, that they should "Get a job, spend less than you earn, and develop a good character so you can have more than one friend" is not an educational statement about hacking or learning to hack. It is simply a caustic remark meant to embarrass and humiliate the recipient.

In addition, Meinel's non-profit status as an "educational organization" was revoked in 2003 by the IRS."

"I too have read the Bible and nowhere in it did I find reference giving any individual the right to insult or make little of another individual," ~Dream Maker (one of Carolyn P. Meinel's victims' statements to Meinel)

So, was there *any* "win" for her vastly meaningless, futile, fool's errand efforts?

Perhaps, for a split second, she felt smug. "I read all about you raping that old lady at the nursing home. How disgusting you are!" she snapped at David Newman during the six-day trial. She walked away, snickering, her mocking laughter echoing in the courthouse halls.

But now, Rebecca Fierle, whom Meinel had been assisting behind the scenes, was arrested; her life of crime, exposed.

Disgraced Florida guardian Rebecca Fierle arrested

"She can never escape her tarred reputation on the internet," said Brian Martin (a.k.a "Jericho"). The Carolyn Meinel "Hall of Shame" erected (no pun intended) by other victims or her libelous statements, remains the top choice in a Google search under her name. "I will never take it down." ~Jericho, author of Attrition.org ("The Carolyn P. Meinel Hall of Shame")

Likewise, Meinel's damaged daughter, Valerie Aurora, also has publicly stated on the world wide web, for the whole world to forever see, that she will never speak to her mother ever again.

Says Valerie Aurora~

I do not speak to or associate in any manner with my parents or any of their spouses, past or present:

- Keith Henson

- Carolyn Meinel

- Arel Lucas

- John Bosma

- Mike Bertin

I will not under any circumstances be in physical proximity to my parents or their spouses, attend any event they are present at, or be associated with any endeavor of theirs. ~Valerie Aurora

For a daughter to make such a public statement about her mother is not only brave, but reveals the deep scars that she (Valerie Aurora) permanently carriers.

I slayed a dragon. Was it worth it?

Here are some of the most bizarre and memorable moments of the 7-year Dancing Penis Lawsuit.

BIZARRE: [1] The Court-Mandated Lunch -- *What?!*

Yep. The loony Judge Huling, after I won on appeal, decided that Meinel and I should have a lunch together. Winning, I discovered, is like swatting at a hornet's nest. The judge was pissed.

"I think the two of you should go have lunch together," the Judge Huling announced in seemingly nonchalant tones.

"What?!" I replied. "I don't want to have lunch with her, Your Honor!" I stated, my eyes wildly wide open.

Carolyn Meinel glanced over at me, snickering and grinning.

"Well, I am ordering that the two of you have lunch together," Judge Huling repeated, slamming down her gavel and exiting the courtroom.

There is nothing more unappetizing than champing on tortilla chips while sitting across from a smiling stalker, who has taken a bizarre interest in your life. In between my nibbles on cheesy quesadillas and spicy bean tacos, there sat Carolyn P. Meinel and her husband, with every copy of every CD I had ever recorded spread across the table. The judge had ordered I provide her with copies of everything I had ever published.

Meinel had brought along a little CD player. As we sat there in one of the lime-colored booths, waiting on our meals, Meinel slipped one of the Idora CDs into the tape machine.

"I love all of the songs from your Remember Idora show!" Meinel announced. "But this one is my absolute favorite!"

Meinel attempted to gently grab my hands as she began singing, but I pulled my hands away.

She wailed out the lyrics to my original song, in Little Anita's Mexican restaurant, with calypso music playing in the background over the restaurant's loud speakers. She emotionally choked on the lyrics with the utterance of every off- key note, as tears began streaming down her cheeks.

She stared at me intensely, and continued singing off key, while dipping a small handful of tortilla chips into the salsa. *"I'll always be your friend! I'll always be your friend! Until the kitchen sinks and Niagara Falls, I'll always be your friend!"*

And then, after singing these lyrics from my own original song from the Remember Idora musical, Meinel looked at me intensely and asked me,

"If you ever stage 'Remember Idora' again, will you put my name in the program? I would love for you to remember me."

In my mind, I was plotting my escape, but there was nowhere to go.

Then, as she whisked back her stringy gray hair, she looked at me intensely and asked, **"How 'bout you come out to my horse ranch and go horseback riding with me?"**

**Where to start unpacking the crazy?**

BIZARRE: [2] The 312 Pages of E-mails

After I had won at the Court of Appeals, I told Judge Huling, "This is no win, Your Honor. Carolyn Meinel has now befriended my ex-husband, the Mascarellas, and even Rebecca Fierle and her attorney. She hacks into my computer every day and then lets all of them know where I am going, and what I am writing."

Judge Huling didn't believe me. She ordered that Carolyn Meinel print out all of her emails on the spot. Meinel's face flushed. She didn't want to do it. But Huling, confident that I was lying, made Meinel spit out all of her emails -- right then and there. Meinel always brought along a printer to the courtroom.

Lo and behold – There were 312 pages of e-mails spit out in all.

The e-mails were immediately damning evidence, proving not only that the Mascarellas were now in cahoots with Meinel, but also that they had even joked about plotting my death. It turns out Meinel's "innocent" invitation at Little Anita's Mexican Restaurant, for me to come ride horses with her had a sinister motive.

p. 57 of 312 pages of e-mails: "It is possible to commit suicide by riding a horse over a cliff ... well, you get my drift." [Meinel to the Mascarellas]

The voluminous pages of emails also proved that Carolyn Meinel was sneakily composing sworn affidavits for the Mascarellas to use in their quest for my inheritance. In return, Meinel would invent additional sworn affidavits that stated anything she wanted her witnesses to state. She carefully crafted numerous sworn affidavits, each statement more aligned to what she wanted her newfound friends to say rather than the truth.

"Look at this, Your Honor!" I showed Judge Huling. "This is illegal! She cannot fabricate sworn affidavits! She cannot evolve sworn affidavits! That is against the law!"

(assortment actual, authentic emails follow)

p. 12 Meinel to Mascarellas and Philpot: "I can create affidavits (for you)."

p. 47 -- Once this evidence has been submitted to the court and is on record, this will be a valuable piece of evidence for Shirley Mascarella in her cases against Ms. Woodhull.

p. 62--"I made some changes to the text. If you'd like to review it first."

p. 100 --Please look this over. I'm trying to not overdo things. Do you feel comfortable with starting out saying nice things about her? I believe it makes you more credible if you can show what you loved about her, and that she wasn't always the way she is now. {Meinel to Philpot]

p. 119--[Meinel to Philpot]--One more revision of affidavit. Please look over this one more revision.

Finally pleased that she got Philpot to say exactly what she wanted, Meinel wrote:

· p. 124--[Meinel to Philpot]--Your affidavit is powerful. I read over your affidavit. It is powerful and does portray yourself as a solid citizen, as contrasted with Woodhull. Let's go with it!

Such revelations should have allowed the judge to immediately halt the entire judicial proceedings in my favor. But Judge Huling did not chastise Meinel.

Instead, the two of them developed a farcical courtroom repertoire reminiscent of the dynamic duo, Lucille Ball and Ethel Mertz.

Meinel, on the witness stand, turned to Judge Huling one day and smiled. "You know, my father was in the Army, and he taught me to be polite to Colored People."

Judge Huling displayed no offense. Instead, like a slapstick sidekick of Meinel, she smiled politely and nodded.

There was even blatant evidence of witness bribery among the e-mails:

p. 47--[evidence of witness bribery] [Meinel] "To make certain Woodhull can't claim I bribed you, all your accommodations will be Government standard rates for lodging and per diem.

Meinel then paid them handsomely in other ways. For instance, she bought David Hansen, my former saxophone player, a $600 saxophone and mailed it to him as a "gift."

BIZARRE: [3] Fake Arm Canes, Rolling Around on the Floor During the Six Day Trial

The Judge also did nothing during the long six-day trial when Meinel showed up wearing double arm canes and faking arthritic distress. Right in the middle of trial, Meinel laid down on the floor and drew her knees up to her chin. Then she began rolling her body from side to side while making loud groaning noises during one of my witness' testimony.

"Your Honor," I interjected. "I cannot hear what my witness is stating with Ms. Meinel down on the floor ready to give birth to a puppy."

Judge Huling simply replied, "Well, if she is feeling pain, I think it's all right for her to stretch her back."

Then Meinel let out one more ominous groan which even caused the bailiff to step forward. I thought he was going to take her pulse.

At one point, Meinel left the courtroom and checked herself into a local hospital's emergency room. We had just returned from lunch, and Mike Bertin, her husband addressed the judge. "Ms. Meinel is very distressed. She has checked into an emergency room."

Meanwhile, during the lunch break, I had found photos on Facebook of Meinel riding horses on her horse ranch and showed them to the judge!

"Okay, I'll ask her about this," Judge Huling stated, nonchalantly. But not a word was spoken about the robust horse rider, now apparently crippled again, the following day in court.

BIZARRE: [4] An Unexpected Witness, Not on the Witness List, Appeared and Was Allowed to Testify On Day Four of the Six Day Trial, we took a lunch break.

When we came back from lunch, there was a man already seated up on the witness stand waiting for court to resume. From far away, I didn't realize "who" the man was, but as I approached the front pew, the man looked at me and chuckled.

"John? John Mascarella?" I proclaimed, stunned. ***All the way from Youngstown, Ohio.***

A litigant cannot simply pull a new witness out of her ass. This is against the court rules. The witness list includes all witnesses and cannot be altered at trial.

John Mascarella belly chuckled, then openly laughed as he eyeballed me.

Soon, Judge Huling appeared from behind the black curtain.

"All rise," the bailiff declared.

Dumbfounded, I couldn't sit back down when Judge Huling stated, "You may be seated." It was a jaw-dropping moment.

"Your Honor! Ms. Meinel cannot do this! John Mascarella wasn't on her witness list!"

But Meinel interrupted. "Your Honor! John Mascarella wasn't sure he could make it 'til the last moment! He has come all this way!"

Judge Huling then allowed him to testify.

Yep. There was John Mascarella up on the witness stand – to verify that all of my shows have "dancing penises" in them!

But at this point, I didn't care about "dancing penises." I decided I would use this opportunity to prove that John and Shirley Mascarella are complete strangers to me, attempting to steal my inheritance. I succeeded in doing that.

MS. WOODHULL: (turning around to look at John Mascarella) Do I know you?

MASCARELLA: Do you know me?? Yeah, you know me.

MS. WOODHULL: How do I know you?

MASCARELLA: You were at my house playing piano one time.

MS. WOODHULL: One time?

MASCARELLA: Yeah. And we met you at your production of

Idora Park in Youngstown, Ohio at Powers Auditorium. We

knew of you for a long time, though.

MS. WOODHULL: So, you've met me twice (during my entire lifetime)?

MASCARELLA: Yes, where I talked to you, yes. Just twice.

MS. WOODHULL: But you feel entitled to my inheritance money?

(John Mascarella shifted uncomfortably, but didn't respond.)

****

In the end . . .

Meinel "won" the libel lawsuit, according to Judge Huling's Final Judgment. But what did she win?

I did not quit in my standing up to the dragons. I used this travesty of justice to alert **all** of the legislators in the State of New Mexico, who had archaic anti-bullying laws even in 2013.

Here's what I passionately wrote them:

••●⬤●••

TO: ALL NEW MEXICO LEGISLATORS

Dear New Mexico Legislators:

I am the victim of cyberstalking by a resident of your state who is also a professional computer hacker and who is also notorious and known for stalking and harassing a multitude of other people, not just me.

Your state laws appear to be archaic, and do not really address the problem of cyberstallking (do not even mention the word "cyberstalking" in your stalking statute), and, as a result, it appears that New Mexico judges are unable to understand or properly determine the (unaddressed) law of cyberstalking.

Additionally, there is not even one case (New Mexico Supreme Court or New Mexico Court of Appeal) on this subject matter, while Florida already has several Florida Court of Appeal written decision regarding cyberstalking.

I have hereby attached a copy of Florida's cyberbullying/cyberstalking laws and a copy of my own horrific experience at the hands of your New Mexico courts and New Mexico judges, and the Defendant.

Hopefully, this eye opening account will assist members of the New Mexico legislature in updating your cyberstalking and cyberbullying laws.

I am also available for speaking on this topic and/or addressing your legislators.

Thank you for your consideration.

 Sincerely,

Angela V. Woodhull, Ph.D.

1920 S.W. 72nd Street * Gainesville, FL 32607 * (352) 327-3665

****

In 2013, New Mexico rewrote their anti-bullying laws to include "cyberbullying."

---•••●•••---

Quiet Justice: An Early Retirement.

I also informed the New Mexico Judicial Commission, in a detail letter, what I had been subjected to at the hands of Judge Valerie Huling. Shortly thereafter, Huling took an early retirement. It is well known that when judges retire early, they have been chastised behind the scenes and quietly forced to retire.

---•••●•••---

The Trampoline Lawsuit – The Conclusion

Back in Gainesville Florida, I was going door-to-door with a petition for all of my neighbors to sign. "I do not wish for the Tower Oaks Homeowners Association to continue." It was amazing how many of them were willing to sign the document. Out of some 400 homeowners, I was able to gather up some 65 signatures. Additionally, 41 of my courageous neighbors who were ready to stand in court, testifying the trampoline's steadfast existence for 14 long years, and my rightful ownership of the side yard. Additionally, since the Tower Oaks Homeowners Association was violating their own covenants due to their negligence and turning the neighborhood into a ghetto pigsty eyesore, the HOA had no right to sue anybody for any reason.

I was also in contact with an attorney from Kentucky who was my ghostwriter of court papers. She was convinced that I would prevail at the trial.

I also hired an expert witness who was willing to testify that the side yard belonged to me by plat map, since the house had been wrongly placed when it had been built.

Also, there was Jan Bergemann. Jan has an anti-HOA organization in the state of Florida. He was prepared to testify that the Tower Oaks Homeowners Association was in violation of its own covenants and that the grass fines were 100% illegal. And that the covenants were actually expired and therefore unenforceable!

The evidence against Tower Oaks HOA was overwhelming.

Jumping for "Joy"! -- The Conclusion of the Trampoline Lawsuit

On the big day, 41 neighbors stood by my side in court, passionately expressing their disdain for the Tower Oaks Homeowners' Association. Our evidence against the HOA was as towering as the oaks in our neighborhood. Also, criminal charges had been written up by John Caravella from Seniors v. Crime. He was ready to testify that the grass violations were illegal. He had submitted his detailed report to the Florida Attorney General.

Jan Bergemann, head of the Florida anti-HOA organization, also came to testify; he was prepared to state that the TOHA covenants were expired, meaning TOHA has no power to sue anybody for anything.

Despite the ***overwhelming*** evidence, Judge Toby S. Monaco decided to **close down the trial three days early** and rule in favor of the Tower Oaks Homeowner's Association. Bergemann and Caravella never even got to testify, meaning a dirty judge gets to do whatever he wants to do.

Instead, while one of my expert witnesses was testifying that the side yard actually belongs to me by plat map, Judge Toby S. Monaco shockingly **<u>hung up the phone on him</u>** and then began laughing hysterically with Tom Daniel and his attorney.

••●●●●••

Fast forward to April 2022

Justice sometimes has a very odd way of coming around.

In August 2021, I decided to write a letter to the Better Business Bureau informing them that the CAM for Bosshardt Property Management was sending out letters, attempting to collect annual dues for TOHA, but that the TOHA covenants had expired and therefore no dues should be collected. It is illegal to demand dues on expired covenants.

Bosshardt responded to the BBB complaint with a carefully crafted statement, "Ms. Woodhull,

The Tower Oaks Homeowners Association, Inc. is an active Florida Not or Profit Corporation that was created and still strives to promote the health, safety, and welfare of the residents within the Tower Oaks Community. The Association is aware the original Declaration for Tower Oaks was recording more than 30 years ago in 1981. The Association has been attempting to properly revitalize the Declaration to make certain that the covenants and restrictions under the Declaration are enforceable as to the entire community for at least another 30 years. The Association received and acknowledges your request to be excluded from any future mailings, notices, etc. as to the operations of the Association and the Association will respect your request at this time."

Eight months passed. I'm sure there were many conversations behind the scenes during that eight month time period, Bosshardt fully aware that they could be sued for attempting to enforce expired covenants. Then, lo and behold – a letter sweeter than a note from Heaven arrived in all of our mailboxes on April 20, 2022. Here's the contents of the actual letter:

April 20, 2022

To: Tower Oaks Owners

Re: Termination of Management Services

Dear Tower Oaks Owner,

Please be advised that Bosshardt Property Management will terminate our Association management services on June 30th, 2022. After this date, we will no longer perform any services for the Association including accounts payable and accounts receivable.

As you may know, the governing documents of the Association have expired. Back in 2020, a revitalization attempt was made that required signatures from the owners. We received very little response. We were gearing up for a second attempt at revitalization but that has fallen apart as well. There seems to be little interest in maintaining the integrity of the Association which has led to our decision to resign as registered agent and terminate our services.

We appreciate the opportunity to have been of service to the Association for many years and wish everyone the best.

Regards,

Bosshardt Property Management
toweroaks@bosshardtcam.com

Neighbors danced in the streets. It was the equivalent of V-E Day, the end of World War II. One of my neighbors immediately took her boat out of storage and parked it in her driveway. Now, she was free to do that, and nobody cared. Another neighbor erected a basketball hoop. All in all, the neighborhood looks better than ever. Freedom has a way of motivating people to keep up their yards.

And what about yours truly? In a grand gesture of victory, I bought myself a brand new trampoline, placed it right in my side yard, and spent the day bouncing to glory, waving at my neighbors, receiving thumbs-up and grins in return.

"Huge congratulations to Angela," declared one neighbor in an email to all, "whose resilient spirit and well-crafted letter to the BBB might have just been the last straw for the TOHA. The victory is as much hers as it is for the entire neighborhood!"

I thought of also buying a huge Statue of Liberty and placing it in my side yard next to the trampoline. But I want to create a new version of Lady Liberty, with the melted expired TOHA covenants dripping from her left hand, and a Tiny Tom Daniel perched on top of her torch, his pants on fire.

Let the celebrations continue, my friends! 🎉🥂 Here's to our newfound freedom and triumph against tyranny!

"There're a few more "dishonorable mentions" who must be included in My Scrap Book," I told my friend Cheryl, the professional crafter.

Here is Attorney A. Brian Phillips, the louse who got the last $250,000 of my stolen inheritance money.

Cheryl looked at his photo and then mocked a vomiting motion.

"We used to refer to him as the 'red-faced fat fuck," I told her.

 We laughed heartily.

As you will recall, I was the kid who was severely bullied in grade school – long ago -- even before the word "bully" existed. Being verbally tormented by one's grade school classmates is something a victim never forgets.

Grade school bullies teased me on a regular, daily basis. They ridiculed my style of dress, my long curly hair, even my name. They called me "Angie Pangie," as they mocked me and pointed at me with derisive laughter. They snickered at me and called me all sorts of derogatory names. Guinea. Wop. Dago. Guido. Goomba. Meatball. They laughed even harder when they succeeded in provoking my tears. I would run home and lock myself in my bedroom. My cat, purring on my lap, as large tears from my eyes rolled onto his fur and made his back twitch.

But six decades later, nothing could have prepared me for the new tormentor in my life.

His name is "A" Brian Phillips. I never learned what the "A" actually stood for, but I had my special own word for his "A".

For those of you seeking a white-collar criminal defense attorney, there is none "better" -- none more crafty, cunning, ruthless, unethical, egotistical, and loathing than "A." Brian Phillips. If you haven't noticed yet, the acronym is CRUEL – a befitting title for "A" Brian Phillips.

Overweight and bald, with a deep crease between his reptilian brows and sagging flaccid jowls, he appears to be a massive heart attack in the making. I imagine that his colossal seizure will swiftly arrive someday while he is in the middle of choking on his own deceptive words.

His frequent outbursts of derisive laughter, as he paces the courtroom floor like a wild beast, lets you know that there is a sickening soul-lessness about his pitiful judicial existence.

Perhaps the Florida Bar, who welcomed him into their arrogant, elitist fold, can award him with more than just their ordinary "Super Lawyer" status. He deserves an extraordinary title. Just what, I don't know. Perhaps the word "creepy" for a start. But something more than just the word "creepy."

Ironically, there is also this goofiness that permeates him. In between his snickering, snorts, and undignified exaggerated belly laughs during court hearings, you come to realize the he is merely a pathetic, sadistic Bozo, the Clown. ***At the end of the day***," "A." Brian Phillips is merely a white collar criminal defense attorney who defends pedophiles with gusto, and applauds, protects, and sanctifies bottom-of-the-barrel lawyers, like the Reverend Nardellas of the world, who rob and torture the elderly.

"Who was A. Brian Phillips before he evolved into this creepy member of the legal profession?" Was he the kid who took pleasure setting ants on fire? Or maybe he was just that kid who steals your marbles and poops in the school bushes out of pure laziness. I visualize his excessive gluttony mixed with the supersized raw steak churning in his gut as his foul breath permeates the courtroom. There is a gust of septic in the courtroom with his every derisive chuckle.

"You see, ***at the end of the day,*** one can Loot an Estate through predictable time-tested judicial tactics that my cunning peers have masterminded over the years. But, ***at the end of the day,*** I add visceral pleasure to my twisted, non-answerable questions."

"***At the end of the day***" is his favorite hackneyed saying, while

"non-answerable questions" is his sickening forte.

"So, when you ***kidnapped*** your mother," he stated multiple times to me over a sickening decade of my life, while staring me down, "where did you take her?"

"I did not 'kidnap' my mother."

"Did you take her back to Gainesville? Or did you immediately drive her to Oviedo, Florida **when you kidnapped your mother**?"

I could feel my blood pressure instantly spiking. "I can't answer that unanswerable question! I **_never_ kidnapped** my mother."

"Just answer the question, or you will be held in contempt of court!" his despicable buddy judge, **Victor Hulslander,** chimed in.

Hul-*Slander*, really?

"Because **at the end of the day**, the court has noted that you kidnapped your mother!" And then he would belly chuckle until he burst into hysterical tears. The extreme pleasure that he was deriving from his courtroom antics actually seemed more pleasurable to him than the extraordinary sums of money he was raking in.

"A" Brian Phillips would proclaim, with an invisible LOL written across his shiny, bald forehead, "Your Honor, please take judicial notice that the witness has just perjured herself!" (even though there was no perjury ever committed by me) There was sheer pleasure in his bulging eyes when he would fire off these twisted malicious statements.

"Your mother hated you! Didn't she? She absolutely HATED you!" he would declare, pacing the floor, chuckling.

"No, she did not hate me," is all I could reply, as memories of her beatings would cross my mind, tears flowing down my cheeks, my head hung low on the courtroom stand.

"She did! She HATED you!" he would repeat, in a loud mocking, shrill voice. And then that sheer look of absolute utter pleasure, mixed with utter contempt and hatred, would come across his face again, as he watched me twist myself into a pretzel and weep hysterically. His belly chuckling would commence. The Despicable Judge Victor Hulslander, Judith Paul, and all of the rest of the obnoxious judicial gang, joined in with his vicarious pleasure watching me so utterly distraught.

As I wept, I could once again visualize the army of grade school children pointing at me and snickering, "Angie. Pangie! Angie! Pangie! You are soooo weird! No wonder everyone HATES you!"

But they had only stolen my lunch money.

In June 2012, "A." Brian Phillips went above and beyond the call of duty in order to loot the final $250,000.00 of my mother's million dollar non-estate (my inheritance).

"A." Brian Phillips scheduled several days' worth of depositions in Youngstown, Ohio. **Youngstown, Ohio.** Yes, we flew all the way from Gainesville, Florida back to Youngstown, Ohio for these unnecessary and excessively costly depositions.

And there we all were in the court reporter's office, downtown Youngstown – the same building where Louise and her sister Antoinette had once had their final words in Attorney Malkoff's office which commenced their 23-year fallout. The same building where Louise had threatened to throw her sister out of the window.

And there was Estranged Cousin Shirley seated cozily next to "A." Brian Phillips, her free attorney. There was also her creepy husband, John Mascarella, and the Youngstown attorney, Charlene Burke, whom John and Shirley Mascarella had taken my mother to see, in order to get her to change her will, while holding her hostage in a nursing home where she didn't want to be – a nursing home that ordered an illegal ankle bracelet that would beep if my mother attempted to leave this smelly nursing home facility where crafty Cousin Shirley had surreptitiously placed her.

By early afternoon, it was time for John Mascarella's deposition.

Although Shirley seemed to have been well prepped by A. Brian Phillips, as she repeatedly stated "I don't know" and "I don't remember" throughout her entire deposition, John Mascarella didn't seem to be so savvy.

When one of my attorneys questioned him, while the court reporter was typing, typing away, with her handy tape recorder at her side for back up, John Mascarella made a major blunder. Major, *major* blunder.

"So, did you happen to be inside the lawyer's office, with the attorney and Louise present, when Louise was executing a new will that favored Shirley?" my attorneys asked him.

"Oh, yes!" the ignorant John Mascarella boasted. "We had all become such close friends! We thought of the attorney, Charlene Burke, as our close friend!"

"And did you advise Louise on what to say to the attorney?"

"Yes, *of course*!" John Mascarella bragged, his voice rising, a twinkle in his eyes. "We wouldn't ever abandon Aunt Lou!"

Shirley was shooting subtle daggers at John during these self-incriminating statements, but ignorant John Mascarella didn't pick up on her devastated body language whatsoever.

"And how did Louise get to the attorney's office?"

"Oh! Shirley and I drove her there, of course!!!"

By this time, my attorneys and I were gently kicking each other under the table with glee. It was hard to conceal our elation. You see, John Mascarella's deposition was an admission of "undue influence" under the law. (If you drag someone to an attorney's office, and you're sitting there in the room while they're making out the new will that disinherits a natural heir, that will is considered, by law, **null and void**.) By law, as soon as Judge Monaco back in Florida would read these self-incriminating admissions from John Mascarella, he would be mandated to purge Shirley Mascarella's bogus will.

I quickly ordered a copy of John Mascarella's damning deposition transcript.

And there it was – one week later --

John Mascarella's self-incriminating words -- ***magically erased*** from the deposition transcript.

Presto.*

It had evaporated.

"A" Brian Phillips deserved a double A at this point.

CORRUPT JUDGES—the root problem of The Guardianship Racket

On June 27, 2021, Dr. Sam Sugar, M.D., the founder of AAAPG.net, authored an article titled "Black Robe Disease." Here are some excerpts from that article.

Black Robe Disease

"Justice is blind; judges are mute. Black Robe Disease?"

Dr. Sam Sugar, M.D., founder of AAAPG.net, underscores a glaring issue within our legal system, something he refers to as the "Black Robe Disease". This refers to the unchecked power, bias, and questionable conduct of judges, especially those in equity courts, such as probate, family, and divorce courts.

Sugar argues that despite the ideal of impartiality in the legal system, equity courts often generate more injustice than justice. They are almost completely unaccountable, due to the lack of checks and balances that are present in other branches of the government.

He provides some alarming statistics; for instance, in fiscal year 2018-19, of the 708 complaints received by the Florida Judicial Qualifications Commission (JQC), only 58 (8%) were investigated. This raises concerns about the effectiveness of self-policing within the judicial branch. Sugar points out that no Florida Circuit Court judge has ever been sanctioned for violating rules or the Constitution, or for routinely approving questionable fees. Complaints from the public, particularly related to equity courts, are largely dismissed, adding to the frustration of those seeking justice.

Sugar describes "Black Robe Disease" as a set of symptoms exhibited by judges that include an inflated ego, lack of empathy, outbursts of rage, and imperious attitudes, among others. These traits lead to inefficiency, waste of time, and a disregard for the very law they are supposed to uphold.

"Unfortunately, there is no known cure for this 'disease,'" says Sugar. Sugar suggests raising public awareness as a possible first step, even if it doesn't solve the problem directly. He acknowledges the difficulty in dealing with this issue due to the significant power vested in judges, and the potential risk of successors falling victim to the same issues.

The four judges who exhibit **Black Robe Disease**, responsible for the demise of my mother and the stealing of my inheritance include:

Judge Nancy Alley, Seminole County. Alley took an "early retirement" after I wrote a formal complaint about her to the JQC. At a hearing on June 5, 2008, Alley allowed Nardella and Fierle to destroy the Payable on Death Bank accounts and place all of my mother's assets into one, large guardianship bank account at Bank of America. This was actually a violation of federal law, to destroy a Totten Trust. But nothing was done about it. I cried out to other state court judges, and to the federal courts. Alley was previously given a public reprimand for dishonesty as a judge, but today, she enjoys the full benefits of being a retired judge.

Judge John D. Galluzzo, Seminole County

This judge is so despicable that multiple victims started an online petition to have him removed as a judge. Instead, Judge John D.

Galluzzo, who signed off on most of the exorbitant attorneys' fees granted to Reverend Nardella, was promoted to Chief Judge of Seminole County.

Judge Victor Hulslander, Alachua County --

Down in the basement of the Alachua County courthouse are the hard copies of court files that are then scanned in to the online court records. One day, based on a hunch, I decided to go down to the basement and ask to see the hard copy of my mother's probate file. And there, to my shock and disbelief, I found a secret document that had been written by Attorney Amy Scully, who was working as an internal attorney for the Eighth Judicial Circuit Alachua Courthouse. In this memorandum, written to Judge Hulslander, Scully informed Hulslander that it was a violation of case law and statutes to give any more money to Reverend Nardella out of my mother's bank accounts. Hulslander had then taken a yellow post-it note and scribbled on it "Do not file." And then Hulslander, ignoring the law and ignoring the advice of the internal attorney, went ahead and granted another $160,000.00 in attorneys' fees to Nardella.

When the clerk in the basement had her back turned, I put the post-it note in my hand and then crumbled it into my pocket. Then I took the secret document and unlatched it from the manilla file folder.

"Hi, could you make a certified copy of this for me, please?" I asked the clerk, trying to remain calm and poker-faced. "Oh, sure," she replied, and soon the document was scanned, stamped, and the certified copy was handed to me.

I then filed it into the court record and called for a hearing. Judge Hulslander was **furious**.

Furious. I had caught him red-handed.

I glared at him during the hearing, holding up the document. "You were advised by your own legal counsel to NOT grant any more money, and you did it anyway?"

Hulslander then recused himself from my mother's probate case and instead appointed his buddy judge, Toby S. Monaco.

Judge Toby S. Monaco, Alachua County

This judge gets top place for being the most despicable judge of them all. If you Google his name, Toby S. Monaco, you'll see that he was sued by other victims in federal court for his corrupt rulings.

Judge Monaco, as you will recall, was the laughing-hysterically, cracking up judge on the TOHA trampoline lawsuit who hung up on my expert witness and cancelled the trial. But he was also the judge who determined that the last $250,000.00 of my inheritance money should be given to Attorney A. Brian Phillips. His courtroom style is unforgettable. He dresses identical to Mr. Rogers, and speaks to the litigants in his courtroom in low, soft, soothing tones. Then, with the stroke of a pen, he allows the most corrupt to prevail. My "favorite" memory of Monaco is the day he took over as judge on my mother's probate after I had caught his recused buddy Hulslander red-handed. He knew that probate was inappropriate since everything had been left Payable On Death in the banks to me. Yet despite this knowledge, he allowed the proceedings to drag on for years and years, lining the pockets of his attorney friends who chuckled each time we left a hearing. "I've gone to the FBI!" I told them one day as we were leaving the courtroom.

"Good luck with that one!" Attorney Judith Paul replied, and they all chuckled and headed for lunch.

Today, both Monaco and Hulslander are retired judges, but they still work at The Resolution Center, as certified mediators, in addition to collecting their permanent -- for life – comfortable judges' pensions from the State of Florida.

CHAPTER SEVENTEEN:

IT'S BUSINESS AS USUAL

This book of tragedies is really not about Rebecca Fierle, Reverend Attorney M. Nardella, Jr., Judge "Sleazy" Galluzzo, Judge Toby S. Monaco (a.k.a "Judge Mr. Rogers"), Attorney "A." Brian Phillips, Attorney Judith Paul or any other of Fierle's despicable cohorts. It's about the Fierles of the world, the Fierles of America, the Fierles of American Greed.

Not long ago, during the 1800s, after the conclusion of the War with Mexico, when most of the West suddenly became the property of the United States, former residents of Mexico were taxed so highly on their properties that they were foreclosed upon by clever attorneys who then robbed them of their real estate.

We are a country founded on slavery, where the White folk mentality believed they were entitled to the free labor of Black people they had kidnapped from their homeland Africa.

When I read stories about the Trail of Tears, in which Native Americans were forced off their lands and mandated to walk barefoot from Ohio to Oklahoma, crying, cold, and hungry, I am moved to tears. Thousands of them died.

So, when I read another petition for emergency guardianship, in which the lifetime savings of an elderly person winds up being in the pockets of the Rebecca Fierles of the world and her unscrupulous, greedy attorneys/social workers/nursing home administrators, et al. friends, I am simply reminded of the tragic, shameful violations of human rights that have been characteristic of the United States of America from the onset.

On February 28, 2020, I met with Attorney Finkbeiner, two agents of the FDLE, and the head of economic crimes for Orange County, Florida. They allegedly wanted to read my detailed 8 year old report on Rebecca Fierle, detailing financial crimes I had written about seven or eight years previously. They were finally taking my report seriously. *Or **were** they?*

One additional noteworthy observation – Fierle committed crimes in more than 13 Florida counties, yet only the Orange County Sheriffs' Department (economic crimes) was present. Seminole County Sheriffs' Department (where a large number of Fierle's victims were placed (or transferred to)), and all other Florida counties, were not present at the meeting.

Best-selling author CARL HIAASEN, said, "Florida really is a magnet. It's a magnet for predators. It's a magnet for scammers. It's a magnet for sleaze. It also makes for [true] stories that are beyond what you would think of writing in a novel." On his website, he states, "Carl Hiaasen was born and raised in a bizarre place called Florida, where he still lives."

All the weird shit always happens in Florida. ~Comedian Rob Schneider, 6/18/2023

"Our society has treated any kind of fraud or deception of the elderly as a civil offense to be handled through the court system by filing a lawsuit. Why doesn't our society recognize that that is theft? And theft is a crime. A guardian that commits a fraud actually commits a crime." Sharon R. Bock, Clerk and Comptroller, Palm Beach County, Florida

"This is supposed to be America. You wonder what's going on in America. I can't believe it. I still can't believe it." ~John Savanovich, Needham, Massachusetts (penniless multimillionaire and ward of the state of Massachusetts) "They took my properties away from me and said it was all legal. They sold it for just over $3 million and to this day, I never received any proceeds – not even two dollars. As it is now, I'm totally penniless. Totally penniless. And the judge said I'm not allowed any financial resources whatsoever. I'm a ward of the state."

~John Savanovich (John fought to have his rights restored, but his fight has been futile.)

"It's estimated there are 1.5 million adults under guardianship in the United States. The rampant abuse of laws meant to protect the elderly has left many seniors penniless, powerless, and isolated from their families." ~Dirty Money "Guardians, Inc." (aired March 11, 2020)

"Guardianship exploitation is the (number one) crime of the 21st Century." ~Dirty Money "Guardians, Inc." (aired March 11, 2020)

FIERLE ARREST TRANSCRIPT

**

[KNOCK ON THE DOOR OF THE RESIDENCE OF REBECCA FIERLE BY MARION COUNTY, FLORIDA DEPUTY SHERIFF]

FIERLE: Hey!

Deputy: Hello, are you Rebecca?

FIERLE: I am.

Deputy: I'm Deputy Young. What's your last name?

FIERLE: Fierle-Santoian.

Deputy: Yeah, I wasn't going to say that.

FIERLE: I know. Right? (laughs)

Deputy: I have a warrant for your arrest.

FIERLE: Yes, I was talking to my attorney today and my plan was we were supposed to go down to Hillsborough to do a walk through. That's what we were promised by FDLE when we um . . . .

Deputy: They called us and said that they have a warrant and come arrest you.

FIERLE: Great! Which is basically the opposite of what they were telling my guy because, like I said, I've already talked to the bail bondsman in Hillsborough. We were told they were going before the judge ten and noon today and then the FDLE guy called my guy and said, "Well, there's no, they haven't been in front of the judge yet."

Interesting. They assured me that they would cooperate. Imagine that.

Well, I'm not a flight risk. I'm not going anywhere, so you don't have to worry about that.

[The deputy then handcuffs her.]

FIERLE: You can keep it (hand cuffs) up front [if] you want.

Deputy: All right. Like I said, I'll put these on the front. You're cooperative.

FIERLE: Yeah, absolutely. I'm not on meth. (cracks up really hard)

FIERLE: This has been an ongoing thing since last year.

I'm a mess (laughs heartily)

Deputy: Well, I'm not . . .

FIERLE: No, I know you're not an asshole.

(FIERLE ENTERS THE DEPUTY'S CAR)

FIERLE: _That's when the FUN starts!!!_

(now inside the deputy's car)

FIERLE: Thank you!!!!

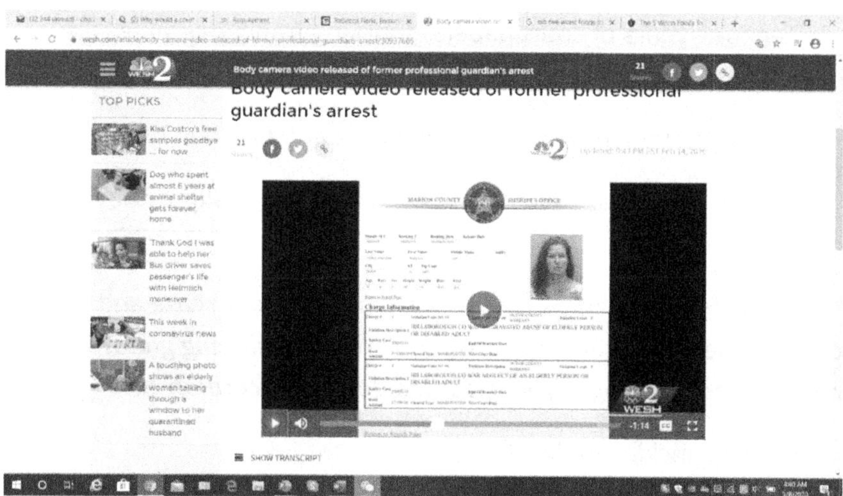

GRAND FINALE:

 On June 8, 2018, I walked into Horst Gasthaus (a German restaurant in North Myrtle Beach), donning my tiara and purple wig.

Clad in my 80's prom dress, I greeted restaurant patrons with my trademark "WEEEE-OOO!!!! It's Polka Time!!!"

Restaurant patrons picked up the maracas I had passed out to them and shook them with vigor. Several children came up to the stage area and jumped up and down – their version of the polka dance.

A couple of drunken patrons came up and performed a comical version of the chicken dance.

And, indeed, I sang my heart out while the restaurant patrons clapped their hands and sang along.

"Oh, Polka Fans!" I said, while brushing away tears. "I'm so happy to be back! It's been a long time."

I was overwhelmed. Overwhelmed with joy.

It had been more than ten years.

Ten long years of court papers, shocking fraud, migraine headaches, and gavels.

And now, I opened my accordion case and brushed off the dust.

Somehow, a magnifying glass had managed to slip its way into my accordion case.

I removed a magnifying glass from my accordion case and carefully peered through it at my audience. **Magnifying glass? Why does she have a magnifying glass inside here accordion case?**

Then I chuckled in delight. . . .

When you play the accordion, you are a one-man band. You are the life of every party. ~Weird Al Yankovick

I put down my magnifying glass and picked up my accordion and strapped it on in delight.

You see . . .

I'm not just a licensed private investigator.

I'm also Angelina, the Polka Queen!

WEEEEE-OOOOOOOH!!!!

AFTERMATH

A few weeks ago, I visited my mother's grave. I walked over to her headstone, where she and my father lay side by side.

I placed a bouquet of yellow flowers on top of her grave.

Yellow was her favorite color.

Here's a song I wrote on the day of my mother's death

Had a dream where I was picking all the poppies in a field
I looked up, and in the sunlight I saw you
You smiled for just a moment, then vanished when I touched you
Then I fell among the flowers, and I cried
I wept for you
Every time the phone rings now, I always wonder if it's you
With a thousand things you want for me do to do.
Every day you're in my thoughts;
You're remembered, not forgotten
And I walk among the flowers and I cry

I weep for you.
So, let me hold your hand, and put your spirit next to mine
While your heart inside still's warm, we can get closer
Let me hear the stories that you've told a million times
For a million times is not enough, when it's all over. Over.
Mama, I'm an orphan now
Mama, I get lonely
Mama, where's your medicines
I wish I'd known, if only
Oh, mama!
Domini y patre y e fili y e tu
Domini y spiritu and God Bless you!
Domini y patre y e fili y e tu
Domini y spiritu and God Bless you!
GOD BLESS YOU! I MISS MY MAMA!
GOD BLESS YOU! I MISS MY MAMA!
GOD BLESS YOU! I MISS MY MAMA!
Oh, Mama!

FINAL THOUGHTS

I know what you're thinking.

I know what you're going to ask me.

You're going to ask me what you can do to make sure that predatory guardianship never befalls upon you or your loved ones.

"Welcome to The Club"

Just the other day, I received yet another phone call from yet another guardianship victim. I have frequently received these types of phone calls for the past 15 years.

"My family is quite wealthy," he stated, sounding very distressed. "The money is going, going, going . . . so rapidly. What can I do? Do you know a good lawyer who can assist me?"

"Nope," I replied. "Welcome to The Club."

"**The Club**?" he asked.

"Yep, you're now part of a club you never asked to join. Welcome."

I always feel rather numb when I say this. I know I sound calloused, unfeeling, unsympathetic, sarcastic...

Not a week passes when I don't receive one of these tragic phone calls.

The Courthouse Vultures

"Vultures circle their prey while flying high in the sky. And when they finally pounce, they strip their victims down to the bone, taking everything, including the dignity of their victims. It's impossible to fight back.

"There are growing complaints across the country about a very different kind of vulture. And their victims? They are disabled. Their victims – they are elderly.

"Ninety-six year old Margaret Landgrebe may spend her final days separated from her family. They will need permission from strangers to even visit.

This is what happens when courts appoint guardians to replace families. This is what happens when the lawyers swarm. It begins with a wealthy parent, a relative who likely wants a bigger cut of the estate than they think they might get. It ends with a collection of doctors and lawyers and experts who can control your mom or dad's every move.

"Imagine strangers eating away at inheritance your mom and dad worked for all their lives – for you. The U.S. Senate Committee on Aging has now issued the warning about the 1.5 million Americans under guardianship control.

"U.S. Senator Bob Casey stated, 'In many cases, guardianship is a blunt tool that transfers ALL decision-making power about the life of a person to someone else. Guardianship can also put a person at risk for abuse, neglect, and exploitation.'" ~Wayne Dolcefino, Dolcefino Consulting, "*The Courthouse Vultures*," Premiered on YouTube, May 16, 2023.

When **The Courthouse Vultures** swoop in, there are three types of reactions from victims.

Type One Victims are people who realize quickly that there is no way to ever triumph over the guardianship hustle. They quickly give up and get back to their everyday, ordinary lives, although they are forever changed from knowing that their loved ones were robbed and tortured by complete strangers through perfectly "legal" maneuvers.

Type Two Victims fight wholeheartedly for a while – for a good, long while. I was a Type Two Victim. I fought more than 12 years, contacting every agency under the sun, to no avail. Eventually, I felt like a wind-up toy banging into the wall. "I just don't want to spend my entire life trying to solve the unsolvable," I told David Newman.

"I don't blame you," he replied. David, a **type one**, got out of **The Club** a long time ago, and is back to happy harmonica playing and enjoying weekend outings with his new lover in Minnesota.

Then, there are **the Type Three Victims.** They never give up. Rick Black. Hillary Hogue. Elliott Bernstein. Dr. Robert Sarhan. They are the True Believers.

I very much admire **The Type Three Victims.** They will always be my heroes, and I am honored to know them.

At the time of this writing, Sarhan is suing the FBI for not listening to us and not acting upon all of our complaints. Sarhan has been in The Club since 2007. "I will **NEVER** give up!" he told me. I am reminded of what Attorney Judith Paul said to me when I announced to her, "I am going to the FBI!"

She scoffed and replied, "Good luck with that one!" And she walked away chuckling.

I love Robert. He is one of my heroes. We will be friends forever. But I, personally, decided to reduce my membership in **The Club** to "alumni" for the sake of my sanity.

Our fiercest leader at the time of this writing, Rick Black, founder of CEAR (Center for Estate Administration Reform), is currently being sued for allegedly "libeling" a crooked guardianship attorney that Black has exposed on his website, CEAR. If Black doesn't end up bankrupt from this despicable and retaliatory litigation, he might continue the fight. His strategy is to find guardianship reform activists in all 50 states who are willing to continuously write and contact legislators in their respective states.

Meanwhile, our former leader, Dr. Sam Sugar after many long decades of fighting and exposing the Guardianship Racket, has thrown in the towel. Despite more than two decades of his extraordinary efforts, Dr. Sam Sugar, age 75, has retired from **The Club.** I don't blame him. He is the author of "Guardianship and The Elderly: The Perfect Crime."

Then there's Elliott Bernstein. He has been fighting the fight for more than 20 years. He now needs open heart surgery. ***Stress.***

"Short of a French Revolution, is there really any progress we are actually making?"

I posed this rhetorical question to Rey Contraras. He's a hardcore, super dedicated, **Type Three** Victim. He's one of the newer members of The Club and has been systematically researching and exposing guardianship fraud for the past four years. He's done one hell of a job. For example, he discovered that a corrupt judge in Polk County, Florida, is ending up with most of the houses that guardians sell after they evict their "wards" from their homes. Convenient, eh?

"And so what has happened with all of your exquisite research?" I asked Contreras.

Rey recently assisted another member of The Club, Lesa Martino, who lost her $450,000.00 home in Florida for writing truth about a corrupt guardian on her Facebook page. The guardian, Traci Hudson, then sued Martino for libel and won, of course. Martino's house was then sold and used to pay Hudson's attorneys' fees. Martino was left homeless.

Ironically, Hudson is now facing 23 felony charges related to guardianship fraud. Like Fierle, Hudson is no longer a guardian.

"So, what is our 'win' in Martino's case?" I asked Contraras. "She lost her $450,000 home – for exposing a corrupt guardian!"

"Well, we kept her from going to jail!"

Then there are some members of The Club who simply vanish from the face of the Earth.

Type Three members of **The Club** generally believe that their approach to end guardianship fraud will be the winning ticket – the ultimate, correct approach.

One of those Type Threes who comes to mind is Lori Bennett. More than a decade ago, I met with Bennett in a restaurant here in Gainesville, Florida. She came across as extremely sophisticated. She was dressed elegantly and had all of her files neatly in order, stacked next to her in the restaurant booth.

Bennett boasted that she holds a paralegal degree. "I'm taking an approach that no one – no victim -- has taken before," she boasted. "I'm taking all of our stories to the FBI!" she stated. She leaned forward in the booth where we were sipping on coffee. "The reason why the FBI hasn't taken this seriously up until now is because none of the victims are organized. I am approaching this in an organized fashion!" she boasted. And then she removed a form from her briefcase. "I want you to fill this form out very precisely. You have to put down your mother's name, your name, the judge's name, a brief description goes here. Answer all of the questions precisely as I have written them here."

"Okay," I replied, taking the form from her.

It's been several years now since any of us have heard from Lori Bennett. It's as though she has evaporated from the face of the Earth. Her website, www.guardianshipmafia.org, no longer exists. Her phone number is disconnected. The e-mails I have sent to her bounce back: ***undeliverable***.

Latifa Ring was our original organizer. She, too, had a well-organized website with thousands of victims' stories in brief. In 2011, Ring took 41 of us to Washington, D.C. where we marched and spoke on the Congressional Record. Shortly thereafter, Ring, who was only 52 years old, died of colon cancer.

Stress.

Then there was Jeff Frazier, a Seminole County deputy, who left law enforcement and started a website, exposing all of the corruption in Seminole county. The evidence he assembled, including guardianship fraud in Seminole County, was overwhelming. Frazier died a few years ago of cancer. His website of damning evidence, SeminoleWatch.Com, no longer exists.

****

I didn't want this book to be just another sad story. Sad stories are boring. Nobody wants to hear someone's sad story. We all have sad stories. Even Brittney Spears has gone on with her life after her guardianship nightmare, and no one seems to even understand what her story was all about.

"Something about her father stealing her money, right?" a checkout clerk at Dollar General hastily speculated when I asked him what the guardianship of Brittney Spears was all about. He had no clue that The Guardianship Hustle is a scam that could happen to anyone.

Anyone.

Anyone, including you, can be snatched from your home, confined to a urine-smelling nursing home, while all of your money and worldly possessions are confiscated, and divvied up among grinning strangers. And then your life snuffed out. The Courthouse Vultures are just a phone call away.

Perhaps this story will finally be the guardianship story that sticks in one's belly and finally makes a difference. That is my ultimate goal.

"It's Raining Lawsuit in My Life, and I Just Wanna Be . . . ANGELINA, THE POLKA QUEEN."

Yesterday, I was in a recording studio singing and recording ***"O Solo Mio!"***

I'm putting samples of my vocals and accordion playing on YouTube. After all, no nursing home wants to hire Her Majesty, The Polka Queen, unless they can hear a few samples of her accordion playing.

I want to go on a national tour, ***The Great American Sing-Along Show!*** My dancers will throw stuff into the audience. Everyone will wear a tiara or crown. Everyone will sing along! And I'll promote this book!

Oh, my mother would be so proud of me!

****

"I wish I were supernaturally strong so I could put right everything that is wrong." ~Greta Garbo

APPENDIX

WHERE ARE THEY NOW?

Reverend Anthony M. Nardella, Jr.. Esq. -- Are you looking for a great guardianship attorney? Perhaps Reverend Anthony M. Nardella, Jr., or his son, are for you. They have formed a family law partnership business, Nardella and Nardella, LLC. They can be contacted here:

If you want to pray with them, or contribute to their ministry, go here: https://www.heartoftitus.org/

Attorney Judith B. Paul -- According to the Florida Bar website, Attorney Judith B. Paul is now retired and sipping on pina coladas as she basks in the sun. Last time I saw her, she was flinging an invoice down Judge Monaco's conference table, demanding more hefty payments out of my inheritance money.

Attorney "A" Brian Phillips – (Orlando) Are you looking to hire an excellent **white collar criminal defense attorney** who will represent you in a will contest? I know it sounds weird, but it's something Attorney "A" Brian Phillips can do for you – at no cost to you! Free of charge! Looking to steal your cousin's inheritance money? **"A" Brian Phillips** and his team might be the right choice for you! They can be contacted here:

Shirley Mascarella -- According to mylife.com, Shirley
Mascarella is 82 years old because Shirley's birthday is on
04/23/1941. Shirley Mascarella lives in Youngstown, OH. Sometimes
Shirley goes by various nicknames including Shirl A. Mascarella.
Taking into account various assets, Shirley's net worth is greater than
$250,000 - $499,999; and makes between $70 - 79,999 a year. (Funny.
When I was investigating her, Chase Bank confirmed she had about
$5,000.00 in her bank account.)

John Mascarella -- According to mylife.com, John Mascarella is 84
years old and was born on 09/08/1938. Youngstown, OH, is
where John Mascarella lives. John also answers to John C Mascarella,
and John Charles Mascarella, and perhaps a couple of other names.
(Loved "a couple other names") We know that John's political
affiliation is currently a registered Democrat; ethnicity is Caucasian;
and religious views are listed as Christian. Taking into account various
assets, John's net worth is greater than $250,000 - $499,999; and
makes between $70 - 79,999 a year.

Attorney Evelyn Cloninger -- Evelyn Cloninger was born on
09/06/1952 and passed away at 67 years old. Oviedo, FL on
09/09/2019 – three days after an article appeared in the Gainesville
Sun, exposing the forgery of Angela Woodhull's signature committed

by Cloninger, which commenced and ignited a predatory
guardianship upon Woodhull's mother.

R.I.P., Evelyn!

"I have never killed a man, but I have read many obituaries with
a lot of pleasure." ~Attorney Clarence Darrow

(Judge, retired) Toby S. Monaco -- now works as a mediator for
The Resolution Center, Gainesville, Florida, and receives a
comfortable lifetime pension for his former excellent work as a judge.

(Judge, retired) Victor Hulslander -- now works as a mediator
for The Resolution Center, Gainesville, Florida, and receives a
comfortable lifetime pension for his former excellent work as a judge.

(Judge, retired) Nancy Alley -- was given a public reprimand by the Florida Supreme Court for running a dirty judge campaign. See: **https://www.tampabay.com/archive/1997/10/19/publicly-tarred-and-feathered/**

Nonetheless, she went on to become a judge in Seminole County and is remembered by Woodhull for signing an Order that violated federal banking laws, allowing Reverend Nardella to destroy Payable on Death bank accounts in trust for Angela Woodhull and using the stolen bank accounts to pay himself, with Judge Nancy Alley's approval. When the JQC was alerted to the illegal order, Alley suddenly took an early retirement. Here's her public reprimand: **http://library.law.fsu.edu/Digital-Collections/flsupct/dockets/90691/op-90691.pdf**

Judge John D. Galluzzo – continues his reign of terror in Seminole County. A petition to get him kicked off the bench is here: https://www.thepetitionsite.com/519/950/829/destructive-and-corrupt-judge-galluzzo-off-the-bench-now/

Read more about Galluzzo here: http://www.therobingroom.com/florida/Judge.aspx?id=2154

After converting most of my inheritance money into attorney's fees for Reverend Nardella, and my informing the JQC, ***Galluzzo was promoted to Chief Judge***!

Read more about Galluzzo here:

Watch a video here, demanding Judge Galluzzo's resignation:

Ira Judson Philpot -- (ex husband, "King Ira") Is now a 50-year-old man who hangs out in skateboard parks, skateboarding on his skateboard.

Judge Valerie Huling (retired) – Judge Huling also took an early retirement.

[Check out https://uglyjudge.com/] Usually, judges are asked to take an "early retirement" when they are caught in the cookie jar. I found out from a fellow victim at a national conference for guardianship victims that Huling was also involved in The Guardianship Racket in many New Mexico guardianship cases. One of the victims at the guardianship conference had lost her inheritance because of Huling.

Huling also got into some hot water here: https://www.afscme18.org/archive which may be another reason why she is no longer a judge. She stated at the DP trial that she is a firm believer in "freedom of speech" and that's why she denied my request for injunction and let the DP case drag on and on for seven years. Ironically, she got in trouble with the city because she ordered public records be sealed, despite the Sunshine Law. Her zeal for "freedom of speech" suddenly became "a right to privacy."

"It is unfortunate that a judge [Huling] has rendered a decision to deny the citizens of New Mexico easy access to public information about how their taxpayer dollars are being spent," Rue said Monday. "This decision is a blow to open and transparent government." The

local government was furious with her.
https://www.afscme18.org/archive

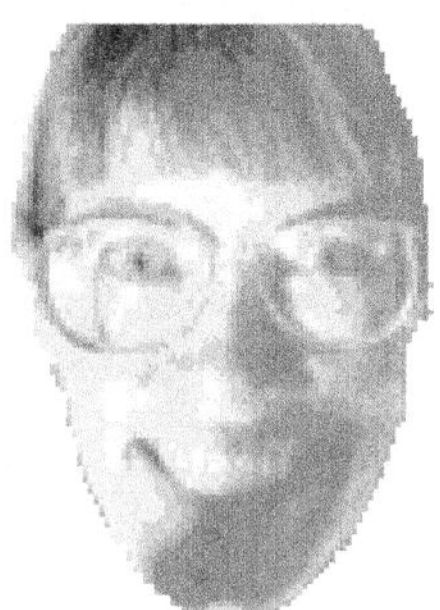

Carolyn P. Meinel – no longer seems to cyberstalk and harasses people. She is Facebook friends with Ira Judson Philpot. She took down her Happy Hacker website. According to her Facebook posts, she now spends her time riding asses on her horse farm. However, the Carolyn P. Meinel Hall of Shame is still up and running on the internet, and Jericho (a.k.a. Brian Martin), one of her former victims that she stalked and harassed for many years, says he will **never** unpost The Carolyn P. Meinel Hall of Shame.

Thomas A. Daniel, Esq. -- retired attorney, who formerly terrorized The Tower Oaks neighborhood for decades and created illegal grass fines. He now enjoys a quiet financially comfortable life as a retiree in Montana.

David A. Newman (my ex boyfriend) – now lives in Minnesota, playing his harps, and enjoying life with his new girlfriend. He doesn't want to hear anything about guardianship fraud ever again.

Rebecca Fierle -- **while awaiting her sentencing, Fierle has reactivated and renewed her business license, Geriatric Care Management, with the State of Florida.**

Detail by Registered Agent Name

Florida Limited Liability Company

GERIATRIC MANAGEMENT LLC

Filing Information

Document NumberL13000085789FEI/EIN Number46-3054349Date Filed06/12/2013StateFLStatusACTIVE

Principal Address

1646 HILLCREST ST.
ORLANDO, FL 32803

Mailing Address

3280 SE 20th Ave
ocala, FL 34471

Changed: 04/14/2021

Registered Agent Name & AddressFIERLE, REBECCA

3280 SE 20th Ave
ocala, FL 34471

Address Changed: 04/14/2021

Authorized Person(s) DetailName & Address

Title MGR

FIERLE, REBECCA

3280 SE 20th Ave
ocala, FL 34471

Annual Reports

Report Year	Filed Date
2021	04/14/2021
2022	07/25/2022
2023	03/17/2023

Document Images

03/17/2023 -- ANNUAL REPORT   View image in PDF format

search.sunbiz.org/Inquiry/CorporationSearch/SearchResultDetail?
inquirytype=RegisteredAgentName&directionType=Initial&searchNa
meOrder=FIERLEREBECCA%20L130000857890&aggregateId=flal-
l13000085789-b577815c-96c0-4b53-8850-
1d9afafc78b2&searchTerm=Fierle&listNameOrder=FIERLEDEBRAR%2
0L110000430680

But there's more. Fierle has also become a *licensed life coach*!

Yep. You heard me right. While Fierle awaits her sentencing, I discovered that Rebecca Fierle has opened her own Life Coach School.

Detail by Registered Agent Name

Florida Limited Liability Company

UNLIMITED LIFE COACH SCHOOL LLC

Filing Information

Document NumberL20000189825FEI/EIN Number85-1757546Date Filed07/06/2020Effective Date07/01/2020StateFLStatusACTIVE

Principal Address

3280 SE 20TH AVE
OCALA, FL 34471

Mailing Address

3280 SE 20TH AVE
OCALA, FL 34471

Registered Agent Name & AddressFIERLE, REBECCA

3280 SE 2OTH AVE
OCALA, FL 34471

Authorized Person(s) DetailName & Address

Title MGR

FIERLE, REBECCA

3280 SE 20TH AVE
OCALA, FL 34471

Annual Reports

Report Year	Filed Date
2021	04/14/2021
2022	07/25/2022
2023	03/17/2023

Document Images

03/17/2023 -- ANNUAL REPORT   View image in PDF format

Remember Rebecca Fierle? Smiling and laughing in the back of a cop car on the day she was arrested? Well . . .

She wrote a letter to Elder Affairs, State of Florida, stating she doesn't want to be anybody's guardian ever again. Here is the letter:

Rebecca Fierle
PO Box 568625
Orlando, FL 32856

July 25, 2019

Via U.S. Mail to:
Richard Prudom, Secretary
Florida Department of Elder Affairs
4040 Esplanade Way
Tallahassee Florida 32399-7000

Via email to:
prudomrm@elderaffairs.org

Re: OPPG Registration Resignation

Dear Secretary Prudom:

Please be advised that I am hereby resigning as a registered professional guardian in the state of Florida. I have instructed all of the attorneys with whom I work to file resignations as guardian on my behalf in my cases. That process is proceeding expeditiously. Successor guardians will be appointed. I will seek a discharge in all of my cases. The exact timing of the appointment of successors and my discharges are not entirely in my control because I rely on my attorneys to prepare the resignations and judges to accept them and appoint successors. I will not be seeking reappointment in any cases nor will I seek future appointments as a guardian.

Sincerely,

Rebecca Fierle

cc: Anthony Palmieri
        apalmieri@mypalmbeachclerk.org

Instead . . . .

She wants to help you ... with your life decisions. Yep.

Between her two businesses, registered in the state of Florida, I can hear the conversation already.

[***Knock. Knock***.]

"Hello, Mrs. Smith! How are you feeling this morning?"

"Oh, I'm doing pretty good!"

(Fierle, checking out her sparkling wedding bands and stunning jade earrings.)

"Do you have a moment to talk with me?"

"Why sure, honey. I'm just sitting here watching TV."

Fierle sits down next to the bed, opens her briefcase.

"I'm a life coach; I can help change your life!"

⸺ ••●❍●•• ⸺

APPENDIX

Judge Nancy Alley's Shocking Illegal Order that Violated Federal Banking Laws

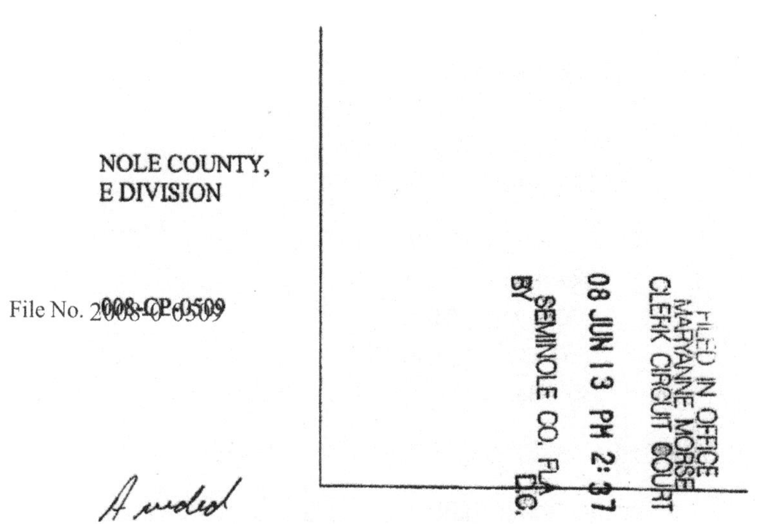

CIRCUIT COURT FOR SEMINOLE COUNTY,

FLORIDA   PROBATE

RE: GUARDIANSHIP OF

LOUISE A. FALVO,

ORDER **incapacitated** ON PETITION FOR ORDER AUTHOR<u>IZ</u>ING LIQUIDATION OF

BANK ACCOUNTS WITH VARYING BENEFICIARY DESIGNATIONS,

DIRECTING NECESSARY THE
DESIGNATION OF BENEFICIARIES
THE DEPOSITORY'S ACCOUNTS AND
DETERMINING THE ORDER OF

PRIORITY FOR SPENDING
MONEY FROM SAID
ACCOUNTS FOR THE
PAYMENT OF WARD'S
EXPENSES, AND

<u>ABSOLVING THE GUARDIAN OF ALL RELATED LIABLITY</u>

On the petition of <u>REBECCA FIERLE,</u> as
Guardian of the Person and Property of
LOUISE FALVO, the Ward, for an Order Petition
For Orda Authorizing Liquidation Of

Bank Accounts with Beneficiary Designations, Directing If Necessary
The **Designation**

Of Beneficiaries in The Depository's Accounts and
Determining die Order Of Priority For

Spending Money From Said Accounts For
The Payment Of Ward's Expenses, and
Absolving the Guardian Of All Related
Liability (the "Petition"), the Com finds that
all interested persons have been served
proper notice of this proceeding or have
waived notice thereof. The Court having
examined the file in this proceeding and
having considered evidence presented
regarding the criteria established by relevant
portions of Florida Statutes, and finding that
the material allegations of the petition are
true and being otherwise fully advised, it is

ORDERED and ADJUDGED as follows:

1. The Petition is hereby granted; and

2.   Ihe Plenary Guardian of the Property is
hereby authorized and directed to:

a.   liquidate all of the Ward's
bank accounts at Bank of America,
Wachovia Bank, and Farmer's
National Bank, without regard to
whet-ha the accounts have
beneficiary designations; and

b.   deliver the proceeds from
the said accounts to the court
appointed depository,

Bank of America, to be
deposited, held and managed
in accordance with this court's
Order Designating Depository
for Assets dated May 5, 2008;
and

3.   The court-appointed depository, Bank of America, is hereby ordered, authorized and directed to receive all of the liquid assets of the Ward from the Ward's accounts at Bank of America, Wachovia Bank and Farmer's National Bank in accordance Wiff this court's Order Designating Depository for Assets dated May 5, 2008.

4.   The Court further finds and determines that the Wad's apparent intentions regarding her estate plan are not currently determinable; and it is therefore

ORDERED and ADJUDGED:

5.   The Plenary Guardian of the Property is hereby ordered and directed to open accounts with the Ward's cash proceeds at the depository, of America, without regard to ITF or POD beneficiary designations on any accounts; and to pay the living expenses of tie and other guardianship expenses without attempting to preserve the alleged intentions or estate plan of the Ward; and

6.   REBECCA FIERLE, the Plenary Guardian of the Property and Person of die Ward, is

hereby absolved of all liability and responsibility for not attempting to preserve the alleged

intentions or estate plan of the Ward, except that records of the accounts at liquidation be maintained for potential distribution should any remain at death.

ORDERED on _______ 11 _______ 2008.

NANCY F. ALLEY
Circuit Judge

AN E-MAIL REGARDING REVEREND NARDELLA'S BILLINGS WITH BLANK PAGES

Angela V. Woodhull <angelavwoodhull@yahoo.com> wrote:

Sent: Friday, July 24, 2009 8:33:46 AM
Subject: Please send reports, etc.

Hello to all~

Please send to me at your earliest possible convenience the reports you would have stated for the record in court.

 I am asking for a recusal and a rehearing.

I found some additional damning evidence in the actual physical records of the court yesterday. The clerks allowed me to look at the actual physical pieces of paper. As you know, Nardella previously had a "sealing" order in effect from Judge Galluzzo that is no longer in effect because it was overturned by the 5th DCA. So, in one of the "sealed" envelopes there appears a cover letter from Nardella to Galluzzo asking him to review a billing statement from October l, 2008 through November 30, 2008 for Galluzzo's review "in camera." The billing statement, which totals $25,718.61, is simply page upon page upon page of blank entries--dates, hours spent, price--but the description part is left totally blank.

Trying to figure out how the judge was supposed to review pages of nothingness. The sealing order (now defunct) stated that anything Nardella billed for had to be looked over and approved by Judge Galluzzo.

———— ••◉••• ————

EMAIL FROM REVEREND NARDELLA TO ME

On Fri, 9/26/08,

Anthony Nardella <anardella@zkslawfirm.com> wrote:

From:

Anthony Nardella <anardella@zkslawfirm.com>

Subject: RE: Fierle,

Rebecca - Falvo, Louise A., Guardianship of: LIABILITY

To:

angelavwoodhull@yahoo.com

Cc: "Rebecca Fierle" <rfierle@msn.com>

Date: Friday, September 26, 2008, 1:25 PM

Ms. Woodhull,

We are and have been

 reviewing the situation regarding the security of the

guardianship assets. I will be discussing some

 options with the guardian

shortly. In the meantime, we recognize that you are likely the ultimate

beneficiary of most if not all of the guardianship assets. We therefore want to take your concerns into consideration. Do you have any preferences for investment of the assets pending their final distribution?

Thank you and I look forward to hearing from you.

Anthony M. Nardella, Jr.

Phone: 407-425-7010

Facsimile: 407-425-2747

315 East Robinson Street, Suite 600

Orlando, FL 32801

••◦●◦••

WOODHULL V. MEINEL – A WIN FOR WOODHULL.

WOODHULL'S MOTION FOR SUMMARY JUDGMENT [ARGUMENTS WHICH HELPED WIN WOODHULL'S APPEAL]

STATE OF NEW MEXICO

COUNTY OF BERNALILLO

SECOND JUDICIAL DISTRICT COURT

No, CV-2007-346

ANGELA VICTORIA WOODHULL, Ph.D.,

 Plaintiff,

v.

 CAROLYN MEINEL,

 Defendant.

I, Angela V. Woodhull, Plaintiff, do hereby move for Summary Judgment in the above mentioned case. Below are my reasons.

1. I have been libeled by Carolyn Meinel. The definition of libel and is include, below, from www.law.com**, the online law dictionary. The words which I have bold faced will also be addressed.**

libel

1) n. to publish in print (including pictures), writing or broadcast through radio, television or film, an **untruth** about another which will **do harm** to that person or his/her **reputation**, by tending to bring the target into **ridicule**, hatred, scorn or contempt of others. Libel is the written or broadcast form of defamation, distinguished from slander, which is oral defamation. It is a tort (civil wrong) making the person or entity (like a newspaper, magazine or political organization) **open to a lawsuit for damages** by the person who can **prove** the statement about him/her was **a lie.** Publication need only be to one person, but it must be a statement which **claims to be fact** and is not clearly identified as an opinion. While it is sometimes said that the person making the libelous statement must have been **intentional and malicious**, actually it need only be obvious that the statement would **do harm** and is **untrue.** Proof of malice, however, does allow a party defamed to **sue** for **general damages for damage to reputation**, while an inadvertent libel limits the damages to actual harm (such as loss of business) called special damages. **Libel per se involves statements so vicious that malice is assumed and does not require a proof of intent to get an award of general damages.**

The rules covering libel against a "public figure" (particularly a political or governmental person) are special, based on U.S. Supreme Court decisions. The key is that to uphold the right to express opinions or fair comment on public figures, the libel must be malicious to constitute grounds for a lawsuit for damages. Minor errors in reporting are not libel, such as saying Mrs. Jones was 55 when she was only 48, or getting an address or title incorrect. 2) v. to broadcast or publish a written defamatory statement.

http://dictionary.law.com/default2.asp?selected=1153&bold=

Key words which were boldfaced in the above definition:

Untruth—Carolyn Meinel wrote, *she was soliciting me to commit a Federal felony. http://www.happyhacker.org/sucks/sucks12-15-03.shtml#angela.*

In what she labeled as an "update" to her information, she reiterated, *Back in 2003, Angela V. Woodhull, PhD wanted me to break into a news website and change the wording of a story about her. I told her over the phone that this would be a crime. Despite this, she offered to pay me to do it. I had no recourse but, muhahaha, to make fun of her on this website.*

Ridicule—Meinel openly admits that her intention is to ridicule when she writes,

I had no recourse but, muhahaha, to make fun of her on this website.

http://www.happyhacker.org/sucks/sucks1-4-06.shtml

2. I have been libeled per se by Carolyn Meinel. Here is the definition of libel per se and the reference.

- **libel per se** n. broadcast or written publication of a false statement about another which accuses him/her of a crime, immoral acts, inability to perform his/her profession, having a loathsome disease (like syphilis) or dishonesty in business. Such claims are considered so obviously harmful that malice need not be proved to obtain a judgment for "general damages," and not just specific losses. The

Defendant claimed that I solicited her to break into a news site (i.e., immoral act, accusation of a crime).

http://dictionary.law.com/default2.asp?selected=1154&bold=

The words in black in the above definition of "libel per se" will now be addressed.

(a) She accused me of a crime-- *she was soliciting me to commit a Federal felony. http://www.happyhacker.org/sucks/sucks12-15-03.shtml#angela.*

(b) Carolyn Meinel does more than just accuse me TWICE of wanting her to commit a federal crime.

She then goes on to collaborate with Mike Jimigiani and accuse me of having an immoral show which contains "dancing penises." She even links this quote to the article, which is now down.

(c) "Malicious"—When the *Independent Florida Alligator* took down the story and Meinel continued to promote the untruths, it became malicious on her part.

(d) "Malicious"—When a nicely worded letter was sent to Carolyn Meinel pointing out to her that the *Independent Florida Alligator* article was unposted and she continued to post her comments, it was malicious.

(e) "Malicious"—Despite Attorney David Peterson attempting to reason with Ms. Meinel for more than one hour by telephone, she continued to post her **malicious statements** about me while simultaneously **admitting** that her purpose was to **"muhahaha" make fun of me.**

3. Meinel wrote, *I had no recourse but, muhahaha, to <u>make fun of her</u> on this website.*

This is a false statement. When a person is solicited to commit a federal crime, they certainly have recourse, such as

(a)   Contact and report to the FBI

(b)   Contact and file a criminal report with the local
authorities, such as city police or sheriffs department

(c)   Contact the state prosecuting attorney's office and
sign a sworn statement, press charges.

However, Meinel chose to do none of the above because:

(a)   She admits on happyhacker.org did she did not even
fully hear or understand what was being requested of her.
She wrote,

*Sorry, I didn't let her get far enough to find out what website she
wanted altered. I cut off any crime request discussion instantly.*

This above statement shows more intention of malice. For,
without even knowing the name of the website, she then goes on
to collaborate with the *Independent Florida Alligator* and link
herself to a libelous article about me (which is now unposted).

Meinel is not claiming opinion or mere speculation when she
quotes Jimigiani,

"About ten minutes of research proved our story correct."
(Jimigiani was probably in junior high school in 2001, so how
would he know about a show at the Florida Theatre? He probably
did not even live in Gainesville, Florida at that time.)

In summary, teaming up with Jimigiani and quoting him, Meinel
purposefully intends to libel a person whom she has never met,
namely me—Angela V. Woodhull.

Under oath, Meinel said that she spoke with someone at the
Independent Florida Alligator who claimed that two news reporters
from the *Independent Florida Alligator* attended my show,
Remember Idora! To which I responded, "This cannot be true
because *Remember Idora!* took place in Youngstown, Ohio at

Powers Auditorium. Why would two college students/reporters from Florida attend one of my shows in Ohio?"

Under oath, Meinel also admitted that I simply contacted her and asked her if there was a way to delink my name in a Google search from the offending article.

But instead of listening to me and responding, "Yes it can be done," or "No, this cannot be done," instead she went into a tirade—"How dare you contact me and try to solicit me to commit a federal crime! Etc. etc." and then she slammed down the receiver while I was in the process of trying to explain myself. Meinel's overreaction and poor listening skills have turned into a nightmare for me. Hence, this lawsuit.

4. PROOF OF LIBEL:

In this section, the proof elements are in black and my supporting statements are in red.

A defamation plaintiff must usually establish the following elements to recover:

***Identification:** The plaintiff must show that the publication was "of and concerning" himself or herself. Yes, Ms. Meinel specifically uses my name, phone numbers, and e-mail address to specifically identify me. As far as I know, I am the only Angela V. Woodhull, Ph.D. on the planet. No one else with this name comes up during a Google search. Nor does anyone else possess those phone numbers and e-mail address (at that time of the original posting).

- **Publication:** The plaintiff must show that the defamatory statements were disseminated to a third party. Yes. Ms. Meinel admitted during the preliminary hearing that she obtained a series of e-mails from (then) editor-for-the-semester Mike Jimigiani and that he conducted a Google search of me in order to obtain information regarding Meinel's libelous post of me, to which she then updated the original post to include quotes from Jimigiani.

• **Defamatory meaning:** The plaintiff must establish that the statements in question were defamatory. For example, the language must do more than simply annoy a person or hurt a person's feelings. Yes, this is actually libel per se. Here is the definition of libel per se. See definition of libel per se, above

***Falsity:** The statements must be false; truth is a defense to a defamation claim. Generally, the plaintiff bears the burden of proof of establishing falsity. Yes, on both statements.

(1)   I did not solicit Ms. Meinel to break into a news website. Ms. Meinel, for the record, admitted this to the court and the court reporter. She admitted that I simply inquired about delinking my name in a Google search. To ask a question is not a crime.

(2)   **I have never had a show that contained "dancing penises." Videotapes of my shows are available for the Court. My mother will be my witness to this. Also, the names of hundreds of activity directors at hundreds of nursing homes who have hired me over the years are available to the court to see if any of my shows ever contained "dancing penises." Also, I am attempting to get in touch with the former owners of the Florida Theatre to see what their policy was regarding nudity and nude dancing, which, I am certain, was never permitted and never occurred at this venue. Since 2001, the establishment has**

switched owners and is now called "The Venue." It is located at 233 W. University Avenue, Gainesville, Florida.

- **Statements of fact:** The statements in question must be objectively verifiable as false statements of fact. In other words, the statements must be provable as false. (Caveat: Expressions of opinion can imply an assertion of objective facts. See _Milkovich v. Lorain Journal._)

- **Damages:** The false and defamatory statements must cause actual injury or special damages

(unless it is libel per se, which, in this case, it is).

5. I am not a public figure. I do not fit the legal definition of a public figure.

public figure

n. in the law of defamation (libel and slander), a personage of **great public interest** or **familiarity** like a government official, politician, celebrity, business leader, movie star or sports hero. Incorrect harmful statements published about a public figure cannot be the basis of a lawsuit for defamation unless there is proof that the writer or publisher intentionally defamed the person with **malice** (hate).

http://dictionary.law.com/default2.asp?selected=1681&bold=

Needless to say, I am not Angelina Jolee or Hillary Clinton or in such a category as either one of them or people of their stature. I do not have access to the media to clear up my name as a public figure would have. I have never been featured on ET or Inside Edition or anything like this. In fact, my primary job is caring for a 91 year old mother.

6.   Carolyn Meinel states that her website is posted for "educational purposes."

Collaborating with the *Independent Florida Alligator* in claiming that I have a show with "dancing penises" in no way is meant to "educate" her clients. This statement has no educational value for people who are interested in learning about hacking into other people's computers.

7.   "Educational Value." In fact, much of what is up on Meinel's website has nothing to do with "educational value." Much of her posts are meant to humiliate people. Here are some examples:

8.   Attorney for Defendant states that Meinel is not responsible for the contents of Jimigiani's e-mail which she intentionally selected to post on her website. He cites, as his proof,

Section 230 of the Communications Decency Act, passed in 1996, specifically states that "no provider or user of an **interactive computer service** shall be treated as the publisher or speaker."

This act does NOT apply to this law suit because:

(a) Meinel's website is NOT interactive. Meinel specifically republishes selected e-mails that are sent to her at cmeinel@techbroker.com, which is a separate location from happyhacker.org. It's completely her show.

Meinel wrote, *Carolyn replies: On this page I don't do anything anyone asks of me. http://www.happyhacker.org/sucks/sucksmarch1.shtml*

(b) Internet users who visit her happyhacker.org do NOT have the option of logging in under a user's name and interacting with other users who are interested in the topic of "hacking."

(c)   There is an option to download a program and then interact one-on-one with Philippe Detournay on a program called PJRC (Plout's Java IRC Client), but this is part of Detourney's deal called "Chat with Hackers."

9.   Therefore, under the rules of "republication libel," Ms. Meinel becomes solely responsible for the content of all e-mail posts and commentary on her website, an NONINTERACTIVE WEBSITE. Meinel creates and selects ALL content on her website exclusively.

Liability for republication of a defamatory statement is the same as for original publication, provided the defendant had knowledge of the contents of the statement. Thus, newspapers, magazines, and broadcasters are liable for republication of a libel or slander because they have editorial control over their communications. On the other hand, bookstores, libraries, and other distributors of material are liable for republication only if they knew or had reason to know the statement was defamatory.

http://www.answers.com/topic/slander-and-libel

Meinel, since December 15, 2006, had reason to know that the *Independent Florida Alligator* article is libelous because (a) she was contacted by e-mail and it was clearly explained to her, (b) she was contacted by phone by Attorney David Peterson and it was carefully explained, (c) it was carefully explained at the preliminary hearing and Judge Huling said, for the record, that it appears there are "no dancing penises" in my shows, and (d) the *Independent Florida Alligator* has unposted the libelous article. But despite all that, Meinel continues to keep up the libelous posts about me.

> 10.   Statute of Limitations. The libelous posts about me on happyhacker.org do fall within the three year statute of limitations for New Mexico because (1) one post is a reiteration of the other, (2) one post is an update of the other, (3) Meinel references one post to the other not once, not twice, but THREE TIMES to show that they are one thought, one link, one post that has been updated in which it has been substantively altered. By updating the post and claiming such:

Some of the most obnoxious experiences of my life are when people phone or email me and beg me to help them commit crime. Rude, huh? Anyhow, in case you were wondering about some of the nastier figures from "It Sucks to Be Me," here is an update.

http://www.happyhacker.org/sucks/sucks1-4-06.shtml

By "updating" the same information, Meinel openly admits that she is reopening the statute of limitations so that the original post and the subsequent post are treated as one post.

In addition, she links one to the other three times:

"Angela V. Woodhull, Ph.D."—links back to the original post, as a footnote

"make fun of her"-- links back to the original post, as a footnote

http://www.happyhacker.org/sucks/sucks12-15-03.shtml--links back to the original post.

Therefore, by substantively altering the original post and linking them together three times, Meinel reopens the statute of limitations of all posts regarding Angela V. Woodhull, Ph.D. on her website, happyhacker.org.

However, a secondary argument can be made by the Plaintiff. The Plaintiff can and hereby does request, if the above explanation is not satisfactory, to implement the delayed discovery rule for the following reasons:

> (a)   Plaintiff, following the production of *Remember Idora!* in May 2003 underwent a serious and life threatening automobile accident.
>
> (b)   As a result, Plaintiff was out of commission for the last three years, recovering from a broken leg, a divorce, loss of her father, and new role as caregiver to her mother.
>
> (c)   It was only when I decided it was time to restart my life that I discovered the libelous post on happyhacker.org after dealing with and resolving the libelous issue with the *Independent Florida Alligator.*
>
> (d)   Defendant was actually contacted on December 15, 2006—the last day of the statute of limitations regarding the original post, which has now become a footnote to the latest updated post of January 4, 2006, which reignites the statute of limitations.

11.   Invasion of Privacy. This lawsuit also fits the definition of "invasion of privacy."

Invasion of privacy is a <u>legal</u> term essentially defined as a violation of the right to be left alone. The right to <u>privacy</u> is the right to control property against search and seizure, and to **control information about oneself.**

One who gives publicity to a matter concerning another that places the other before the public in a false light is subject to liability for invasion of privacy, if:

1.   The false light would be highly offensive to a reasonable person; and

2.   The actor acted with *malice* -- had knowledge of or acted with **reckless disregard** as to the falsity of the publicized matter and the false light in which the other would be placed.

See Section 652D of the Restatement (Second) of Torts.

The tort of false light involves a "major misrepresentation" of a person's "character, history, activities or belief." See *Gannett Co., Inc. v. Anderson*, 2006 WL 2986459 at 3 (Fla. 1st DCA Oct. 20, 2006.)

Meinel selected to publish false informtion about me without my permission. In addition, she invaded my privacy by including my personal e-mail and phone numbers for the whole world to see.

Highly offensive to a reasonable person: By republishing the statement that I have a show that includes "dancing penises," this is absolutely, without a doubt, HIGHLY OFFENSIVE to a reasonable person. By accusing me of soliciting her to commit a federal crime, this is HIGHLY OFFENSIVE to a reasonable person.

Reckless disregard: Meinel did little to discover whether or not I have a show that contains "dancing penises," and so this is RECKLESS. All she did was link yet another *Independent Florida Alligator* to her website about the time I was on America's Funniest Home Videos as "Wedgie Woman." Her statement about this matter shows firsthand her **propensity for exaggeration and reckless disregard for the truth**. She stated,

I did a little more research on Dr. Woodhull and learned that she's been on America''s Funniest Home Videos and says she is proud to be known as <u>*Wedgie Woman*</u>*. She owns a website,* <u>*http://www.polkaqueen.com*</u>*, but it seems to be defunct nowadays.*

NOWHERE in this article does it state that I am "proud" to be known as "Wedgie Woman." In fact, like the *Alligator,* I am misquoted in this article. America's Funniest Home videos dubbed me "Wedgie Woman."

That is the extent of her research on me. This is the extent to what Meinel calls "a little more research." Before claiming that a person has a show with "dancing penises," I certainly would do A LOT MORE RESEARCH. Then again, what would be the MOTIVE for spreading such lies? Since there is no "hacker" "educational value" to claiming I have a "dancing penis" show, this shows MALICE—INTENTIONAL MALICE, which is also acknowledged by Ms. Meinel when she writes, "I had no choice but to make fun of her . . ." "muhahaha." All of this combined shows (a) reckless disregard for the truth and (b) intentional MALICE.

Out of all of my many positive accomplishments, this is all she chooses to say about me—DANCING PENISES AND SOLICITOR OF FEDERAL CRIMES.

 In reality, I have been a published author, a musician, a songwriter, a mother, a caretaker of a senior citizen (my mother and my present job), a seminar leader, a produced playwright. Meinel was accurate in stating that www.polkaqueen.com is defunct nowadays, which would indicate that a person is no longer performing shows. But instead of concluding the obvious or attempting to contact me and get the truth from me, Meinel chose to add more to her libelous information about me for NO APPARENT GOOD REASON EXCEPT TO EMBARRASS, LIBEL ME, AND HUMILIATE ME EVEN THOUGH I HAVE NEVER, EVER DONE ANYTHING TO HER TO DESERVE THIS HORRIBLE TREATMENT. DURING THE THREE YEARS THAT ACCUSED ME OF COMMITING A FEDERAL CRIME, I NEVER ONCE CONTACTED HER OR ATTEMPTED TO HARASS HER. SO, WHY WOULD SHE UPDATE INFORMATION ABOUT ME ON JANUARY 5, 2006 EXCEPT TO EMBARRASS AND HUMILIATE AND DEFAME ME?

In addition, you will find no other negative posts about me anywhere on the internet or anywhere else. My polka shows were always clean cut and in good taste. Most of my shows were performed for the elderly at nursing homes, retirement centers, assisted living facilities.

Meinel has been given plenty of opportunities to simply UNPOST her libelous statements about me but she has selected to move forward with this law suit.

I am therefore asking for a 12 member jury on this trial.

I will also be asking for **damages.**

I kindly ask the Judge to determine the amount of **damages.**

I do not know what to ask for, Judge, as I have always been very terrible about asking for money; hence, all of my life I have been poor.

However, I found two very similar cases, and here is what the Plaintiffs were awarded:

Damages--$3 million (Minnesota)
In May 2003, the Associated Press reported that the North Dakota Supreme Court upheld a $3 million libel verdict against a former University of North Dakota student accused of using an Internet site to spread lies about a physics professor.

Glenda Miskin, of Crookston, Minn., argued that a North Dakota court did not have jurisdiction over her Web site because its content was not "directed uniquely to the state of North Dakota." The state's highest court disagreed, in a unanimous decision written by Chief Justice Gerald VandeWalle.

Miskin's Web site included links to articles about UND issues and staffers, VandeWalle wrote, along with items about physics professor John Wagner and Wagner's attorney, William McKechnie. And the state chief justice said that in any case, a North Dakota court could assert jurisdiction over Miskin personally because she lived in North Dakota when many of the allegedly defamatory incidents occurred.

Miskin is a former UND student. She took a physics class from Wagner in the fall of 1998, but was suspended from school the following year after a university student-relations committee concluded she was stalking and harassing Wagner. Miskin contended she and Wagner exchanged a number of sexually explicit e-mail messages. Wagner denied Miskin's claims.

Wagner sued Miskin in June 2000, arguing **she was trying to ruin his reputation and interfere in his business relationships. In April 2002, a jury awarded Wagner $3 million in damages, which the state Supreme Court upheld in 2003.**

Damages: $11.3 million (Florida)

In another case, the jury awarded $11.3 million to the Plaintiff. The details are very similar to the Woodhull v. Meinel case.

http://www.firstamendmentcenter.org/news.aspx?id=17527

CONCLUSION: In conclusion, Carolyn Meinel's website is more about shaming and embarrassing people than informing and educating. To back up this premise, see the selected quotes of Meinel's that appear below. Meinel is like a sting operation. She announces to the world that she can hack into people's computers. She waits for requests and then, after baiting people, exposes them for their "crimes" on her website. Telling someone, for instance, that they should "Get a job, spend less than you earn, and develop a good character so you can have more than one friend" is not an educational statement about hacking or learning to hack. It is simply a caustic remark meant to embarrass and humiliate the recipient. In addition, Meinel's non-profit status as an "educational organization" was revoked in 2003 by the IRS. This needs to be explained to the 12 person jury.

EXAMPLES OF CAUSTIC AND CONTRADICTORY QUOTES FROM
CAROLYN MEINEL ON www.happyhacker.org ("It Sucks To Be Me")

*Carolyn replies: Peterson is the first person ever who has demanded
that I call him a criminal. Normally a person would get really upset,
and have reason to sue, if I were to publicly claim that he or she had
been arrested for computer crime without any evidence that it was
true. That's one reason I'm not claiming that Peterson is an arrested,
perhaps convicted criminal. I have no evidence that this ever
happened*

http://www.happyhacker.org/sucks/sucks1-13-04.shtml

From: "dream maker"
Subject: it sucks to see you
Date: Sun, 5 Mar 2000 05:43:26 -0000

Im pretty sure that you wont publish this letter and chances are that
after the first couple of lines you delet it, however i am still going to
continue typing regardless.

Having recently visited the happhacker website, i decided to read
some of the letters sent in by visitors to your site. The majority i will
agree are outragous to say the least and so too are your replies. Take
for example the letter sent to you on January the 26th by "Bob
cratchet", this was a letter sent to you by what would appear to be a
curious individual who for reasons unknown is unable to afford to
have a land line installed. "Bob" politely asked if there was a way that
he/she could make free phonecalls he/she also added that they
would understand if you could not publish any information that may
be able to help them. But you did publish a reply and here it is

"Carolyn replies: Because you have been financially irresponsible, you
think I would help you commit a crime? Here's how to solve your
problem. Get a job, spend less than you earn, and develop a good
character so you can have more than one friend.".

When i first read this i was confused, i thought maybe im taking this up the wrong way, so i showed it to some friends of mine who found it to be "insulting, degrading and upsetting to the individual to whom it was addressed". You have basically implied that this individual is stupid, unlikeable and irresponsible. I mean this from a woman who, in the reply to the previous letter lays claim to being a bible reader. Well i too have read the bible and nowhere in it did i find refernce giving any individual the right to insult or make little of another individual. As i stated earlier im sure you have no intention of either publishing this letter or replying to it so im quite sure that my next comment will be in vain, however i am going to voice that comment regardless. Miss Meinel, you should really take a step back from your workstation and take a good look at yourself and your attitude.

Now though it may seem ironic im going to quote you, just to help you understand my point, here it is the saying that has helped you rise to your position of fame "I promise, I will not make fun of anyone for asking a "stupid" question. There are no stupid questions, only teachers who haven't figured out how to teach things well enough to help you".

Well im sure you will either delete this letter after having a good laugh at it with your comrades at the happyhacker but that doesnt bother me in the least as i know that if youve gotten this far, then you have read it, which is more then enough for me.
http://www.happyhacker.org/sucks/sucksmarch3.shtml

Now, on to the topic of revenge. "In taking revenge, a man is but even with his enemy; but in passing it over, he is superior." -- Francis Bacon, writing in "Of Revenge." This is from the man who invented the scientific method, the most revolutionary development in history since the coming of Jesus Christ. The Bible is full of commands to NOT commit revenge. For example, "Thou shalt not avenge," Leviticus 19:18.
http://www.happyhacker.org/sucks/sucksmarch.shtml

Carolyn replies: My beliefs that crime and violation of privacy is wrong come from the <u>Holy Bible</u> and my relationship with God. Try it -- you'll like it!

http://www.happyhacker.org/sucks/sucksfeb.shtml

SUMMARY

It was extreme and intentional and reckless disregard for the truth when Carolyn Meinel republished an e-mail from Mike Jimigiani claiming that I have a show that features "dancing penises" when all she had to do was look up the civil codes for Gainesville, Florida, available on the internet which, probably apply to ALL municipalities across the entire United States (except maybe Las Vegas).

http://municode.com/resources/gateway.asp?pid=10819&sid=9

Municipal Code 17-15 states:

Sec. 17-15. Nudity, sexual conduct prohibited in establishments dealing in alcoholic beverages.

The following prohibitions and criteria shall apply within existing and/or newly created establishments dealing in alcoholic beverages and the curtilages thereof:

(a) No person shall knowingly, intentionally or recklessly appear, or cause another person to appear, nude, or, expose to public view his or her genitals, pubic area, vulva, anus, or any simulation thereof.

Even if Meinel did not know that the Florida Theatre was a place that sells alcoholic beverages, she would still read the part of this municipal code that states:

(h) *Public place:* Any location frequented by the public or where the public is present or likely to be present, or where a person may reasonably be expected to be observed by members of the public. Public places include, but are not limited to, streets, sidewalks, parks, forests, lakes, business and commercial establishments (whether for profit or not for profit and whether open to the public at large or where entrance is limited by a cover charge or membership requirement), bottle clubs, hotels, motels, restaurants, night clubs, country clubs, adult cabarets, and meeting facilities utilized by any religious, social, fraternal or similar organization. Premises, or portions thereof such as hotel rooms, used solely as a private residence, whether permanent or temporary in nature, shall not be deemed to be a public place.

(Ord. No. 4080, § 1, 5-22-95)

Therefore, to make such a horrible claim about me on the internet (that my shows contain "dancing penises") AND refuse to unpost it when she was given several opportunities shows MALICE.

It also dawned on me that if Carolyn Meinel wanted to settle this lawsuit and then changed her mind when I said I don't want her to write anything more about me ever again, then the ONLY reason she is continuing this lawsuit is to have the right to WRITE MORE ABOUT ME. There is nothing else for her to gain! This shows additional malicious intent, for I am certain that what she wants to write about me is nothing positive.

The court cautioned that application of this so-called "first publication rule" is not without its limitations. "[A] republication of the plaintiff's likeness can constitute a new cause of action if the publication is altered so as to reach a new audience or promote a different product." *Lehman v. Discovery Communications, Inc.*, 332 F.Supp.2d 534, 539 (E.D.N.Y.2004).

I therefore petition the Court for Summary Judgment based on these findings.

[The above arguments prevailed on appeal, on a case of first impression; Woodhull (who wrote her own appeal) won against the largest law firm in the state of New Mexico, the Rodey Law Firm, on appeal.]

EMAIL FROM WOODHULL TO REVEREND NARDELLA

From: Angela V. Woodhull [mailto:angelavwoodhull@yahoo.com]
Sent: Tuesday, September 30, 2008 8:50 PM
To: Anthony Nardella
Subject: RE: Fierle, Rebecca - Falvo, Louise A., Guardianship of: LIABILITY

Believe me, I am trying my best to understand you. But this makes no sense. As long as Shirley Mascarella is contesting my being appointed the personal representative claiming that Louise A. Falvo was incapacitated at the time that she created her March 22, 2008 will, then I have a problem, do I not? This problem, however, could be ended if it were acknowledged that this guardianship violated guardianship statutes and that the money was POD and ITF to me and then the whole probate mess would go away if you would simply put in a motion to the Seminole County court to terminate this irregularly taken guardianship.

I try my best to understand you, Mr. Nardella, but do you see that you wanted to sue me for something I didn't do, accused my fiance of sleeping with 90 year old women, helped yourself to my mother's estate ex parte, kept a guardianship going that creates a probate nightmare for me, and now you want me to drop my appeals? This makes no sense.

Imagine for a moment what it might be like to spend a lifetime dealing as patiently as possible with a difficult mother who adored me but did very strange things to me, a greedy cousin who whisked my mother off for 2 1/2 months to a very bleak town and also slandered me and called DCF on me over the years without cause, which can easily be proved, and now expects my inheritance, and then all the nightmare that follows when by now I should simply have what is entitled to me as my mother's only child. Given all that has happened I now feel that I have earned more than my inheritance. You know, out of that cast of characters down there in Seminole County , I only have some hope for you. I keep waiting for you to do the right thing. How did you get involved with such a group of thugs to begin with? And as for Rebecca "Fierle," I certainly would represent other guardians in the future to limit personal liability if I were you. In the end, it's only money and there are times when I am torn between justice and just wanting a life of comfort and perhaps in the end there will be both. Mr. Nardella, the cards will fall where they fall as we both proceed. I'm always willing to be open to communication but I also have a very definitive sense of justice.

Angela W.

••●●●••

PARTIAL TRANSCRIPT, ATTORNEY AL FLEMING, YOUNGSTOWN, OHIO, QUESTIONING AND VIDEOTAPING LOUISE A. FALVO, MARCH 3, 2008

LOUISE A FALVO: "THEY WANT MY MONEY"

ATTORNEY FLEMING: It's not what your daughter wants. It's not what your niece wants. It's what YOU want.

LOUISE FALVO: I know.

ATTORNEY FLEMING: Okay, well, I'm not going to belabor that. You make your decision wherever you want to – if you want to stay here in Youngstown at Meridian Arms . . . .

LOUISE FALVO: Well . . .

ATTORNEY FLEMING: If you want to go back to Florida . . .

LOUISE FALVO: I know there's gonna be trouble . . .

ATTORNEY FLEMING: Why is that?

LOUISE FALVO: With my niece and her husband . . . . I'll probably have a court case out of that . . .

ATTORNEY FLEMING: Why is that?

LOUISE FALVO: Because they want my money.

ATTORNEY FLEMING: Who wants your money?

LOUISE FALVO: My niece and nephew.

ATTORNEY FLEMING: Well, it's your decision on where your money goes.

LOUISE FALVO: And they're going to contest anything I do.

ATTORNEY FLEMING: Oh, really?

LOUISE FALVO: They will. They will contest any decision I make.

ATTORNEY FLEMING: Well, do you want to give your money to your niece and nephew?

LOUISE FALVO: Well, no. I think I explained to you that if there's anything left after all my bills are paid from Bank of America.

ATTORNEY FLEMING: From Bank of America?

LOUISE FALVO: Yes, but if I'm already in Tampa that would change then.

ATTORNEY FLEMING: Oh, I see. Then you would not want that to happen?

LOUISE FALVO: Well, if I'm in Tampa, I'm sure that Angie will be taking care of all of my affairs then.

ATTORNEY FLEMING: Tampa or Gainesville?

LOUISE FALVO: Gainesville.

ATTORNEY FLEMING: Okay. Well, I'm sort of . . . I didn't . . . You made mention that your niece and nephew want your money?

LOUISE FALVO: Oh, that's what it's all about.

ATTORNEY FLEMING: Do you want them to have your money?

LOUISE FALVO: I want them to have "some" of it for the trouble they went through of bringing me here and taking care of me. I don't feel they shouldn't have "something" but . . .

ATTORNEY FLEMING: I don't want you to think that anyone is forcing you anywhere. You go where you want to go. That's very important. You want to stay? You can.

Think about that but if you'd like to stay in Youngstown, that's fine.

LOUISE FALVO: No. I really don't like the cold. I do like warm weather.

ATTORNEY FLEMING: Especially on a day like this?

LOUISE FALVO: Yeah.

ATTORNEY FLEMING: Well, is that what you want to do—to go back to Florida? Or do you want to stay in Youngstown?

LOUISE FALVO: No.

LOUISE FALVO: So, does Angie and my niece both have Power of Attorney over the account at Bank of America? Who has authority to withdraw over there in case I pass away?

ATTORNEY FLEMING: I don't know what Shirl Mascarella has. I don't have those documents. I don't know what you signed. And you don't have copies, either.

LOUISE FALVO: No, I don't.

ATTORNEY FLEMING: It's your decision. I don't want to dwell on that so . . . What we'll do, we'll ...

LOUISE FALVO: Well, I guess I'll have to give Angie Power of Attorney over my funds which will cause a disruption with my niece, I am sure. Oh . . . her husband and Angie. Angie never met her husband until the day you made the will.

ATTORNEY FLEMING: Yes?

LOUISE FALVO: And they got into an argument. She never met him before but he strongly wants my money. He strongly wants it.

ATTORNEY FLEMING: Who is that?

LOUISE FALVO: Shirl's husband. They got into a battle and I'm sure when he finds out Shirl isn't going to have Power of Attorney, there's going to be a lawsuit against me. He's not going to stop. He's a very strong fellow.

ATTORNEY FLEMING: Okay. And do you want him to have your money? What is his name?

LOUISE FALVO: His name?

ATTORNEY FLEMING: Yeah.

LOUISE FALVO: John Mascarella.

ATTORNEY FLEMING: John Mascarella.

ATTORNEY FLEMING: You think that Mr. Mascarella is going to sue you?

LOUISE FALVO: I believe so. Yeah, he won't stop.

ATTORNEY FLEMING: Why would he sue you?

LOUISE FALVO: Because he wants the money!

ATTORNEY FLEMING: He wants your money?

LOUISE FALVO: Oh, yes. Yes. He made that almost clear that he's entitled to it.

ATTORNEY FLEMING: He made it clear that he's "entitled" to it?

ATTORNEY FLEMING: Why did he say that he's "entitled" to your money?

LOUISE FALVO: Well, I don't know. They just want the money to spend it and have a good time. I don't know what people want my money for. I thought they should at least wait until I die, but they're fighting before I die about my money.

ATTORNEY FLEMING: Apparently.

LOUISE FALVO: That's kind of unusual, isn't it? Can't they wait until I'm in a coffin at least? I don't know. I think if my husband was able to see this, he'd be shocked.

••●●●••

RE: The Florida Bar v. Evelyn Watts Cloninger, TFB#210382 Case No. 1995-31,876(18A)

DISCIPLINE BY THE FLORIDA BAR OF EVELYN WATTS CLONINGER

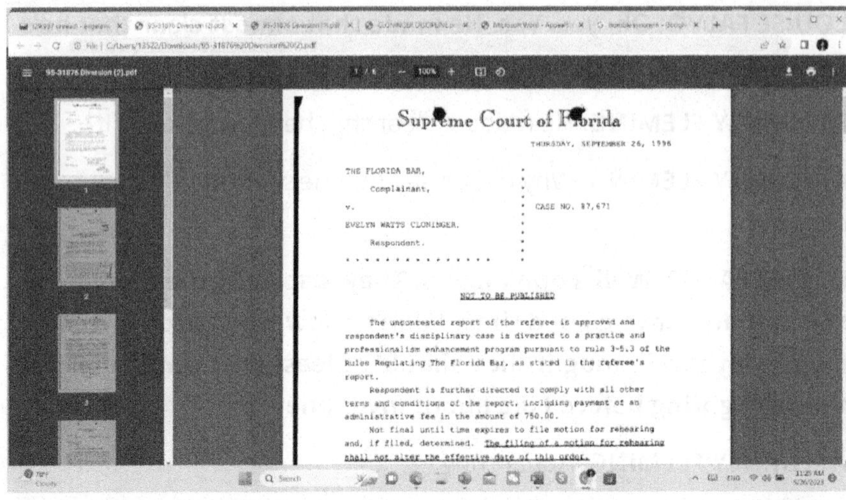

Supreme Court of Florida

THURSDAY, SEPTEMBER 26, 1996

THE FLORIDA BAR,

    Complainant,

v.   CASE NO. 87,671

EVELYN WATTS CLONINGER,

    Respondent.

NOT TO BE PUBLISHED

The uncontested report of the referee is approved and respondent's disciplinary case is diverted to a practice and professionalism enhancement program pursuant to rule 3-5.3 of the Rules Regulating The Florida Bar, as stated in the referee's report.

Respondent is further directed to comply with all other terms and conditions of the report, including payment of an administrative fee in the amount of 750.00.

Not final until time expires to file motion for rehearing and, if filed, determined. The filing of a motion for rehearing shall not alter the effective date of this order.

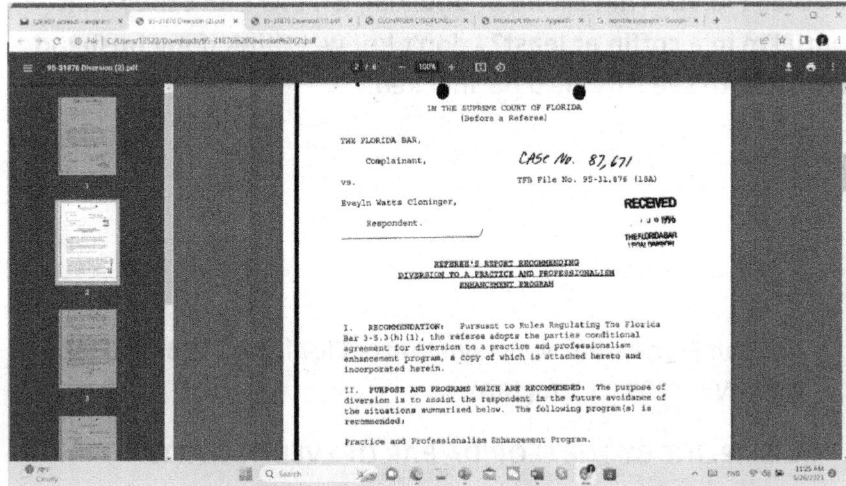

IN THE SUPREME COURT OF FLORIDA
(Before a Referee)

THE FLORIDA BAR,

    Complainant,   CASE No. 87,671

vs.   TFB File No. 95-31,876 (18A)

Eveyln Watts Cloninger,

    Respondent.

RECEIVED

THE FLORIDA BAR

REFEREE'S REPORT RECOMMENDING DIVERSION TO A PRACTICE AND PROFESSIONALISM ENHANCEMENT PROGRAM

I. RECOMMENDATION: Pursuant to Rules Regulating The Florida Bar 3-5.3(h)(1), the referee adopts the parties conditional agreement for diversion to a practice and professionalism enhancement program, a copy of which is attached hereto and incorporated herein.

II. PURPOSE AND PROGRAMS WHICH ARE RECOMMENDED: The purpose of diversion is to assist the respondent in the future avoidance of the situations summarized below. The following program(s) is recommended:

Practice and Professionalism Enhancement Program.

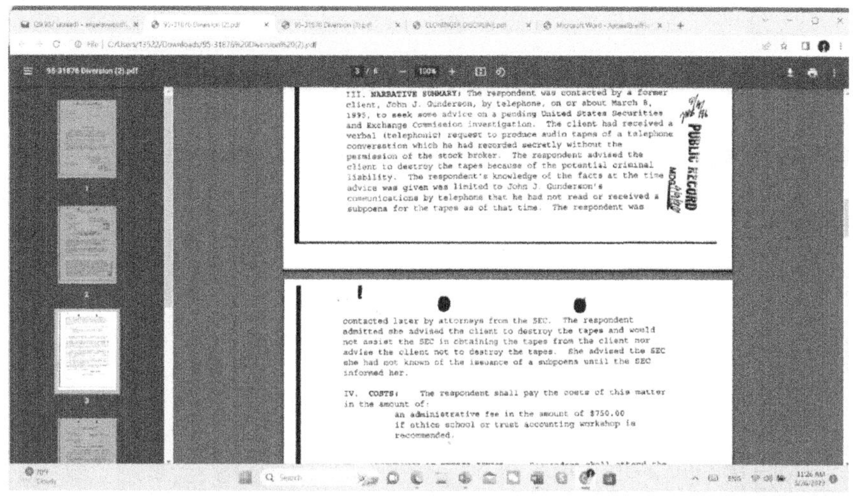

III. **NARRATIVE SUMMARY:** The respondent was contacted by a former client, John J. Gunderson, by telephone, on or about March 8, 1995, to seek some advice on a pending United States Securities and Exchange Commission investigation. The client had received a verbal (telephonic) request to produce audio tapes of a telephone conversation which he had recorded secretly without the permission of the stock broker. The respondent advised the client to destroy the tapes because of the potential criminal liability. The respondent's knowledge of the facts at the time advice was given was limited to John J. Gunderson's communications by telephone that he had not read or received a subpoena for the tapes as of that time. The respondent was

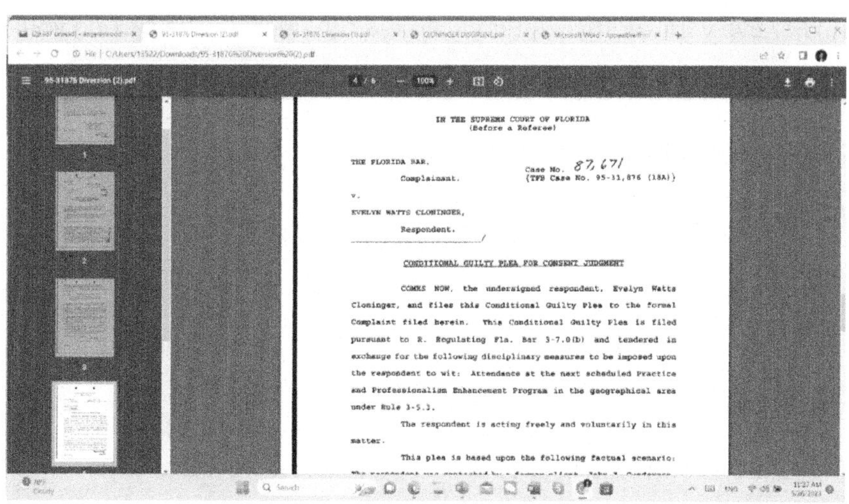

contacted later by attorneys from the SEC. The respondent admitted she advised the client to destroy the tapes and would not assist the SEC in obtaining the tapes from the client nor advise the client not to destroy the tapes. She advised the SEC she had not known of the issuance of a subpoena until the SEC informed her.

IV. **COSTS:** The respondent shall pay the costs of this matter in the amount of:

an administrative fee in the amount of $750.00 if ethics school or trust accounting workshop is recommended.

ANGELINA, THE POLKA QUEEN'S RECIPE FOR HAPPINESS

[15 things you can do to be happy and make a difference.]

[1] Buy a purple wig.

[2] Dance the polka.

[3] Learn to play a musical instrument.

[4] Be sassy sometimes.

[5] Dare to slay a dragon.

[6] Forgive your mother. After all, no matter what . . . she carried you.

[7] Avoid most lawyers.

[8] Learn to write your own court papers.

[9] Avoid court at all costs.

[10] Kiss your cat.

[11] Walk to the Farmer's Market and devour some delicious, fresh

tomatoes.

[12] Start a court watch. Let the predators know we are always

watching.

[13] Thank the Divine.

[14] Whenever possible, buy a house where there's no HOA. Make
that always possible.

[15] Respect yourself and all living things.

[IT'S SING ALONG TIME! THE "THANK YOU!" POLKA

NOW, GET UP OFF YOUR FAT ASS AND TELL OTHERS ABOUT THE
GUARDIANSHIP HUSTLE! THE MORE PEOPLE WHO ARE INFORMED,
THE LESS LIKELY THE GUARDIANSHIP RACKET CAN HAPPEN TO
ANY ONE OF US. THANKS!

~Angelina, the Polka Queen

[IT'S SING ALONG TIME! THE WORLD IS GOOD, BAD

Made in the USA
Monee, IL
07 July 2026